STUDY GUIDE TO ACCOM

INTRODUCTION TO FINANCIAL MANAGEMENT

MW01166176

STUDY GUIDE TO ACCOMPANY SCHALL/HALEY

SIXTH EDITION

INTRODUCTION TO FINANCIAL MANAGEMENT

THOMAS E. STITZEL

College of Business   **Boise State University**

Boston, Massachusetts   Burr Ridge, Illinois
Dubuque, Iowa   Madison, Wisconsin   New York, New York
San Francisco, California   St. Louis, Missouri

To Gladys, in appreciation for her friendship

McGraw-Hill

A Division of The McGraw·Hill Companies

Study Guide to Accompany Schall/Haley
INTRODUCTION TO FINANCIAL MANAGEMENT

3 4 5 6 7 8 9 0 BKM BKM 9 9 8 7

ISBN 0-07-055119-7

This book was set in Times Roman by J. M. Post Graphics, Corp.
The editors were Judy Motto and Bob Greiner;
the production supervisor was Louise Karam.
The cover was designed by Joan Greenfield.
R. R. Donnelley & Sons Company was printer and binder.

CONTENTS

To the Student   vii

CHAPTER 1	Financial Management and Goals	1
CHAPTER 2	The Financial System: Domestic and International	7
CHAPTER 3	The Legal Environment: Business Organization, Taxes, and Bankruptcy	25
CHAPTER 4	The Time Value of Money	45
CHAPTER 5	Security Prices	61
CHAPTER 6	Risk and Return	73
CHAPTER 7	The Cost of Capital	85
CHAPTER 8	Fundamentals of Capital Budgeting	99
CHAPTER 9	Capital Budgeting: Special Topics	117
CHAPTER 10	Risk Analysis and Capital Budgeting	125
CHAPTER 11	Raising Intermediate- and Long-Term Funds	139
CHAPTER 12	Financing Decisions and Capital Structure	167
CHAPTER 13	Dividend Policy and Retained Earnings	185
CHAPTER 14	Financial Statement Analysis	201
CHAPTER 15	Break-Even Analysis and the Measurement of Leverage	221
CHAPTER 16	Financial Forecasting and Planning	237
CHAPTER 17	Inventory and Accounts Receivable Management	253
CHAPTER 18	Cash Management	275
CHAPTER 19	Short-Term Financing	283
CHAPTER 20	Working Capital Management	295
CHAPTER 21	Leasing	303
CHAPTER 22	Convertibles and Warrants	315
CHAPTER 23	Holding Companies, Mergers, and Consolidations	329

Solutions to Crossword Puzzles   341

TO THE STUDENT

This book has been written to support your efforts to learn finance principles and their applications. The pages that follow are a *guide* to your *study*—material to help you better understand *Introduction to Financial Management,* sixth edition. Each *Study Guide* chapter distills concepts and major points from the textbook and gives you another pass through the subject matter.

Most people make progress in their learning by reading from or by listening to more experienced sources. The process is similar to the situation one faces in acquiring some new skill, such as hitting a golf ball or playing tennis. Your mastery of these skills suddenly improves once you "see how" by having someone else demonstrate and explain. The *Study Guide* fills this role. It presents the material covered in the textbook in a different, more concise manner. The concepts and principles are explained in the most straightforward way possible. The purpose is to give you "someone in your corner."

Quintessence Each chapter begins with the *Quintessence* (according to Webster, "the essence of a thing in its most pure and concentrated form"), a paragraph describing the theme and highlights of the material covered. Read these sentences several times—at the outset, after going through the other parts of the chapter, and again to refresh your memory before an exam.

Outline The next section of each *Study Guide* chapter is an *Outline* of the text chapter. These brief sentences offer a summary of the text discussion and tie things together. The outlines begin with *what* the chapter is about, follow with *why* the topics are important, and end with *how* to understand and use the theory and techniques presented in the textbook. Major information is restated in an abbreviated form and elaborated upon where appropriate.

Keys Key terms and concepts are printed in **boldface** type in the margins of the outlines. Skimming these words will be helpful as a last-chance review before exams.

Completion The *Completion Questions* are part of each *Study Guide* chapter. They help test your recall and comprehension. Use this section by covering up the answers and writing in your own solutions. Another approach is to complete the questions while looking at the answers provided, and then carefully reread the entire statement. Many of these sentences are direct quotes of key points made in the text, and the additional impression will further cement the idea or concept in your mind.

Problems   Much of finance can be best learned by problem solving. The last section of each chapter contains *Problems,* based on those given in the textbook, to help you learn by **doing.** The detailed solutions to the problems are an important learning aid. Each step is part of the thought process that has been carefully organized and developed to illustrate the principles outlined in the text. But remember, you must **do,** to learn. Try for your own answer before studying the solutions. This is why space has been left just after each question. If you become stuck, look at the beginning of the solution for a hint to get started.

To get the most from the following pages, first read and study Schall and Haley's book. This is essential. The *Guide* is a condensation of the text presentation; it is less than one-third the length of *Introduction to Financial Management.* After working with the text material:

Summary   1. Read the *Quintessence.* It should help affix the overall picture in your mind.
2. Ask yourself while going over the *Outline,* "How would I explain this point to a friend who knows nothing about finance?"
3. Try the *Fill-in Questions* for a quick review.
4. Work the *Problems* for mastery of the material, covering up the answers at first. When you come up against a tough one, review the solution carefully and watch for the **reasoning.**
5. For last-minute reviews before an exam, read the key terms and concepts found in the margins of the outlines.

Constructive criticisms from readers of earlier editions of the *Study Guide* have improved it. Their assistance is gratefully acknowledged, and yours is invited to further strengthen the material.

Finally, please remember that the objective of this book is to help you "get it all together." GOOD LUCK!

Thomas E. Stitzel

CHAPTER ONE

FINANCIAL MANAGEMENT AND GOALS

QUINTESSENCE The goal of most firms is to maximize the value of their shares while operating within laws and restrictions that protect the interests of society. Management, stockholders, and members of society may have different interests (i.e., salaries, profits, and pollution control). The resulting conflicts may be minimized by an understanding of the potential problems and by careful financial planning. The function of the financial manager is to raise and employ funds.

OUTLINE

I. What
   A. Purpose of the book:
      1. To identify and explore the factors that are relevant to financial decision making for both large and small businesses.
      2. To identify goals and policies and develop a framework using problem solving tools of effective financial management.
   B. Topics discussed in this chapter:
      1. Areas of mutual benefit or conflict between:
         a. Owners (stockholders) and managers.
         b. The firm and the rest of society.
      2. Ways to resolve the interests of conflicting groups.
      3. Finance as a discipline and the key role of the financial manager in raising money and putting it to work.

II. Why
   A. Money is the lifeblood of most activities. It is the scorecard for our financial endeavors. Principles of finance apply to most situations—individual, business, and governmental.
   B. Financial decisions affect all segments of our society; it is important to understand potential conflicts between groups and to offer suggestions for settling these problems.

III. How
   A. Set corporate objectives (goals):

Maximizing Wealth
      1. Maximize the owners' wealth.
      2. Establish policies (strategies) to achieve this.

**Owners vs.
Managers**

B. Potential conflicts

    1. Owners and managers may have different interests; **agency theory** helps explain the interrelationships. Differences can be minimized by:

        a. Encouraging management through performance bonuses or having them become part owners through stock purchase plans.

        b. The increased legal accountability of the board of directors.

        c. The threat that an outside group may gain control. The potential for a **takeover** encourages management to strive to keep the owners happy.

**Business vs.
Society**

    2. Corporations and society

        a. According to one view, an active government is needed to ensure that companies behave (Galbraith and Nader).

        b. Others feel free competition serves the best interests of everyone (Friedman and Kristol).

**Ethical
Considerations**

    3. Ethical principles

        a. Consider the impacts of decisions on:

            i. Shareholders.

            ii. Employees.

            iii. Customers.

            iv. Other people.

        b. Theories or principles for ethical behavior

            i. Utilitarianism—greatest good for the greatest number.

            ii. Egalitarianism—strive for equal benefits for everyone.

            iii. Individual rights—individual people are the key.

            iv. Libertarianism—free choice; keep promises.

            v. When in Rome . . .—recognize cultural differences.

C. The solution for most firms is to maximize the value of their shares, operating within laws and economic considerations that protect the interests of society.

    1. This means maximizing earnings, part of which are reinvested in the business and part of which are used to pay dividends.

    2. The trade-offs between riskiness and the level of future earnings must be considered in setting policies.

    3. Maximizing share values is a long-run goal. Day-to-day price fluctuations are not of vital concern.

Role of Finance

D. Finance plays a key role in and for:

    1. Business, where there is a need to know:

        a. How best to obtain financing.

        b. How best to use money and control financial activities to ensure success (maximize wealth of the owners).

        c. How the financial vice president or manager is responsible for:

            i. Fund raising and usage (treasurer).

            ii. Accounting and control (controller).

    2. Individuals, who can maximize their well-being by making intelligent choices between consumption and investment:

a. Finance aids in the process of selecting investments.

b. It also helps to know how to raise money so that consumption and/or investment can be increased.

3. Financial markets and institutions, where a knowledge of opportunities, attitudes, and limitations helps one to play a more effective role in business, government, or personal life.

E. Outline for *Introduction to Financial Management*

1. Part 1 provides the background for the individual and corporate financial decision-making process. The financial environment is described. Fundamental concepts, including the time value of money and the effect of risk on asset values, are developed.

2. Part 2 deals with the basic techniques for investment, financing, and dividend decisions. Key issues include the cost of money, capital budgeting, internal and external sources of long-term funds, and how each of these issues is affected by uncertainty.

3. Part 3 presents tools to analyze past performances and to aid in planning for the future.

4. Short-term sources and uses of funds are emphasized in Part 4.

5. Part 5 covers the special topics of leasing, convertible securities, and mergers.

F. Check this blank ____ if you can recall the main points discussed under "To the Student." That material was written to explain the philosophy of the *Study Guide* and to offer suggestions for getting the most effective use from this book. You can maximize the value of the *Guide* by a careful reading of "To the Student"; therefore, if you didn't check the above space, please take a few minutes to go back and digest that section.

COMPLETION QUESTIONS

small, individuals, governmental

1. Principles of financial decision making apply to large firms as well as to _____ firms and to _____ and _____ units.

owners, managers, society, company

2. Potential conflicts of interest exist between _____ and _____ and between the rest of _____ and the _____.

Agency

3. _____ theory is used to help explain relationships between the owners and the managers of a firm.

maximizing common stock

4. The objective of a corporation is usually stated in terms of _____ the value of the corporation's (*assets/common stock*).

strategies goals

5. The policies of a company are the _____ it employs to achieve its _____.

board	6. The goals and policies of a firm are determined by the elected _____
directors	of _____, which is responsible for representing the (*credi-*
shareholders	*tors/shareholders*).
owners	7. In most small businesses the _____ are the same people as the
objectives	managers, and so the _____ of both groups will be identical.
owners	8. A method of minimizing potential conflicts between _____ and
	managers involves creating opportunities for the managers to become part
owners, stock option	_____ through _____ _____ plans.
owners	9. Increased interest of (*owners/managers*) in company affairs and the threat
takeover, directors	of a _____ by outsiders or the election of new _____
	encourages managers to align their interests with those of the stockholders.
corporations	10. A view that many large _____ are unscrupulous and antisocial
Galbraith, Nader	has been expressed by _____ and _____.
government	11. Their solution is to impose strict control by _____.
Friedman, Kristol	12. An opposing view offered by _____ and _____
free	places reliance on a _____ marketplace.
society	13. Their position is that _____ is best served when individuals and
corporations, interests	_____ are allowed to serve their own _____ within
	general rules of conduct.
	14. A return to a philosophy of "What's good for General Motors is good for
unlikely	the country" is (*likely/unlikely*).
	15. The action to deregulate the airlines would be applauded by (*Galbraith/*
Friedman	*Friedman*).
share	16. The goal of maximizing (*share/asset*) value is translated to maximizing
earnings, dividends	(*sales/earnings*), which are used to pay _____ and
reinvest	to _____ in the company.
	17. Ethical considerations for the share value maximization objective include a
shareholders,	review of the impacts a decision may have on _____,
employees, customers	_____, _____, and other people.
utilitarianism,	18. When theories or principles of ethics are incorporated into decision making
egalitarianism	_____ and _____ are concerned with the results of
rights, libertarianism	decisions whereas individual _____ and _____ are
	concerned with the reasons or process for making the decisions.

19. While stockholders prefer higher earnings, companies may pass up some

profitable, risk   potentially very _____ projects because the (*return/risk*) is too

great.

long   20. Management is concerned with maximizing share values in the (*short/long*)

daily   run but is not vitally interested in (*daily/yearly*) stock price fluctuations.

raising   21. The duties of the financial manager include _____ funds and

allocating   _____ these moneys to their best use.

Money   22. _____ is often called the lifeblood of a company.

controller   23. The (*controller/treasurer*) of a firm is responsible for maintaining financial

planned   records and identifying deviations from _____ actual perfor-

mance.

treasurer   24. The _____ of a firm is involved in overseeing the firm's cash

planning   and other liquid assets and in short- and long-range financial _____.

Finance   25. _____ is the body of facts, principles, and theories dealing

using, individuals   with the raising and _____ of money by _____,

businesses, governments   _____, and _____.

consumption,   26. Individual financial problems involve decisions of allocating resources be-

investment   tween _____ and _____.

27. A knowledge of financial markets and institutions is necessary to under-

limitations   stand the opportunities, attitudes, and _____ that, in turn, in-

individuals, firms   fluence financial decisions of _____, _____, and

government   _____.

CHAPTER TWO

THE FINANCIAL SYSTEM: DOMESTIC AND INTERNATIONAL

QUINTESSENCE   The well-developed global financial system has played a major role in the achievement of a high standard of living. Transforming savings into investment is accomplished by the creation and transfer of financial assets. The key components in this process are (1) competing institutions (deposit types, insurance firms, and finance companies), (2) markets (primary, secondary, money, and capital), and (3) securities (federal funds; Treasury bills; banker's acceptances; commercial paper; certificates of deposit; corporate, federal, and municipal bonds; mortgage securities; and common stock). Prices of financial assets are determined by interest rates, which, in turn, are influenced by the supply of and demand for funds and the expected inflation rate. Understanding each piece and how and why it fits into the system is important to financial decision making. International financial markets serve savers and users of funds all around the globe. Spot and forward currency exchange rates are determined by the levels of interest rates and inflation in different countries and by governmental policies in each nation.

OUTLINE   I. What

    A. The American financial system consists of the institutions and markets that serve individuals and companies in financing the acquisition of goods and services, in investing capital, and in transferring the ownership of securities.

       1. Money, debt, and stock are the types of financial assets described in this chapter.

       2. The roles of financial institutions, including deposit-type institutions (banks, savings and loans, and credit unions), insurance operations, finance companies, pension funds, and mutual funds, are discussed.

       3. Primary and secondary markets are defined as well as money and capital markets (bond, mortgage, and stock markets).

    B. The level of interest rates is explained in terms of the supply of and demand for loanable funds and the expected rate of inflation.

II. Why

A. A well-developed financial system is essential to a healthy economy.

B. An understanding of the financial environment is of crucial importance to the study of the role and functions of a financial manager.

III. How (Study hint: Because of the large number of terms introduced in this chapter, it would be most helpful to make up a glossary [like that at the end of the text] for review purposes. Use this list to aid in recalling where each of the pieces [terms] fits into the system.)

Financial Assets

A. The financial system provides services to transform savings into investments via the creation and transfer of **financial assets** (these are pieces of paper as opposed to tangible assets such as buildings, trees, and oil wells).

1. Types of financial assets (claims against future income and assets)

    a. **Money** comprises:

    i. Currency and coin issued by the federal government. (Counterfeiters don't help the system, even though they may be creative.)

    ii. Checking accounts, demand deposits, **NOW** and **share draft accounts.**

    b. **Debt** is:

    i. IOUs, or promises to pay specific amounts in the future.

    ii. Issued by everyone—individuals, firms, and governments.

    c. **Stock:**

    i. Is a claim on future income *after* debtholders receive what is owed them.

    ii. Is issued only by business firms.

    iii. Includes **preferred stock,** which is like debt; it has limited claims on future income, but its claims must wait until debtholders have been paid.

    iv. Is mainly **common stock,** which represents ownership of the firm. Stockholders are last in the line for claims on the firm's earnings and assets, but they are entitled to everything that is left over.

2. Creation and transfer of financial assets which are claims against future income and assets

Primary Markets

    a. The origination occurs in **primary markets.**

    i. The most direct method is for a "have-not" (borrower) to give a piece of paper (a financial asset such as a stock or a bond) to a "have" (investor) in exchange for money.

    ii. Funds more typically flow indirectly from savers to users through financial intermediaries.

    iii. The key function of the primary market involves the transfer of money from savers to users.

Secondary Markets

    b. The **secondary markets** are where the buying and selling of previously issued financial assets take place.

i. **Brokers** are go-betweens, bringing savers and users together, like real estate agents.

ii. **Dealers** buy from one party and sell to another, like car dealers.

iii. Primary and secondary markets offer investors a wide range of opportunities to buy and sell, just as the used-car market complements the new-car market. (This is a good analogy; think about it until you have a firm understanding of the separate and yet interdependent roles of the primary and secondary markets.)

Advantage of Financial Institutions

c. Financial intermediaries (**financial institutions**), e.g., banks, help transfer funds by:

i. Collecting money from savers and investing it with users.

ii. Providing *flexibility* by accumulating small amounts into large pools of funds.

iii. Offering opportunities for investors to sell their securities for cash. This gives investors greater *liquidity* since they can sell their securities more easily.

iv. Providing more safety by spreading investments out to many different places (*diversification*). Also, many of the institutions offer government insurance on deposits.

v. Providing *convenience* by offering a variety of financial services—"one-stop shopping."

vi. Offering investment *expertise*—skills and knowledge of full-time professionals—and economies of large-scale operations.

d. Other services of the financial system include insurance, consumer loans, and the monetary system for clearing consumer and business transactions.

B. Financial institutions are of crucial importance to the financial system because they help create the markets for funds.

Deposit Types

1. In the United States, **deposit-type** financial institutions accept deposits from, and lend to, individuals, businesses, and governmental units.

Commercial Banks

a. The 12,000 **commercial banks** are the largest and most diversified type of financial institution.

S and L's

b. **Savings and loan associations** are the second largest group. Most of their funds come from individual deposits. This money is lent back to individuals for real estate needs, i.e., loans for homes and apartments.

Savings Banks

c. **Savings banks** are similar to savings and loans, but they are located mainly in the Northeast. They and the S and L's have become more like banks in recent years.

Credit Unions

d. **Credit unions** outnumber banks, but as a group (18,000) they have the smallest aggregate amount of assets. They concentrate on providing services to individuals, receiving money from some and relending it for consumer credit.

Insurance Firms

2. **Life insurance firms** and **property and casualty companies** collect premiums, in advance, from a large number of people and firms to provide money to pay the smaller number who actually have losses.

    a. Insurance companies invest the premiums mainly in home mortgages and other debt forms.

    b. Most life insurance companies sell policies that have a savings element to build cash values. These plans make this type of company much larger and very similar to deposit-type financial institutions.

Pension Funds

3. **Pension funds** take in money to provide retirement and disability payments for persons in private and government employment. The major investment is in corporate stock, especially for the private pensions.

Mutual Funds

4. **Mutual funds** take in money from individuals and invest it in a diversified list of securities. They sell and buy back their own shares. This repurchase arrangement is unique to this group, so there is no secondary market in mutual fund shares. (Can you think why this is so?) Different funds choose their investments to emphasize current income, growth, tax-free returns, and various combinations and other special objectives. The dominant type of mutual fund was begun in 1974 and is called the **money market fund.** Money market funds invest in short-term, low-risk debt securities.

Finance Companies

5. **Finance companies** raise money by selling securities and borrowing from banks. They make short-term and intermediate-term loans to individuals and businesses.

    a. **Sales finance companies** concentrate on consumer installment loans, especially for cars.

    b. **Personal finance companies** make small loans to individuals.

    c. **Commercial finance companies** make large loans to business firms—particularly those who have high risks.

C. **Financial markets** and **securities** involve virtually every financial transaction. There are two general classes of markets in the United States.

Money Markets

1. **Money market** securities have little or no risk of loss. This means that they must be short-term, typically one year or less, and top-quality securities.

    a. The money market is the link that ties the local and regional money costs (interest rates) together in a national system.

Federal Funds

    b. **Federal funds** are reserves of depository institutions held at the Federal Reserve banks. These deposits can be loaned for very short periods. For example:

        i. Banks with excess reserves lend to banks having shortages.

        ii. These loans are at the federal funds rate, which is a very sensitive indicator of money market conditions.

Treasury Bills	c. **Treasury bills** are short-term (less than one year) debt of the U.S. government.
	   i. They are sold at a discount and redeemed at par value; the difference amounts to interest.
	   ii. Because of their safety (they are backed by the U.S. government and have short maturities), they are the most popular money market security.

Banker's Acceptances	d. **Banker's acceptances** are short-term notes, issued by firms and guaranteed by large banks.
	   i. They typically arise out of foreign trade.
	   ii. They are issued at a discount.

Commercial Paper	e. **Commercial paper** is soft and absorbent and comes in easy-to-tear rolls. Not really! It is short-term IOUs issued at a discount by firms or financial institutions. The equivalent interest rates are above the rates on Treasury bills.
CDs	f. **Negotiable certificates of deposit (CDs)** are large interest-bearing deposits having fixed maturities of typically less than one year.
	g. Other money market securities include soon-to-mature bonds of governments and companies. No hard-and-fast time line separates the money market from the bond market; the distinction is between one and three years.
Capital Markets	2. The **capital markets** are comprised of intermediate- and long-term securities issued by individual firms and governmental units. These markets are subdivided into bonds, mortgages, and stock.

Issuing Securities	a. The securities are "born" in the following ways:
	   i. Most money is raised by the user going *directly* to the sources of funds and borrowing or selling stock.
	   ii. In the **auction** approach, the securities are sold to the highest bidder. For example, the U.S. Treasury sells bills to investors who offer their money at the lowest competitive interest rates.

Investment Banking/ Underwriting	iii. State governments, local governments, and some utilities (e.g., telephone and electric firms) rely heavily on **underwriting through competitive bids.** In this procedure, a group of financial institutions form a **syndicate** to bid on the issue. The winning group actually buys the securities and resells them to investors. Firms specializing in underwriting are called **investment bankers.** iv. Most companies raise funds by going to a particular investment banker for assistance in planning the terms of the offering. This method is called **negotiated underwriting.**
Bonds	b. **Bonds:** i. Are debts of the federal government, state and local governments, and large firms.

Governments

Agencies

Municipals

Industrial
Development

Corporate Bonds

Mortgage Market

       ii. Are issued in units of $1000 or more, with an interest rate that stays the same throughout the life of the bond.

      iii. Offer total yearly interest called the **coupon** rate. Payments are semiannual.

  c. The two groups of **federal** securities are:

       i. **Governments,** which are notes (up to 10-year maturities) and bonds (over 10 years) issued by the U.S. Treasury and guaranteed by the government.

      ii. **Agencies,** which are debt securities issued by federal units to raise money for extending credit, primarily in real estate and agriculture.

  d. **Municipal bonds** (also called **munis** or **tax exempt bonds**) are obligations of various state and local governments. Interest received by investors holding them is not taxable by the federal government, and so these issuers can typically borrow money at the lowest rates.

       i. The most common munis are **general obligation bonds,** which are backed by the taxing power of the issuing governmental body; school bonds are an example.

      ii. Interest and principal payments for **revenue bonds** are paid out of the revenues generated from the project that was built from funds obtained in the original bond sale. For example, revenue bonds are used to raise money to build a turnpike; interest and principal payments are made from the tolls collected.

     iii. **Industrial development bonds** are sold to finance construction of plants that are then rented to firms. The rental payments are used to repay the bonds. This arrangement results in a company's having financed its facilities with low-cost funds since tax exempt bonds were used.

  e. **Corporate bonds** are issued by the larger firms and usually have long maturities.

3. The **mortgage market** has historically been limited to primary market operations.

  a. However, a national secondary market has developed, aided by the following federal agencies, which buy mortgages from financial institutions (banks, savings and loans, etc.) that originally made the loans:

       i. **Federal National Mortgage Corporation,** or Fannie Mae, as it is affectionately called.

      ii. **Government National Mortgage Association** (Ginnie Mae).

     iii. **Federal Home Loan Mortgage Corporation (Freddy Mac).**

  b. **Mortgage companies** act as investment bankers to provide services to borrowers and lenders in the mortgage market.

Stock Market	4. The **stock market** is a secondary market for trading shares among investors (recall that the primary market involves the initial sales of securities to investors).
Exchanges	a. The purpose of **organized exchanges** is to bring together investors who wish to buy and/or sell securities. The New York Stock Exchange dominates the other national exchange (the American Stock Exchange) and the ten regional exchanges.
O-T-C	b. Smaller firms and some large companies that choose not to be listed on an exchange are traded in the **over-the-counter market.**
Interest Rates	D. **Interest rates** are the prices of credit, the cost of money, or the earning rate on financial assets. While different for different financial assets, rates tend to vary together over time.
Loanable Funds	1. The **loanable funds theory** of interest rates is based on fluctuations in the supply of and demand for loanable funds.
	a. The supply of loanable funds comes from the savings of individuals and firms plus any changes in the money supply provided by banks and the Federal Reserve System.
	b. The demand for loanable funds comes from individuals, firms, the federal government, and state and local governments.
	c. Interest rates rise or fall until supply and demand come into balance.
Inflation Effect	2. The expected rate of future **inflation** influences interest rates.
	a. Anticipated high rates of price increases encourage people to spend more. This reduces their savings, which are a part of the supply of funds.
	b. Lenders seek higher rates of return to compensate them for the reduced purchasing power of the dollars they receive when the debt is repaid.
Fisher Equation	i. The **Fisher equation** states that the observed interest rate equals the real interest rate plus the expected rate of inflation.
	ii. The real interest rate is determined by the productivity of investment and individuals' preference for consuming today versus waiting until later.
	iii. Over time, the real interest rate has been about 2 percent.
	c. The result is that interest rates rise as inflationary expectations increase.
International Finance	E. **International financial** markets
	1. Various domestic markets are being integrated together (**globalization**).
	a. Companies, banks, brokers, etc., have worldwide operations.
	b. Funds are raised and used globally.
	2. Money and capital markets

a. Dollar deposits held abroad are called Eurodollars, Asiadollars, etc.

b. Interest rates are often tied to the London interbank offer rate (**LIBOR**).

    i. The specific rates are slightly higher on deposits and lower on loans.

    ii. Loans for longer than one year are Eurocredits; Eurobonds may have fixed or floating rates.

Foreign Exchange

3. Currencies of different countries are bought and sold in **foreign exchange** markets.

a. The exchange rate is the price of one currency in units of another.

b. Rates are determined by supply and demand.

    i. Demand for a currency is created by exports, foreign travel, purchases of securities as well as plant and equipment abroad, speculation that the currency will appreciate, and governmental actions to support the price of its currency.

    ii. Supply is created by the opposite actions such as imports.

    iii. Supply and demand are, in turn, influenced by inflation—countries with higher inflation will have declines in their currency price, by interest rates—higher rates cause currencies to increase in value—and by governmental policies such as tariffs, quotas, foreign exchange restrictions, and political stability.

Spot Rate
Forward Rate

c. The current exchange rate is the **spot rate.**

d. The currency price in the future is the **forward rate** which may be more or less than the spot rate.

F. To review this material, go back and see whether you can identify the meaning and role of each term in the outline printed in bold type. Then reread the first sentence under "What." It should be pregnant with meaning.

COMPLETION QUESTIONS

institutions

markets

1. The American financial system consists of the _____ and _____ that serve individuals and companies.

financial assets

2. Money, debt, and stock are types of _____ _____.

current

3. The financial system provides ways to transfer money saved from (*current/ future*) income to someone who needs funds today.

4. The creation and transfer of financial assets involve the transformation of

savings, investments

_____ into _____.

currency, demand

NOW

5. Money mainly comprises _____, coins, _____ deposits, and _____ accounts.

Debt	6. (*Debt/Stock*) can be issued by everyone, but only corporations can issue
stock	_____.
Preferred stock	7. _____ _____ claims are after debtholders' claims but
common stockholders'	before _____ _____.
primary	8. Financial assets are created in the (*primary/secondary*) market.
savers	9. In this creation process money is transferred from _____ to
users	_____.
Investment bankers	10. _____ _____ assist organizations in raising funds.
Brokers	11. (*Brokers/Dealers*) are intermediaries bringing buyers and sellers together, much like real estate agents.
Dealers	12. (*Brokers/Dealers*) buy securities from one party and sell to another, operating much like Hi Dollar Joe from St. Louis, Mo., the friendly secondhand furniture store.
secondary	13. The analogy of used-car markets applies to the (*primary/secondary*) market.
secondary	14. The activities of brokers and dealers in the _____ markets do
investors	not involve the securities issuers but instead are restricted to (*investors/ dealers*) who trade securities among themselves.
Financial	15. _____ _____ collect money from savers and invest
intermediaries	it with users.
financial	16. Other functions of (*financial/mental*) institutions include accumulating small
safety, convenience	amounts of funds and providing _____, _____, and
liquidity	_____ as well as investment expertise.
commercial	17. Examples of deposit-type financial institutions include (*investment/
savings, loan	commercial*) banks, _____ and _____ associations,
savings banks, credit	mutual _____ _____, and (*labor/credit*) unions.
	18. Two types of financial institutions that collect premiums from a large number
life	of persons to pay losses for a smaller number are _____
insurance, property	_____ and _____ and casualty companies.
Mutual	19. (*Mutual/Federal*) funds offer investors a means of obtaining (*concentration/
diversification	diversification*) and professional management at low cost.
mutual, income	20. The objective of some (*loanable/mutual*) funds is current _____,
capital	while others may stress _____ gains or a combination of these returns.

Money market	21. _____ _____ mutual funds invest in short-term, low-risk securities.
Sales *personal* *commercial*	22. (*Sales/Personal/Business*) finance companies concentrate on car loans; _____ finance companies, on small loans to individuals; and _____ finance companies, on large loans to businesses.
long	23. Capital markets deal in (*short/long*)-term securities.
primary *secondary*	24. Securities are first sold in the (*primary/capital*) market; trading thereafter occurs in the (*money/secondary*) market.
Money, high	25. (*Money/Bond*) market securities are short-term and of (*high/low*) quality.
excess *federal*	26. A bank with (*federal/excess*) reserves can lend them to another bank at the (*mutual/federal*) funds rate.
Treasury bills, discount	27. _____ _____ are sold at a (*premium/discount*) and redeemed at par by the U.S. government.
	28. If ABC, a U.S. firm, wants to import goods, payment might be arranged
a banker's acceptance	through the creation of (*a banker's acceptance/commercial paper*).
Commercial paper *discount, financial*	29. _____ _____ is a short-term IOU issued at a (*premium/discount*) by a firm or (*governmental/financial*) institution.
certificates, deposit *commercial banks*	30. Negotiable _____ of _____ are issued by large (*credit unions/commercial banks*).
debt *capital*	31. All money market securities are types of (*stock/debt*) with maturities of one to three years or less; longer-lived issues are traded in the _____ markets.
directly *investment bankers* *underwriting* *competitive, negotiated*	32. The initial offerings of securities can be sold _____ to investors or to _____ _____ , who buy the issue and resell it to investors. The latter method is known as a(n) _____ and may be done through _____ bids or on a _____ basis.
auction *lowest*	33. U.S. Treasury bills are sold by the (*auction/negotiated*) approach to the bidders willing to accept the (*lowest/highest*) interest rates.
coupon *35, six*	34. If XYZ, Inc., issued a 7 percent (*dividend/coupon*), $1000 par bond, it would probably pay $_____ interest every _____ months.
governments	35. Notes and bonds issued by the U.S. Treasury are called (*governments/agencies*).
	36. Funds for federal programs to finance real estate and agriculture are often
agencies	raised by selling (*agencies/corporates*).

Municipal	37. (*Municipal/Treasury*) bonds are issued by state and local governments. Their
income	unique feature is that investors do not have to pay _____
tax	_____ on the interest they receive.
general obligation	38. School bonds are examples of (*industrial development/general obligation*) munis.
revenue	39. Toll bridges are often built with funds raised through the sale of (*revenue/ agency*) bonds.
	40. Some firms rent plants financed with low-cost funds raised from selling
industrial	(*municipal/industrial*) development bonds.
mortgage	41. An important improvement in the (*stock/mortgage*) market has been the
secondary	development of _____ market operations, which has been pro-
agencies, Fannie	moted by federal _____ having the nicknames of _____
Mae, Freddy Mac	_____ and _____ _____.
	42. Firms acting as investment bankers in the real estate financing area are called
mortgage	_____ bankers.
stock, stock	43. A major separation in the _____ market is organized _____
over-the-counter	exchanges versus the _____ - _____ - _____ market.
	44. The New York Stock Exchange (NYSE) is an example of a (*primary/
secondary	secondary*) market.
loanable, fall	45. According to the (*federal/loanable*) funds theory, a (*rise/fall*) in interest rates would be likely if people and firms decided to reduce their levels of spending relative to their incomes.
demand for	46. A large federal deficit adds to the (*supply of/demand for*) loanable funds.
	47. If a decline in the rate of inflation were forecast, interest rates would probably
fall	(*rise/fall*).
Fisher	48. The (*Schall/Fisher*) equation equates actual interest rates to the real rate plus
inflation	the expected rate of _____.
London	49. LIBOR is the (*Lincoln/London*) interbank offer rate.
	50. If country A's inflation rate was higher than country B's, A's currency
decrease	would (*decrease/increase*) in value.
	51. Crossword puzzle. This puzzle will not appear in *The New York Times*, but it provides a helpful exercise in using the terminology of this chapter. Answers to this and other crossword puzzles are at the back of the *Study Guide*.

ACROSS

2 The amount of annual interest paid on a bond.

8 In some places an individual can obtain a share draft account at a credit ____.

9 This often occurs when interest rates are high.*

11 The market where unlisted securities are traded.

12 ____finance companies lend to car buyers.

13 The market where new issues are offered.

14 All corporations must issue common ____.

15 The amount that will be paid when bonds mature.

17 Bonds are equivalent to a ____from an investor to a user.

18 This causes debtors to suffer.

20 The ____funds theory helps explain interest rate movements.

23 Commercial finance companies concentrate on making large loans to high risk ____.

27 A few companies sell preferred _____.

28 These help finance international trade.

30 ____stock claims are the lowest priority.

32 ____are transferred into investments by financial institutions.

33 These individuals bring buyers and sellers together.

34 The name for checking accounts offered by some S and L's.

35 London interbank offer rate is the _____ rate.

36 A type of municipal bond.

37 ____savings banks.

DOWN

1 These funds provide for an individual's retirement.

3 Bonds issued by state and local governments.

4 The most liquid of all money market instruments.

5 ____institutions offer money as their product.

6 These institutions serve savers and users of funds.

7 ____Reserve System.

9 These people buy from some and sell to others.

10 ____stock claims are senior to common shareholders'.

16 This market deals in short-term securities.

19 These finance companies concentrate on making small loans.

21 The process of guaranteeing funds to a security issuer.

22 These bankers assist organizations in raising funds.

24 Securities are traded between investors in these markets.

25 A short-term IOU issued by the most creditworthy businesses.

26 ____ paper.

29 A special type of revenue bond.

31 Money ____funds.

38 The current foreign exchange rate is the _____ rate.

*The answer is **disintermediation,** a term that is not widely used any longer.*

PROBLEMS

Use the following data for solving problems 1 through 4.

Country	Currency name	Exchange rate, United States dollars
Australia	Dollar	1.2359
Austria	Schilling	0.0540
Britain	Pound	1.7850
Canada	Dollar	1.0286
France	Franc	0.2065
India	Rupee	0.1421
Italy	Lira	0.0007
Japan	Yen	0.0034
Mexico	Peso	0.0800
Netherlands	Guilder	0.3664
South Africa	Rand	1.1483
Spain	Peseta	0.0147
Sweden	Krona	0.2238
Switzerland	Franc	0.4024
West Germany	Deutschemark (mark)	0.3884

1. From the exchange rates given above, calculate the amount of United States dollars received in exchange for each amount of the following currencies:
   a. 10,000 French francs

Solution

Step one To convert currency A into currency B, multiply the units of currency A times the amount of currency B that can be purchased with one unit of currency A.

Step two To convert French francs to United States dollars, multiply the number of francs (10,000) by the dollars per franc (0.2065).

$$10,000 \times \$0.2065 = \$2065$$

   b. 100 rands

Solution   **Step one**

$$100 \times \$1.1483 = \$114.83$$

    c. 1000 deutschemarks

Solution   **Step one**

$$1000 \times \$0.3884 = \$388.40$$

    d. 10,000 krona

Solution   **Step one**

$$10,000 \times \$0.2238 = \$2238$$

    e. 100,000 lira

Solution   **Step one**

$$100,000 \times \$0.0007 = \$70$$

2. Upon returning from a world voyage, you are asked by U.S. customs to declare all foreign goods purchased. You've recorded your purchases as follows:

Item	Cost
Bone china tea set	20 pounds
Sombrero	375 pesos
Black Forest cuckoo clock	193 marks
Sterling souvenir spoon	20 krona
Fancy leather boots	1,700 pesetas

What is the total value in U.S. dollars of your purchases?

Solution

Item	Country	Exchange rate, United States dollars	Cost In local currency	Cost In United States dollars
China	Britain	1.7850	20 pounds	35.70
Sombrero	Mexico	0.0800	375 pesos	30.00
Clock	Germany	0.3884	193 marks	74.96
Spoon	Sweden	0.2238	20 krona	4.48
Boots	Spain	0.0147	1,700 pesetas	24.99
Total				170.13

3. Use the exchange rate table to calculate the following:
   a. How many Spanish pesetas can be purchased for $10 U.S.?

Solution

Step one When the exchange rate is expressed as United States dollars per unit foreign currency and when the conversion is into Spanish pesetas, divide the amount of United States dollars by the exchange rate.

Step two

$$\frac{\$10}{\$0.0147} = 680.27 \text{ pesetas}$$

b. How many Canadian dollars can be acquired for $25 U.S.?

Solution

Step one

$$\frac{\$25}{\$1.0286} = \$24.30 \text{ Can}$$

c. How many South African rands can be acquired for 10 French francs?

Solution

Step one Remember the property of transitivity from grade school math, which states that if $A = B$ and $B = C$, then $A = C$. Using similar reasoning, the French francs (A) are converted into United States dollars (B), and then these United States dollars are converted to South African rands (C) to determine the number of South African rands that can be acquired with 10 French francs.

Step two

$$10 \text{ francs} \times \$0.2065 = \$2.065$$

Step three

$$\frac{\$2.065}{\$1.1483} = 1.7983 \text{ South African rands}$$

d. How many West German marks can be acquired with 20 Netherlands guilders?

Solution

Step one

$$20 \text{ guilders} \times \$0.3664 = \$7.328$$

Step two

$$\frac{\$7.328}{\$0.3884} = 18.8671 \text{ West German marks}$$

4. Compare the exchange rates for January 1989 listed in Table 2-1 in the text with the exchange rates given in the *Study Guide* for the following currencies. If the rates in the *Study Guide* are more recent, determine if the dollar has gone up or down. What effect would this have on the U.S. consumer?
   a. Rupee

Solution

Step one The quote in the text for rupees equaled $0.066 U.S. The later price in the *Study Guide* was $0.1421 U.S.

Step two The rupee had increased in value relative to U.S. dollars. As a result of this change, United States consumers would find that Indian-made products had become more expensive.

   b. Lira

Solution

Step one The lira decreased in value relative to the United States dollar, from $0.00074 to $0.0007.

Step two This would make Italian items cheaper to U.S. consumers.

5. Suppose the following exchange rates in dollars for the British currency were quoted recently:

British pound	1.6770
30-day futures	1.6605
90-day futures	1.6327
180-day futures	1.5972

a. Is the forward rate on the pound at a discount or premium relative to the dollar?

Solution

Step one   The forward rate is at a discount because the pound will buy fewer dollars in the future than at the present, or spot, rate. *End of solution.*

b. Do the exchange rates given indicate a strengthening or weakening of the dollar relative to the pound?

Solution

Step one   Because the pound is worth less in the future than present, the rates indicate that the dollar is strengthening or, to put it another way, that the pound is weakening. *End of solution.*

c. How many pounds would you get 180 days from the present if you purchased that futures contract with $100,000?

Solution

Step one

$$\frac{\$100,000}{\$1.5972} = 62,609.6 \text{ pounds}$$

CHAPTER THREE

THE LEGAL ENVIRONMENT: BUSINESS ORGANIZATION, TAXES, AND BANKRUPTCY

QUINTESSENCE   The form of business organization chosen by the owners of a business affects many aspects of its operation, particularly the way profits are taxed. Proprietorships and partnerships are relatively easy to start and operate, but corporations offer the advantages of limited liability and ease of transferring ownership and raising money. Proprietorships and partnerships pay no income taxes directly since all profits "flow through" to the owners, who then pay the taxes. Corporations pay taxes on earnings, and their owners pay taxes on the part of earnings paid to them in the form of dividends. Taxable income for individuals equals total income less exemptions, deductions, and exclusions. A variety of expenses, including depreciation, are deductible for corporations. Another part of the legal environment impacts when firms experience financial failure. They can then make an adjustment to satisfy the creditors by postponing the claims, by reorganizing, or by liquidating the venture. Settlements can be handled out of court through an extension, a composition, creditor management of the firm, or liquidation. The formal treatment is a bankruptcy proceeding. Multinational corporations set up subsidiaries for operating and tax benefits.

OUTLINE   I. What

    A. Taxes are paid by everyone, but the *amounts* paid are affected by the form of business organization, namely, a **proprietorship,** a **partnership,** or a **corporation.**

    B. Other factors that influence the choice of a type of organization include liability, continuity, transfer of ownership, legal requirements for start-up and operation, and ability to raise money.

    C. Taxes affect investment decisions through the tax rates, depreciation, and treatment of gains and losses.

    D. Firms that fail are either reorganized for another try or liquidated.

    E. There are known causes and specific remedies for failure.

    F. Firms do business abroad through subsidiaries.

II. Why
   A. The need for this chapter is illustrated by a saying of Benjamin Franklin—something about the certainty of death and *taxes*. Everyone must pay, but it is not a sign of patriotism to pay more than what is required. It is prudent to minimize taxes, just like any other cost, using legal means. The principle is tax avoidance, not tax evasion. (Those who can't make this distinction often have an opportunity, at government expense, to reflect on their decisions in the solitude of prison.)
   B. Taxes affect investment decisions. Income taxes on companies and individuals, as well as special provisions such as depreciation and the treatment of gains and losses, are key factors in the analysis of investment proposals.
   C. Things don't always go as expected, which can result in business failure.
   D. The financial manager must be able to recognize impending disaster and take appropriate actions if the firm is in trouble or to protect the interests of the firm if it is an investor in a failing company.
   E. International trade is becoming more important all the time.

III. How
   A. Types of business organizations

Proprietorship

   1. A **proprietorship:**
      a. Is owned by one person.
      b. Is the most popular form (71 percent of all businesses) because it is easiest to start and runs with the least governmental regulation, but it dissolves when one partner leaves or dies.
      c. Is considered one and the same with the owner's personal life for income tax and liability purposes. For example, profits from the business are taxed as personal income of the owner, and debts of the business are considered personal debts.

Partnership

   2. A **partnership:**
      a. Is owned by two or more people.
      b. Is easy to establish after the partners agree on their shares of time, money, etc. It operates under relatively little government regulation.
      c. May be a **general partnership,** in which each partner is responsible for debts of the business. A **limited partnership** has at least one general partner; the others have a liability that is **limited** to their investment in the operation.

Corporations

   3. **Corporations** are the most important type of organization, accounting for 90 percent of the revenues, and yet they constitute only 19 percent of the number of businesses.
      a. The corporation is an entity separate from its owners (called **shareholders** or **stockholders**). It is a legal "person" with advantages over proprietorships and partnerships:
         i. The liability of owners is limited to their investment in the

business. For example, if a company goes bankrupt, stock-holders won't have to cough up any cash.

      ii. The corporation has an unlimited life.

     iii. It is easy to transfer ownership; in a proprietorship or part-nership, the death of an owner or a need to sell out threatens the continuation of the operation.

   b. Corporations are started by seeking a charter from a state. By-laws and other documents specify operating rules for such items as shareholder rights and election of directors.

   c. Corporations pay income taxes, as their owners do. Proprietor-ships and partnerships don't pay these taxes, but their owners do.

Taxes

B. **Federal income taxes** are the major revenue for the federal government.

  1. The tax is figured as percentage of taxable income (gross income less exemptions and deductions).

   a. State and local income taxes follow patterns similar to the federal provisions.

   b. The Sixteenth Amendment authorized taxation of incomes (this woeful beginning was, with minor exceptions, in 1913).

   c. Taxpayers may contest rules of the IRS in the Tax Court.

Individuals

  2. **Individual income taxes**

   a. Interest received from securities issued by state and local gov-ernments (municipal bonds), life insurance proceeds, and all but large gifts are not counted as taxable income.

   b. Business and personal deductions, in addition to the $2000 in-dividual exemption, reduce taxable income. Examples of per-sonal deductions include:

      i. Interest on home mortgages.

     ii. Property taxes.

     iii. Charitable contributions.

   c. As an alternative individuals can take a standard deduction of $3100 in 1989.

   d. The amount of the standard deduction and individual exemption is indexed to inflation.

Capital Gains

   e. **All capital gains,** regardless of whether they are categorized as short-term (one year or less) or long-term, are added to gross income. They result from buy-low, sell-high events (these are happy occasions).

   f. The tax rate is *progressive* up to 28 percent and depends on marital status. (A 5 percent surtax allows a marginal rate of 33 percent, but the average tax rate will not exceed 28 percent.)

Alternative Minimum Tax

   g. All taxpayers are subject to an **alternative minimum tax** (AMT). This prevents using "tax preferences" to reduce taxes below a certain point.

   h. In many cases owners of small businesses that are incorporated can elect to be taxed as a partnership or as a proprietorship (one owner). Unless income is small and the owners are in high tax brackets, the corporation is not a tax minimizing form of organization.

3. The **corporate income tax**

Corporations Marginal Tax Rates

    a. It is figured as 15 percent of the first $50,000 of taxable income, 25 percent of the next $25,000, and 34 percent of amounts in excess of $75,000.

    b. A 5 percent surtax (total of 39 percent) is applied to taxable incomes between $100,000 and $335,000. For incomes in this range, the average tax rate is below 34 percent.

    c. The marginal rate and average rate for companies earning over $335,000 is 34 percent.

    d. Corporate taxes are paid each quarter on a current basis.

Alternative Minimum Tax

    e. In a manner similar to individuals, corporations are subject to an **alternative minimum tax**. This keeps tax payments from being reduced too far as the result of favored income (municipal bond interest) or special deductions (depreciation and depletion).

Capital Gains

    f. All **capital gains** are added to taxable income.

    g. Taxable income equals revenues less expenses, just as in the case of individual taxes.

       i. Interest received on municipal bonds is not included in revenues.

Dividends

       ii. Taxes on intercorporate dividends depend on the amount of ownership which the receiving company has in the paying company.

         (a) If 20 percent or less, 30 percent of the dividends received are taxable.

         (b) If more than 20 percent but less than 80 percent, only 20 percent of dividends received are taxable.

         (c) No tax on dividends received is due if the receiving firm owns 80 percent or more of the paying firm. (See problem 2 at the end of this chapter for an illustration.)

Business Losses

       iii. Expenses include **carryforward** of losses from fifteen years and **carryback** of current losses for three years. Losses must be deducted, to the extent possible, from the earliest year first, and then remaining losses are applied to each succeeding year.

4. Tax factors in business investment decisions

Depreciation

    a. **Depreciation** is the allocation of the cost of an asset, spread over time. (**Economic depreciation** is the decrease in the *market value* of an asset over time, but this is not of concern for tax purposes.)

       i. It is deductible from taxable income.

ACRS

ii. The Economic Recovery Tax Act of 1981, including the changes in 1986, calls depreciation "cost recovery" and prescribes it by the **Accelerated Cost Recovery System (ACRS).** This divides personal property into six classes (e.g., three years for racehorses, five years for vehicles and computers, and fifteen years for some utilities). A table specifies the allowable percentage of cost for deduction purposes. The factors of salvage value and expected useful life used in the old depreciation system are ignored in ACRS. Real estate has a separate table for percentage deductions. Taxpayers have the choice of using ACRS or straight-line depreciation.

Accelerated Depreciation

iii. Optional methods for computing depreciation include **straight-line, 200 percent declining balance,** and **sum-of-the-years'-digits;** the latter two procedures are **accelerated** methods, which means higher depreciation in the early years with decreasing amounts in later years. While the total depreciation is the same under all methods, the accelerated forms benefit a firm because the higher charges in early years mean lower taxes. Later the expense is lower, and so taxes will be higher. This pattern amounts to deferring, or postponing, the tax bill, which is a pretty good deal—if you can ever call paying taxes a good deal. (Detailed calculations showing the different methods are in Appendix 3A of the textbook.)

Gains/Losses on Assets

b. Gains or losses may be realized when depreciable assets are sold.

i. All or part of some gains may be treated as long-term, and may be taxed at low rates. Losses can be used to offset ordinary income. This means low rates for gains and high rates of deductions for losses, which is a pretty good arrangement.

ii. When personal property (anything but real estate) held for more than one year is sold for more than book value (cost minus depreciation or the ACRS), the gain is treated as ordinary income. Any amount received above the original cost is a long-term capital gain. When the asset is sold for less than its book value, the difference is deductible from ordinary income.

iii. For nonresidential real estate, all of the gain becomes a capital gain or all of the loss is deductible from ordinary income if straight-line depreciation has been used. If accelerated depreciation has been applied in determining book value, the treatment will be the same as for personal property as described in part *ii* above.

iv. For residential real estate all of the gain is a capital gain if straight-line depreciation was used. However, if accelerated depreciation was used, only part of the gain is a capital gain; the balance is treated as ordinary income (see footnote 13 in the textbook).

    v. Losses on any real estate that has been used for business purposes are deductible from ordinary taxable income.

    vi. For all real property acquired after 1986, depreciation must be straight-line.

C. There are two types of failure:

Economic Failure

    1. An **economic failure** occurs when a firm cannot be operated profitably even if it had proper management and had no debts.

Financial Failure

    2. **Financial** or **contractual failure** (these are interchangeable terms) occurs when a firm breaks its contractual promises made to its creditors.

Liquidation

    3. Whenever a firm is "worth more dead than alive," **liquidation** is justified. This is an economic failure even though it may not be a contractual failure. A firm failing in both respects should be dissolved and liquidated.

A New Start

    4. A company that is a financial failure but not an economic failure may be given another chance at life through a voluntary **adjustment** or under a **reorganization.**

Bankruptcy

    5. Contractual failure leads to **bankruptcy.**

        a. Assets are liquidated to pay creditors, or

        b. An **arrangement** or reorganization is made to keep the firm going.

    6. Failures are most frequent:

        a. Among newer firms.

        b. Among smaller firms.

        c. In periods of recession and depression.

    7. Causes of failure:

        a. Inability to effectively promote and sell enough of the product.

        b. Poor collection and expense controls.

        c. Recessions, high interest rates, and a liberalized bankruptcy law. Since 1978, these three causes have contributed to a sharp increase in failures.

Voluntary Remedies

D. Bankruptcy can be averted by *voluntary* agreements between the firm and its creditors.

    1. Any one of the creditors can hold out and force bankruptcy.

    2. Small claims are often paid off to get them out of the way.

    3. Solutions to the financial distress of the firm are:

Extension

        a. An **extension,** whereby creditors *postpone* payments due them. This gives the company some time to work its way out of the hole it is in.

Composition

        b. A **composition,** in which creditors agree to accept less than their claim because under a liquidation they expect to receive even less. To help attain creditor cooperation, security may be pledged.

c. A committee of the creditors may temporarily take over the firm. The **creditor management** hopes to get the business back on the right track.

E. The **Bankruptcy Code** provides for **reorganizations** and **liquidations** for individuals and businesses.
   1. Under Chapter 11 of the code, the court supervises adjustments to keep the firm going.
      a. Debt claims are classified and satisfied by making partial payments now and perhaps more later.
      b. When the company is **insolvent** (not paying its debts as they become due), a custodian takes charge of the property.
      c. A plan for solving the financial distress is filed, and everyone is bound to this plan if it has been adopted by a two-thirds vote of each class of claimholders.
   2. Chapter 13 provides a remedy for *small businesses* to repay up to $100,000 in unsecured claims and $350,000 or less in secured claims within 36 months.

   3. When a **reorganization** plan under Chapter 11 is being evaluated, the crucial issue is whether it is really worthwhile to give the firm another chance. The test is to determine whether the value as a going concern exceeds the liquidation value.
      a. New securities are issued to reduce the debt burden so that the firm can operate for a while.
      b. Stockholders and perhaps unsecured creditors are left out in the cold.
      c. The firm must honor senior claims in full before junior claims receive anything.
      d. The decision to accept a reorganization plan or to liquidate is based on an evaluation of the alternatives by the courts, the security holders, and perhaps the SEC.
         i. Future revenues and costs are forecast to estimate the likelihood that the company can become an economic success.
         ii. If the firm is thought to be "worth more alive than dead," it should be reorganized; if not, it should be liquidated.

F. A **liquidation** occurs in one of two procedures:

   1. A **nonjudicial liquidation** is a private (out-of-court) settlement.
      a. The creditors select a trustee to:
         i. Sell the assets.
         ii. Distribute the proceeds.
      b. *All* creditors must agree to the terms.
         i. The absolute priority rule is usually followed.
         ii. Only cash payments are made. No securities are involved, as in a reorganization.
      c. This procedure, compared with a court-supervised demise, is less costly in terms of:

Bankruptcy

　　　　　　　　　　　i. Legal and accounting expenses.

　　　　　　　　　　　ii. Time.

　　　　　2. Liquidation under **bankruptcy** (Chapter 7 of the Code) can be *voluntary* if the firm files the petition or *involuntary* if the creditors file—either way, the following steps are taken:

　　　　　　a. A referee is appointed by the court to oversee the proceeding.

　　　　　　b. The creditors meet to:

　　　　　　　　i. Prove their claims.

　　　　　　　　ii. Elect a trustee to liquidate the assets and distribute the cash.

　　　　　　c. The priority of claims is established according to the following criteria:

　　　　　　　　i. Expenses for bankruptcy.

　　　　　　　　ii. Certain payments to company employees and their benefit plans.

　　　　　　　　iii. Small consumer claims.

　　　　　　　　iv. Taxes due.

　　　　　　　　v. Secured and unsecured creditor claims in order of priority. (See the problems at the end of the chapter for an illustration of the ordering process.)

　　　　　　　　vi. Preferred stockholder dividends.

　　　　　　　　vii. Last and least, the residual people, the common stockholders.

　　　G. The chart below summarizes the treatment of failure problems:

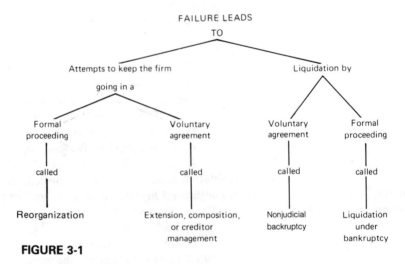

FIGURE 3-1

Multinational Corporation

　　H. The international legal environment and the **multinational corporation** (MNC)

　　　　　1. The MNC sets up subsidiaries in different countries to:

　　　　　　a. Avoid government imposed tariffs and trade sanctions that would apply to exporting and importing.

b. Allow sharing of technical and managerial expertise.

c. Take advantage of tax law differences.

2. Tax considerations include:

a. Income earned abroad through branch operations is taxed in the home country but not if a subsidiary was doing the business in the foreign country.

Foreign Tax Credit

b. The **foreign tax credit** (FTC) helps to keep the MNC from being taxed twice, i.e., a tax credit in the United States is given for every dollar paid abroad.

c. The IRS seeks to prevent MNCs from shifting profits to lower tax rate countries by using unjustified transfer prices.

COMPLETION QUESTIONS

corporations, propri-etorships, partnerships

1. Three major forms of business organizations are _____, _____ , and _____.

proprietorship, cor-poration, partnership

2. A _____ or a _____ can be owned by one person, but at least two people must own a _____.

limited, general

liable

3. A (*limited/general*) partnership must have at least one (*limited/general*) partner, who is _____ for any debts of the firm.

Corporations

4. _____ account for the vast majority of business sales even though this form represents a small minority of the number of organizations.

$2000

5. If Lisa bought 100 shares of General Motors stock for $20 per share, the most she could lose if GM went bankrupt would be _____.

unlimited

6. If Bill paid $10,000 to become a general partner in an organization, his personal liability would be _____.

corporation

7. The owners in a (*partnership/corporation*) will normally find it easier to sell their interest, compared with the owners of a business organized as a (*partnership/corporation*).

partnership

corporation

8. The form of business having the greatest number of restrictions is the (*corporation/proprietorship*).

corporation

9. The _____ is favored over other types of organizations when the ease of raising money is considered.

proprietorships, partnerships

10. Neither _____ nor _____ pay income taxes, but their owners do.

average

34

11. The maximum (*marginal/average*) federal income tax for corporations is (*34/50*) percent.

municipal	12. Interest received by either companies or individuals on (*municipal/ corporate*) bonds is tax exempt.
20	13. If one company received $100 of dividends on the stock it held in another U.S. corporation in which it owns 60 percent, $_____ would be taxable.
three	14. Corporation losses can be carried back _____ years and forward
fifteen	_____ years.
higher	15. The individual income tax is progressive, which means the _____ the taxable income, the higher the tax rate.
28	16. For individuals the maximum average federal income tax rate is _____ percent.
corporation	17. Owners of a small unincorporated business who wish to retain profits for expansion would likely choose to be taxed as a (*partnership/corporation*).
cost recovery	18. Depreciation, which is also called _____ _____, is
cost	an allocation of the (*cost/current market value*) of the asset spread over its class life.
Accelerated	19. The amount of depreciation on personal property is figured as a percentage specified in the _____ Cost Recovery System.
larger	20. In accelerated depreciation, the total amount is unchanged, but the annual amounts are (*smaller/larger*) at the beginning.
lower	21. Accelerated depreciation makes it possible to postpone taxes because taxable income is (*lower/higher*) in early years.
minimum	22. An alternative (*maximum/minimum*) tax applies to individuals as well as to companies.
transfer	23. Multinational corporations have an incentive to set _____ prices so as to minimize income taxes.
economic, financial	24. Failure can be _____ or (*financial/no-fault*).
economic	25. Earning a fair rate of return, even if the firm had proper management and no debt obligations, is considered necessary to avoid being a(n) (*economic/ financial*) failure.
financial	26. Missing a sinking fund payment would be a cause of (*economic/financial*) failure.
liquidation	27. When a firm is worth more dead than alive, (*liquidation/reorganization*) is justified.

sales	28. A major cause of failure is insufficient (*sales/employment*).
Insolvency	29. _____ occurs when liabilities exceed assets.
reorganization	30. When a company is worth more alive than dead, _____ or a voluntary agreement is justified to keep the firm going.
financial	31. Another term for a contractual failure is _____ failure.
newer, smaller	32. Failures are most frequent among (*newer/older*) and (*smaller/larger*) firms.
expansion	33. Failures are less frequent in periods of (*expansion/recession*).
easier	34. Since 1978, bankruptcy has become (*easier/less easy*) to obtain through the courts.
voluntary	35. Bankruptcy proceedings can be avoided by _____ agreements
creditors	by the (*creditors/stockholders*).
extension	36. In a(n) (*extension/liquidation*), payments to creditors are postponed.
composition	37. In a(n) (*assignment/composition*) creditors accept a fraction of their claim and, often, promissory notes on the remainder.
creditors	38. The third alternative to a private proceeding to help keep the firm going is to have the (*creditors/stockholders*) take over the management of the company.
is	39. In a formal bankruptcy proceeding the plan adopted (*is/is not*) binding to all parties.
advises on	40. The Securities and Exchange Commission (*advises on/approves*) reorganization plans for large bankruptcies.
going-concern	41. The decision to stay alive or to liquidate is influenced by a comparison of (*going-concern/book*) value with liquidation value.
absolute	42. The rule of (*relative/absolute*) priority forces the honoring of senior claims completely before any payments are made to junior creditors.
nonjudicial	43. A(n) _____ liquidation occurs in a private voluntary settlement.
voluntary	44. Bankruptcy can be initiated by the stockholders in a (*voluntary/involuntary*) filing.
common	45. Last on the list of priorities for claims are the _____
stockholders	_____.

PROBLEMS

1. Jennifer purchased 100 shares of ABC common stock 10 months ago for $2500. She has received one dividend of $0.50 per share. Her income tax rate is 28 percent. Ignoring commissions:

a. How much tax would she pay if she sold her stock today for $30 per share?

Solution

Step one   The gain on her transaction would be short-term since she owned the stock for less than one year.

She receives	$30 × 100, or $3,000
She paid	2,500
Her capital gain is	$ 500

which is taxable at ordinary income rates.

Step two   The dividend of $0.50 × 100, or $50, would also be taxed as ordinary income.

Step three   Her tax would be $0.28 × (\$500 + \$50) = \$154$.

b. What would her tax be if she waited three more months to sell the stock for $30 per share and if no additional dividends were received?

Solution

Step one   In this case she has owned the stock for at least one year, so it would be a long-term capital gain. However, the tax would be the same as for short-term gains because the preferential treatment was eliminated by the Tax Reform Act of 1986. Therefore, the tax due is $154. *End of solution.*

c. How much more tax would Jennifer pay if she had received $200 in interest from state of Vermont bonds?

Solution

Step one   None: These are municipal bonds; owners pay *no* taxes on interest received from municipal bonds. *End of solution.*

2. MNO, Inc., a hat manufacturer, has taxable income from operations of $80,000.
   a. What is the federal income tax due?

Solution

Fifteen percent of the first $50,000,	or .15 × $50,000 = $ 7,500
plus 25 percent on the next $25,000,	or .25 × $25,000 = 6,250
plus 34 percent on the remainder,	or .34 × $5,000 = 1,700
	Total tax = $15,450

   b. If MNO also received $125,000 of dividends from stock it owned in XYZ, Ltd., how much in taxes would MNO pay if MNO owns 75 percent of XYZ's stock?

Solution

Step one   Taxes due on dividends received by one corporation from another depend on the share of the paying company's stock that is held by the receiving company. Since MNO owns 75 percent of XYZ, it pays tax on 20 percent of the dividends received.

Step two   This means that only $25,000 (20 percent of $125,000) is taxable, and so the total taxable income is $105,000.

Step three   The tax on $80,000 (from part *a*) is $15,450. The marginal tax (remember that term?) on the next $20,000 is 34 percent, or $6800. The marginal tax rate on the next $5000 is 39 percent, or a tax of $1950. The total tax is $24,200.

3. Helena's Health Foods, Inc., experienced a disastrous year in 1991. The preceding four years' operating results (all figures are in thousands of dollars) were:

	1987	1988	1989	1990	1991
Taxable income	25	50	55	0	(200)
Tax	3.75	8.25	9.75	0	0

The firm can file amended returns to account for the loss carryback and carryforward provision. What would be the result?

Solution

Step one Losses can be carried back three years and forward fifteen years.

Step two The loss must be applied to the earliest year first and then to each subsequent year until it has been exhausted.

Step three Compute taxes on reported income in the years 1987 to 1989 and compare your figures with the reported tax to check your understanding of this procedure.

Step four Applying these steps will produce the following amendments to previously filed tax returns:

	Reported				
	1987	1988	1989	1990	1991
Taxable income	25	50	55	0	(200)
Tax	3.75	8.25	9.75	0	0

	Restated				
	1987	1988	1989	1990	1991
Adjusted taxable income	25	0	0	0	(95)
Tax due	3.75	0	0	0	0
Less amount actually paid	3.75	8.25	9.75	0	0
Equals tax rebate (to be returned)	0	8.25	9.75	0	0

Step five The 1987 return will not be amended because the 1991 loss can be carried back only to 1988, even though 1990 had zero taxable income.

Step six The company can apply $95,000 in losses to taxable income for 1992 through 2006. In other words, its next $95,000 of taxable income will be tax-free.

4. MATT Airlines purchased an airplane four years ago for $21 million. It was expected to last ten years and be worth $1 million at that point.

a. What would be the annual depreciation charges using the straight-line method?

Solution

Step one   Straight-line depreciation equals the difference between initial cost and salvage value, divided by the asset life, or ($21 − $1)/10, which equals $2 million per year. *End of solution.*

b. Suppose the plane could be sold for $15 million today. What would be the net amount received if the effective tax rate to the company is 34 percent?

Solution

Step one   The book value of the plane after four years of depreciation would be $21 − (4 × $2) = $13 million.

Step two   Since the market price is above book value, the company must pay income taxes on the difference: tax = ($15 − $13)0.34, or $0.68 million.

Step three   In effect, this is like saying that the company has depreciated its plane too fast; i.e., the excess depreciation charges of $2 million have resulted in the firm's underpaying its taxes by $680,000. This must be paid when the plane is sold.

Step four   The net proceeds on the sale would be $15,000,000 − $680,000, or $14,320,000.

Step five   If the company had received more than the original cost, it would have had to pay two types of tax: regular income tax on the difference between original cost and book value and capital gains tax on the excess of selling price over original cost.

c. What would have been the book value of the plane after two years of ownership using 200 percent declining balance depreciation?

Solution

Step one   Depreciation under this method is twice the rate of straight-line. With a 10-year life the straight-line rate each year is 1/10, or 10 percent.

Step two   200 percent of that rate is 20 percent. This rate is applied to the book value of the beginning of each year.

Step three   The first-year depreciation would be 20 percent of $21 million, or $4.2 million. Notice salvage value is ignored.

Step four   The depreciation in year two would be 20 percent of ($21 − $4.2), or $3.36 million, leaving a book value of $16.8 − $3.36, or $13.44 million.

5. Edith, Maria, and Pan are planning to open a paint and wallpaper store that they estimate will return $60,000 before taxes per year. Each of them will be in the 28 percent tax bracket.
   a. Which form of organization should the women select to minimize their taxes?

Solution

Step one   If the business were taxed as a partnership, each of them would pay 1/3 × $60,000 × 0.28 = $5600, or total taxes of $16,800.

Step two   Taxes to a corporation would be

$$0.15 \times \$50,000 = \$\ 7,500$$
$$0.34 \times \$10,000 = \underline{\quad 3,400}$$
$$\text{Total tax} \quad = \$10,900$$

In addition, the owners would pay taxes on any dividends the firm paid, so if 50 percent of the earnings were retained for expansion purposes and the rest were paid as dividends, the women would pay additional taxes of $0.28 \times \$30,000 = \$8400$. The total tax under the corporate form would then be $\$10,000 + \$8400 = \$18,400$.

Step three If the individuals were in higher personal tax brackets, the tax advantage of the partnership would be less or none at all. Thus, if the women had substantial outside income or if the business generated significantly higher profits, the corporation form might minimize taxes.

Step four A major advantage of the corporate form is the limited liability feature. For the smaller operation this benefit might outweigh the additional tax cost. Recall the subchapter S provision, which allows owners of some small businesses to form a corporation and elect to be taxed as a partnership (or vice versa). This might be the best choice for the women—they could have their cake and eat it too.

b. How would the decision concerning organizational form be affected if each owner was in a different tax bracket?

Solution

Step one It would make the choice more difficult because the corporate form might minimize taxes for one owner; the partnership would be favored by another (the woman in the lowest tax bracket).

Step two The situation could be resolved by adjusting compensation to the owners so that their *aftertax* earnings would be what they each deserved.

6. Tried Hard, Inc., is in bankruptcy. Apply the rule of absolute priority in determining the amounts paid if the firm were liquidated for $12.5 million as opposed to $25 million. The subordinated debentures are junior to the bank loan. The balance sheet, at the time of bankruptcy, is presented below (figures are in millions of dollars).

Assets	Liabilities	
$50	Accounts payable	$ 5
	Bank loan	5
	Subordinated debs.	15
	Stockholder equity	25

Solution

Step one   The claims of each group of creditors are based on their percentage of the total liabilities *plus* adjustment for the subordination provision.

Step two   The stockholders will receive nothing so long as any of the creditors have unsatisfied claims.

Step three   The amounts received by each creditor group, according to the two different proceeds, are as follows (figures are in millions of dollars):

Type of credit	Amount of claim		Payments if $12.5 million is available		Payments if $25 million is available	
	$	%	Without subordination	With subordination	Without subordination	With subordination
Accounts payable	5	20	2.5	2.5	5	5
Bank loan	5	20	2.5	5.0	5	5
Subordinated debentures	15	60	7.5	5.0	15	15

Step four   Notice that if there is not enough to go around, the subordination provision is most helpful to the bank. If the assets are sold for $12.5 million, the accounts payable creditors receive 50 percent of their claims, the debenture holders receive 33 percent, and the bank receives 100 percent.

7. A proposal to reorganize NEVRFALE Company, which is in a bankruptcy proceeding, has been offered that the judge feels is *fair* and *equitable*. The expected income before interest and taxes is at least $500,000 annually, and the capital of the reorganized firm is as follows:

Bank loans (9%)	$1 million
Subordinated debt (11%)	$3 million
Common stock	$1 million

Do you think this is a *feasible* plan?

Solution

Step one The interest payments would be:

Bank loan: $1 × 0.09 = $0.09, or $90,000

Subordinated debt: $3 × 0.11 = $0.33, or $330,000

Step two These fixed payments amount to $420,000 for a coverage of 1.2 (500/420). This does not allow for any repayments of the debt, and so the earning power in relation to the debt service costs seems inadequate.

Step three The other test of adequacy relates to the debt-equity ratio, which is 4 (4/1). This is quite high. If the assets shrink by 20 percent, the debt principal would be impaired. Thus the asset protection is minimal at best and raises a further question as to the feasibility of the reorganization plan.

8. Success, Limited, has failed and is in bankruptcy. It owes $2 million in income taxes from prior years, and the fees for the liquidation proceedings are estimated to be $1 million. The company has $9 million in cash, and its other assets, which are covered by an $11 million mortgage loan, are being sold for $9 million. The claims of general creditors amount to $8 million. How would the proceeds from the liquidation be distributed?

Solution

Step one The proceeds will be $18 million—$9 million from the sale of the property and the $9 million in cash.

Step two Expenses associated with the bankruptcy are paid first, and so this would leave $17 million (18 − 1).

Step three The next priority claim is for back taxes, which leaves $15 million (17 − 2).

Step four The holders of the mortgage loan would receive $9 million, and their remaining claim of $2 million (11 − 9) would be included with those of the other creditors.

Step five The amount left now is $6 million (15 − 9). This is to be apportioned to the remaining claims of $10 million (2 + 8); the mortgage loan creditors will receive $1.2 million ($\frac{2}{10}$ × 6) and the general creditors will receive $4.8 million ($\frac{8}{10}$ × 6).

CHAPTER FOUR

THE TIME VALUE OF MONEY

QUINTESSENCE   Money (cash flow) must be recognized not only in terms of the amounts involved but also in terms of *when* these dollars occur. A dollar received today is not the same as a dollar received two years in the future because money can be put to work to earn a return. This is related to the price of credit, or interest rate. The ability to convert cash flows in different time periods to a common denominator is one of the most important skills taught in finance. Calculating the equivalent amounts of funds that occur at different time periods enables one to solve a variety of cost-benefit problems in business and in personal life, e.g., return on investment and home purchase (mortgage) loans.

OUTLINE
    I. What
        A. Money has a time value. The sooner it is received, the better.
        B. This chapter teaches how to compare money at different time periods by using calculations involving interest rates. In essence, the procedure converts oranges to apples so as to be able to make *valid* comparisons between apples and apples.
        C. Annuities
    II. Why
        A. Money received today can be invested to earn a return so that more will be available later.
        B. The other side of the coin is this: Money borrowed today must be repaid with a larger amount in the future.
        C. The reason why money has an earning power and why more must be repaid than is borrowed is the existence of a charge for the use of money, which is called the **interest rate.**
    III. How
        A. **Compound interest**

Compounding
           1. Growth begins with a present or initial amount P, expands at an interest rate i, for a period of time n, to yield a future amount F, according to the formula

$$F = P(1 + i)^n \qquad (4\text{-}1)$$

45

2. The columns headed "*F/P*" in the tables in Appendix 4A of the text list solutions for *F* given *i* and *n* when *P* = $1. This is a very *useful tabulation:*

    a. When *P* is not $1, multiply the table value for *F* by the actual amount *P* to get the appropriate compound future value.

    b. Any combination of three variables—for example, *P, F,* and *i*—can be used to solve for the fourth variable, in this case *n*.

    c. Time periods vary, and the corresponding interest rate will be for days, months, quarters, years, or whatever other interval is chosen.

Rule of 72

3. You could astound your friends by memorizing the tables in Appendix A. This really isn't very practical, but you could amaze them a little by learning the **rule of 72,** which states that the number of years required for a sum to double equals 72 divided by the growth rate.

    a. In effect you would then have memorized a part of the tables.

    b. Check this out by seeing that the *F/P* column values closest to 2 are in locations where the product of the row and the interest rate is approximately 72.

Present Value

B. **Present value**

1. This is simply the inverse of compound amount. (Note that "value" and "amount" are interchangeable terms, as are "compound" and "future.") Solving Eq. (4-1) for *P* gives

$$P = F\frac{1}{(1 + i)^n} \tag{4-2}$$

2. The columns headed "*P/F*" in Appendix 4A present solutions for *P* in a manner similar to the values of *F* listed in the columns headed "*F/P*." Check corresponding numbers in these two columns to prove that one column is the reciprocal of the other. Go ahead; it'll take only a few minutes. It's important to appreciate the relationship of these factors since you can use *either* one in solving problems *if* you are careful to choose between multiplying and dividing.

3. The shorthand notation for the factor developed is:

    a. (*F/P, i, n*). The slash (/) can be read as "from," and so the expression means "future value from present value, given *i* and *n*."

    b. (*P/F, i, n*) reads "present value from future value, given *i* and *n*."

Annuity Factors

C. **Annuities**

1. Two requirements must be met:

    a. The cash flows must occur at regular (uninterrupted) intervals.

    b. The cash flows must be equal in amount.

Compound Amount

2. When these conditions exist, it is easier and faster to solve problems by using four other columns in the tables in Appendix 4A.
   a. **Annuity compound amount factor**
      i. This tells the sum that a regularly occurring deposit, beginning one year from today, of $1 will grow to, up to and including the last deposit.
      ii. $(F/A, i, n)$ means "future value from an annuity, given the interest rate and the number of periods."
      iii. Multiply the actual amount by the F/A factor to determine the cumulative balance.
      iv. The factor can help solve problems such as "How much can be accumulated if one saves a fixed amount on a regular basis?" (Ads for IRAs use this calculation.)

Sinking Fund

   b. **Sinking fund factor**
      i. This is the reciprocal of the F/A factor and is expressed as $(A/F, i, n)$.
      ii. It is the annuity needed to accumulate to a future value of $1.
      iii. For future values other than $1, multiply the A/F factor by the future value amount.
      iv. The sinking fund factor is used to find out how much must be set aside regularly in order to build up to a certain goal. (This would determine how much should be saved each month to provide a target amount for retirement.)

Present Value

   c. **Annuity present value factor**
      i. This tells the amount of today's dollars (present value) that is equivalent to an annuity of $1.
      ii. $(P/A, i, n)$ means "present value from an annuity of $1, given an interest rate and the number of periods."
      iii. For an annuity of other than $1, multiply the actual amount by the P/A factor.
      iv. This factor is used to compute the total sum needed today in order to yield a specified amount for each of a certain number of periods. (One can determine how much it would cost to buy an annuity.)

Capital Recovery

   d. **Capital recovery,** or **loan repayment, factor**
      i. This is the inverse of the P/A factor and is expressed as $(A/P, i, n)$.
      ii. It is the annuity with a present value of $1. This future amount can be considered a capital investment being recovered or a loan being repaid.
      iii. For annuities other than $1, multiply the A/P factor by the actual amount.
      iv. The loan repayment factor is used to determine how much must be paid periodically in order to retire a certain amount

of debt. (Use this factor to calculate mortgage payments required to buy a house.)

Perpetual

e. **Perpetual annuities**

   i. The cash flows are expected to continue indefinitely.

   ii. The present value of a stream of payments to be received forever is obtained by dividing the payment by the interest rate. Thus

$$P = \frac{A}{i} \qquad (4\text{-}3)$$

   iii. This means that a bank could offer to pay you $10 per year forever if you deposited $200 today and the bank could earn 5 percent because

$$\frac{\$10}{0.05} = \$200$$

Think about that: you and your heirs would receive an *infinite* amount for a mere $200!

Summary

D. Summary of interest factors

  1. In the table below remember to read the slash (/) as "from":

Time period	Type of cash flow		
	Single payment	Annuity with amount known	Annuity with amount unknown
Future	F/P	F/A	A/F
Present	P/F	P/A	A/P

  2. Confusion as to which factor to use in solving problems is minimized simply by asking: "Are single or annuity-type amounts involved?" and "Does the cash flow (or do the cash flows) being solved for occur in the present or future?" A suggested procedure is as follows:

    a. Is a single amount involved? If so, use *F/P* or *P/F* and skip to item *c* below.

    b. If an annuity is involved, ask: "Is the amount of the annuity given?"

      i. If so, use *F/A* or *P/A* and skip to item *c*.

      ii. If the amount of the annuity is to be found, use *A/F* if the future value is given or *A/P* if the present amount is given.

c. Now ask: "Is the future amount what is being solved for?" If so, pick the factor that gives F from P if it's a single-payment problem or the factor that gives F from A for the annuity problem.

3. The best way to master time-value-of-money problems is to learn by doing. Two examples will be given below; problems at the end of this chapter should also be instructive.

  a. How much will $200 grow to in ten years if it grows at the rate of 7 percent per year?

   i. This is a single payment, and a future amount is being sought.

   ii. Looking in Appendix 4A in the 7 percent table for the F/P factor in the ten-year row, we find 1.9672.

   iii. $F = \$200(1.9672) = \$393.44$ (note that the rule of 72 would indicate the answer should be close to $400).

  b. What *equal annual* deposit is needed to accumulate $600 in four years if the deposits earn 7 percent per year?

   i. This is an annuity that must be solved from a future amount, and so the sinking fund factor (A/F, 7%, 4) is required, i.e., 0.2252.

   ii. $$A = \$600(0.2252) = \$135.12$$

  c. When the interest rate is known and cash flows vary each year, solve for unknown present or future values by treating each yearly amount separately—annuity factors won't work. (See problem 9.)

  d. When the interest rate is unknown:

   i. There are three situations in which i can be readily found without tables or complex calculations.

    (a) For a perpetuity,

$$i = A/P$$

    (b) For repayment of a loan in one year,

$$i = F/P - 1$$

    (c) For a loan when interest only is due each year and the principal is due at the end of the loan period,

$$i = A/P$$

   ii. In other cases with constant cash flows, solve for the factor and look in the appropriate table for i. (See problem 6.)

   iii. When cash flows vary, use a trial-and-error method. (See problems 7c and 8.)

COMPLETION QUESTIONS

time 1. Money has a (*book/time*) value because there is a charge for its use, which
interest is the _____ rate.

amount, interest 2. Growth begins with an initial _____ and expands at a(n) _____
$F = P(1 + i)^n$ rate for a period of time according to the formula _____.

3. The single-payment compound interest factors are based on an initial amount
1 of $_____.

multiply 4. When the initial amount is not $1, (*multiply/divide*) the actual amount by
F/P the (*P/F / F/P*) factor.

future, from 5. *F/P* means _____ value (*from/divided by*) present value.

72 6. The rule of (*27/72*) is a handy device for showing combinations of time
growth rate period and _____ _____ required for an amount to
double (*double/triple*).

regular 7. To be an annuity, the cash flows must occur at _____ intervals
equal and be _____.

8. To determine the balance in an account which had annuity-type deposits,
multiply, F/A (*multiply/divide*) the amount of the annuity by the (*F/A / F/P*) factor.

sinking fund 9. The *A/F* factor is also called the _____ _____ factor
deposit and is used to determine the amount of the (*annuity/deposit*) necessary to
future accumulate to a (*present/future*) value.

P/A 10. To compute the amount required to buy an annuity, use the (*P/A / F/P*)
factor.

loan repayment 11. The capital recovery factor is also called the _____ _____
factor because it can be used to determine amount of payments necessary
principal, interest to pay back (*annuity/principal*) and (*dividends/interest*), as in a home mortgage.

12. In solving time-value-of-money problems, determine whether the cash flow
single amount, annuity is a(n) _____ _____ or a(n) _____. Then
present check to see whether the cash flow being sought is in the _____
future or _____.

decreases 13. As the interest rate rises, the present value of an annuity (*increases/*
increases *decreases*), and the future value of an annuity (*increases/decreases*).

PROBLEMS

1. Friendly Shirl the Cycle Girl found her lost passbook for a savings account she had opened with a $100 deposit twelve years ago. If the bank paid 6 percent interest compounded annually over this period, what would the balance in the account be now?

Solution

Step one   This is a single-payment problem because only one deposit was made.

Step two   A future amount is being sought because the compound growth process started with a known amount, i.e., the $100 deposit.

Step three   The factor needed is (F/P, 6%, 12), which is 2.0122.

Step four   The balance will be $100 × 2.0122 = $201.22.

Step five   An approximate answer could have been arrived at using the rule of 72. Because the product of the interest rate and the time period is 6 × 12 = 72, the initial amount would have about doubled, i.e., grown to $200.

2. Parsimonious Pete claims his dad cheated him by offering $133.82 to repay a $100 loan extended five years ago from Pete's paper route savings. If Dad said he would pay 6 percent compounded monthly, what do you think of Pete's allegation?

Solution

Step one   The future amount from a present value is being sought.

Step two   With monthly compounding for five years, the rate is 0.5 percent for 60 periods. The factor needed is (F/P, 0.5%, 60), which is 1.3489.

Step three   The amount due is $100 × 1.3489 = $134.89.

Step four   Since Dad offered $133.82, Pete was indeed shortchanged. (Actually, Dad had figured 6 percent compounded annually—can you find this amount using the 6 percent table?)

3. Marilyn and Ron Doe are planning to buy a $100,000 home. ABC Savings and Loan Association agrees to make them an 80 percent loan at 15 percent to be repaid monthly over twenty-five years. What are the loan payments? How much interest will the Does pay?

Solution

Step one   The loan is for 80 percent of $100,000 = $80,000.

Step two   The monthly payments are an annuity.

Step three   The present value is given, i.e., the loan amount of $80,000.

Step four   There will be 12 × 25, or 300, monthly payments, and the interest rate is 15 ÷ 12, or 1.25 percent.

Step five   The factor needed is the loan repayment factor (A/P, 1.25%, 300), which is 0.0128.

Step six   The monthly payments are 0.0128 × $80,000 = $1,024.

Step seven   The total amount of interest paid is ($1,024 × 300) − $80,000 = $227,200. Wow!

4. Not too long ago, the city of London was looking for a site on which to build a third airport. One location would have involved demolishing the twelfth-century Church of St. Michael's. Suppose this edifice had been built for $240 and had increased 5 percent per year in value. What would it be worth today, 800 years later?

Solution

Step one   This is a single-payment problem involving the construction cost of $240.

Step two   A future amount is being sought.

Step three   The factor needed is (F/P, 5%, 800).

Step four   At the end of 100 years $1 would grow to $131.5013.

Step five   After 800 years $1 would grow to $(\$131.5013)^8 = \$894 \times 10^{14}$.

Step six   The original $240 would amount to $\$240 \times 894 \times 10^{14} = \$214 \times 10^{17}$, which is an astronomical figure. Better locate the airport elsewhere!

5. Greasy Rock State College has an enrollment of 10,000 persons today. When will the student population reach 30,000 if the rate of growth is 6 percent?

Solution

Step one   This is a single-payment problem. Note that compound growth applies not only to money but also to students, fruit flies, and other forms of life and things.

Step two   Both the present and future amounts are given, as well as the growth rate that relates one to the other.

Step three   The time period can be found from the table of factors, but either the *F/P* or the *P/F* factor can be used.

Step four   Suppose we select *F/P*. Then 30,000 = 10,000 × *F/P*.

$$F/P = 3.0$$

Step five   With a 6 percent growth rate this number (3.0) occurs in just under nineteen years.

Step six   If the *P/F* factor were chosen,

$$10,000 = 30,000 \times P/F$$

$$P/F = 0.333$$

Step seven   With the 6 percent growth rate, this number (0.333) occurs in just under nineteen years. Surprised? Don't be. Remember that the *P/F* and *F/P* factors are reciprocals.

6. Suppose tuition at Greasy Rock tripled in the last decade. What was the rate of increase?

Step one This is a single-payment problem.

Step two Both present and future amounts are known, as well as the time period.

Step three The growth rate can be found using either F/P or P/F.

Step four Using P/F and assuming the original tuition was $100,

$$\$100 = \$300 \times P/F$$

$$P/F = 0.333$$

Step five In ten years this number (0.333) occurs at slightly less than 12 percent.

Step six Check this answer using the F/P factor instead.

7. Compute the annual compound rate of return in each of the following cases (ignore taxes and commissions):
   a. A stamp collection was purchased for $250 and sold for $300 one year later.

Solution

Step one The present value is $250, and the future value is $300.

Step two Recall that $i = F/P - 1$ for problems involving one year; thus $i = (\$300/\$250) - 1 = 0.2$, or 20 percent.

Step three The tables could have been used in a manner similar to the way they were used in problems 4 and 5. Thus

$$\$300 = \$250 \times F/P$$

$$F/P = 1.2$$

Then $i = 20$ percent.

b. The Canadian Pacific Railway has a perpetual bond outstanding that is selling for $44 and pays annual interest of $4.

Solution

Step one   This is an annuity of $4 per year and a present value of $44.

Step two   In this case,

$$i = A/P$$

$$i = \$4/\$44 = 0.91, \text{ or } 9.1\%$$

c. Bonnie purchased 100 shares of XYZ Company common stock for $25 per share five years ago. She received annual dividends of $2 per share, and today she could sell the stock for $28.

Solution

Step one   This is a combination of an annuity, the $2 dividend, and a single payment, the future selling price of $28.

Step two   The return sought is the interest rate, which equates the initial selling price to the present value of the future returns.

Step three $\$25 = \$2 \times (P/A, i, 5) + \$28 \times (P/F, i, 5)$.

Step four   This must be a trial-and-error solution.

Step five   The dividends have provided an 8 percent return (2/25), and the current market price is above the original selling price; thus the total return must be above 8 percent.

Step six   Try 12 percent:

$$\$25 \stackrel{?}{=} \$2 \times 3.6048 + \$28 \times 0.5674$$

$$\stackrel{?}{=} 23.0968$$

Step seven   Since this is below $25, the trial rate was too high. Try 10 percent.

$$\$25 \overset{?}{=} \$2 \times 3.7908 + \$28 \times 0.6209$$

$$\overset{?}{=} \$24.97$$

This is almost equal to the initial cost, $25, and so the rate of return is 10 percent.

Step eight   If the dividends had increased each year, this problem would still be solved in a similar manner. However, it would be more complex since the annuity term would not apply and, instead, individual present value calculations of the dividends would be necessary.

8. A bond that matures fifteen years from today can be purchased for $870. The coupon rate is 11 percent. Compute the rate of return.

Solution

Step one   The rate of return in the case of a bond is called the **yield to maturity (YTM).** It is the interest rate that will equate the present value of the future returns from the bond to the bond's current price. In other words

$$\text{Bond price} = \frac{\text{present value of}}{\text{interest payments}} + \frac{\text{present value of}}{\text{principal payment}}$$

Step two   In this problem the equation is

$$\$870 = \$110(P/A, \ i\%, \ 15) + \$1000(P/F, \ i\%, \ 15)$$

Step three   This is a trial-and-error solution as in 7c. Because the investor will receive 11 percent interest plus the gain in principal of $870 to $1000, we know the YTM is above 11 percent.

Step four   Try 14 percent.

$$\$870 \overset{?}{=} \$110 \times 6.1422 + \$1000 \times 0.1401$$

$$\overset{?}{=} \$815$$

Step five   Since this is below the market price, the trial rate was too high. Try 13 percent.

$$\$870 \stackrel{?}{=} \$110 \times 6.4624 + \$1000 \times 0.1599$$

$$\stackrel{?}{=} \$871$$

This is very close to $870 so the yield to maturity is just over 13 percent.

9. Gary was offered a new $6000 sign for his business for a down payment of $3000 with additional payments of $2000 and $1000 one and two years later. Another supplier will sell him a similar sign for $5700 cash. Which offer should Gary accept if money is worth 12 percent to him?

Solution

Step one   This problem involves converting payments to a present value so that a valid comparison of the costs can be made.

Step two   The future cash flows occur at regular intervals, but because they are unequal, they are not an annuity and thus must be treated as separate single payments.

Step three

$$P = \$3000 \times (P/F, 12\%, 0) + \$2000 \times (P/F, 12\%, 1)$$

$$+ \$1000 \times (P/F, 12\%, 2)$$

$$= \$3000 \times 1.0 + \$2000 \times 0.8929 + \$1000 \times 0.7972$$

$$= \$5583$$

Step four   Since this is less than the $5700 cash offer, the three-payment plan should be chosen.

10. Jeff has $100,000 and hopes to live twenty-five more years. If he could earn 6 percent per year from municipal bonds, how much could he spend each year?

Solution

Step one   The problem is to find how much of an annuity he could spend annually.

Step two   The factor is (*A/P*, 6%, 25), which is 0.0782.

Step three   Jeff would thus have $100,000 × 0.0782 = $7820 each year.

11. Suppose Jeff felt he could live on $7000 annually for the next twenty-five years. How much would be left?

Solution

Step one   Jeff would reinvest the excess from what he earned over the amount he actually needed, or $7820 − $7000 = $820 per year for twenty-five years.

Step two   The future value of an annuity of $820 for twenty-five years earning 6 percent is calculated by multiplying the factor (*F/A*, 6%, 25) by the annuity.

$$54.8645 \times \$820 = \$44{,}988.89$$

(Recall the earnings were from munis, so there is no need to adjust for income taxes.)

12. A savings and loan association recently advertised for persons to open Individual Retirement Accounts. It showed a table that indicated that if a twenty-five-year-old person made $2000 deposits each year until retirement at age 65, the account balance would be $1,534,183 if an interest rate of 12 percent per year applied. Given the assumptions, do you believe the ad was correct?

Solution

Step one   The future value of an annuity of $2000 per year for forty years at 12 percent is sought.

Step two   The account balance would be

$$\$2000 \times (F/A, 12\%, 40), \text{ or } \$2000 \times 767.0914 = \$1{,}534{,}182.80$$

The ad is correct. Just think! College-age students can become millionaires by simply saving a modest amount every year until they retire *if* a double-digit rate of return can be earned. The big problem concerns how much those millions of dollars will buy. For example, gasoline originally selling at $1.50 per gallon would sell for almost $100 per gallon if the price increase averaged 12 percent a year during the forty-year span—try using the rule of 72 to check this assertion.

CHAPTER FIVE

SECURITY PRICES

QUINTESSENCE   The value of a security is determined by analyzing the amounts and timing of future cash returns and the uncertainty of these expected returns. The present value of the estimated cash flows is computed using a discount rate that depends on the current level of interest rates, the riskiness of the future payments, and investor attitudes toward risk. Since security prices tend to reflect existing information, it is difficult for investors to outperform the market averages.

OUTLINE

I. What
   A. A security's price equals the present value of future payments to its owners.
   B. The appropriate discount rate depends on the:
      1. Current level of interest rates.
      2. Riskiness of the payments.
      3. Investor attitudes toward risk.
   C. Security prices tend to reflect existing information, which means extraordinary profits cannot be consistently achieved by most investors.

II. Why
   A. The decisions of investors and financial managers are based on security values.
   B. These people need to know what information is relevant and how it is incorporated into prices.

III. How

Price Equals Present Value
   A. A security's price (value) is determined by the present value of its future cash flows.
      1. Assuming the discount rate (market interest rate) is the same for all securities, their prices will differ only because the cash payments differ in *timing* or *amount*.

Prices and Discount Rates Are Inversely Related
      2. For identical streams of future payments, the higher the discount rate, the lower the price.

Bond Valuation
   B. The price of a bond (a type of fixed-income security) equals the present value of the interest payments plus the present value of the principal.

61

1. Using terminology from Chapter 4, this is:

$$\text{Price} = \text{interest} \; (P/A, \; i, \; n) + \text{principal} \; (P/F, \; i, \; n) \qquad (5\text{-}1)$$

2. Work problems 3 and 4 at the end of this chapter to gain familiarity with this important equation. These problems illustrate the relationship that bonds sell at:

Premium
   a. A **premium** when their coupons are higher than their yields to maturity.

Discount
   b. A **discount** when their coupons are lower than their yields to maturity.

Par
   c. **Par** when their coupons are equal to their yields to maturity.

Higher Bond Ratings Mean Lower Yields
3. Bonds of different firms offering the same coupon and maturity date may sell for different prices, thus offering different yields. Why? Primarily because investors view one company as less likely to actually meet its promises to pay interest and principal. This doubt will be reflected in the price; people pay less for riskier assets. Bonds are classified into risk groups by expert rating agencies (Standard & Poor's and Moody's). Baa-rated bonds are riskier than Aaa bonds, and so investors pay less for the Baa securities, which results in higher returns.
   a. Bonds of the same rating won't necessarily have the same yield because the classifications are approximate.

Full Faith and Credit
   b. The least risky bonds are issued by the U.S. government. Remember that Uncle Sam can always pay debts by raising taxes and/or printing money.

Yield Spreads Vary
   c. The rates of return for risky bonds vary over time. The **spread** between different ratings widens during periods of heightened economic uncertainty (risky times).

Risk and the Discount Rate
   d. The appropriate discount rate equals the riskfree rate plus a premium to allow for the riskiness of a security's future cash flow.

Valuing Common Stock
C. Income expected by common stockholders is not promised. It can vary, so valuation is more difficult.
   1. The basic principle is still the same as for fixed-income securities. Future cash flows are forecasted dividends and a future stock price.

Forecast Future Dividends
   2. Mathematically this is:

$$P_0 = \frac{D_1}{1 + i} + \frac{D_2}{(1 + i)^2} + \cdots + \frac{D_n + P_n}{(1 + i)^n} \qquad (5\text{-}2)$$

   3. More frequently today's stock price is viewed as the present value of all future dividends discounted at a rate (k) that is the rate required

to compensate stockholders for the time value of money and the risk associated with the expected dividends. Thus,

$$P_0 = \frac{D_1}{1 + k} + \frac{D_2}{(1 + k)^2} + \cdots + \frac{D_m}{(1 + k)^m}$$

(5-3)

4. Since the last dividend payment, at time *m,* is a long and very uncertain time away, the typical method of handling this dilemma assumes a specific pattern for future dividends.

No-Growth Model

    a. When payments are expected to continue at the present amount into perpetuity (that's a long time from now), the valuation formula becomes:

$$P_0 = \frac{D}{k}$$

(5-4)

       i. This is okay for preferred stock.

      ii. Most people expect companies to expand, so they buy common stock to participate in the increased prosperity, which means a model that incorporates growth is usually more appropriate.

Constant Growth Model

    b. Assuming a steady dividend growth, the formula becomes:

$$P_0 = \frac{D_1}{(k - g)}$$

(5-5)

       i. Note that if dividends are not expected to grow, $g = 0$ and Eq. (5-5) becomes that used in the no-growth model.

      ii. The constant growth model is often expressed as:

$$k = \frac{D_1}{P_0} + g$$

(5-6)

This is relatively easy to remember by thinking of the yield investors expect as being comprised of the dividend yield (D/P) plus the growth in dividends. Dividend growth is assumed to be the same as the expected rate of price appreciation, or the capital gains rate.

Variable Growth Rates

    c. Most firms are not expected to grow at the *same* rate throughout their lives.

i. Extraordinarily high or low rates due to a technological innovation or a downturn in the company's fortunes can be anticipated by adjusting the growth rate to a long-run growth pattern.

ii. These variable trends can be valued by using the different forecasted growth rates in the constant growth model. (See problem 6 for an example calculation.)

Efficient Markets Hypothesis

D. Financial theorists have developed the **efficient markets hypothesis,** which states that information spreads quickly among investors and is reflected immediately in security prices.

No One Can Beat the Market

1. This means no investor can consistently outperform others by acting on public information.

Insider Information

2. The use of nonpublic information, or **insider information,** might allow someone to beat the market.

3. A better way to understand the concept of efficient markets has been offered by Eugene Fama:

Weak Form Efficiency

a. **Weak form efficiency** holds that past price trends can't be used to accurately predict future prices. Most studies support this.

Semistrong Efficiency

b. According to the **semistrong efficiency** adherents, knowledge of past prices plus all other publicly available information won't help in picking stocks.

i. In other words, no amount of analysis using every piece of public information can lead an investor to extraordinary gains.

ii. Empirical tests tend to support this argument for the stock market. Other research indicates some markets aren't as efficient, e.g., real estate.

Strong Form Efficiency

c. Markets are **strong form efficient** when even inside information won't help.

i. Mutual funds haven't consistently outperformed randomly selected portfolios having similar risk.

ii. Some evidence suggests exchange specialists and company officers do better.

iii. The mixed results of these studies indicate that *reliable* inside information is useful but it's hard to tell what is reliable.

Implications of Market Efficiency

4. So what?

a. Only real performance counts. In other words, no accounting manipulations will affect stock prices.

b. Investors and financial managers can't outguess the market unless they do indeed know something that others don't.

c. Mergers are justified only if they will produce synergies.

Random Walk

d. Stock prices follow a **random walk.**

e. Stock price information is a good leading indicator of economic activity.

COMPLETION QUESTIONS

present 1. The market price of a security is the _____ value of its future

cash flows (*cash flows/profits*).

discount rate 2. The _____ _____ used to determine the present value

interest rates depends on the current level of (*interest rates/stock markets*), the (*amount/*

riskiness *riskiness*) of income provided by the security, and attitudes of investors

risk toward (*profits/risk*).

cannot 3. In investing in marketable securities, one (*can/cannot*) be expected to achieve

above-average profits from having information that is widely available.

decrease 4. If the level of interest rates rises, asset values will (*increase/decrease*) if

everything else remains constant.

directly 5. Risk and return can be said to vary (*directly/inversely*), whereas asset values

inversely and levels of expected returns vary (*directly/inversely*).

6. The promised stream of cash payments from fixed-income securities is the

maximum (*minimum/maximum*) amount that the issuer will pay.

interest 7. The price of a bond is equal to the present value of the (*dividend/interest*)

principal plus the present value of the (*principal/principle*).

8. The interest rate used in the bond valuation equation is also known as the

yield to maturity _____ _____ _____ .

higher 9. The lower the rating for a bond, the (*lower/higher*) will be its yield to

maturity.

10. The safest available securities with respect to guaranteed payment of prin-

U.S. cipal and interest are those issued by (*municipal/U.S.*) government.

varies 11. The spread between yields on Aaa bonds and Baa bonds (*varies/is constant*)

over time.

12. The discount rate used in valuation calculations depends on the riskless rate

premium of interest plus a (*premium/discount*) to compensate for the risk of the

security's cash flows.

higher 13. The risk premium is (*lower/higher*) for stock than for corporate bonds.

dividends 14. The value of a stock is equal to the present value of future (*interest/dividends*)

price plus the future (*price/par value*) of the stock.

15. The rate used to discount future dividends is the amount necessary to com-

money pensate owners of the stock for the time value of _____ and

risk the (*amount/risk*) of those expected dividends.

16. If investors expect dividends to remain at the same level indefinitely, the

perpetual

present value is like a (*perpetual/variable*) annuity and is equal to the div-

divided

idend (*multiplied/divided*) by the discount rate.

17. When dividends are expected to grow at a constant rate, the price of a stock

difference between

is equal to that dividend amount divided by the (*sum of/difference between*) the discount rate and the growth rate.

18. In the constant growth model, the required rate of return on a stock is equal

yield

to the dividend _____ plus the growth rate.

information

19. The efficient markets hypothesis states that market prices reflect _____ fully and immediately.

20. The hypothesis that use of price history alone to select stocks won't be of

weak, form

help is the basis for _____ _____ efficiency.

semistrong

21. The argument for _____ efficiency implies that a knowledge of all publicly available information will produce no advantage.

insider

22. Advocates of strong form efficiency include _____ information as well as that which is publicly available.

weak

23. A large body of empirical evidence favors the (*weak/strong*) form of market efficiency.

are not

24. An implication of the market efficiency arguments is that investors (*are/are not*) fooled by accounting manipulations that do not affect the real assets and cash flows of a company.

25. It is also implied that unless the financial manager has inside information

is not

it (*is/is not*) possible to provide superior results by timing issues of securities.

26. In the absence of inside information, it appears that the market is unpre-

random walk

dictable and that it follows a(n) _____ _____ .

1. What price will you pay for a $1000 U.S. Treasury bill due one year from today if the going rate on riskfree money is 7 percent?

Solution

Step one Price = present value of interest + present value of principal.

Step two Treasury bills pay no interest, and so the return comes from paying a price below that which will be repaid at maturity.

Step three

$$Price = \$1000 \times (P/F, 7\%, 1)$$
$$= \$1000 \times 0.9346$$
$$= \$934.60$$

2. Suppose you paid $942.40 for a $1000 U.S. Treasury bill due one year from today. What would be the yield to maturity (rate of return)?

Solution

Step one Price = $942.40 = $1000 × (P/F, i, 1).

Step two The factor $(P/F, i, 1) = 0.9424$.

Step three Look in the "P/F" columns in the one-year row in different tables until you locate 0.9424. Read up to see that the return is 6 percent.

3. Compute the prices (present values) of the following:
   a. XYZ Corp. bond with a 10 percent coupon (interest) and a 10 percent yield to its maturity in twenty years.

Solution

Step one

$$\text{Price} = \text{PV of interest} + \text{PV of principal}$$

$$= \$100 \times (P/A,\ 10\%,\ 20) + \$1000 \times (P/F,\ 10\%,\ 20)$$

$$= \$100 \times 8.5136 + \$1000 \times 0.1486$$

$$= \$999.96, \text{ or say } \$1000$$

   b. ABC Co. bond with a 6 percent coupon and a 6 percent yield to maturity, which occurs in five years.

Solution

Step one

$$\text{Price} = \$60 \times (P/A,\ 6\%,\ 5) + \$1000 \times (P/F,\ 6\%,\ 5)$$

$$= \$60 \times 4.2124 + \$1000 \times 0.7473$$

$$= \$1000.044$$

which is again close enough, "for government work," to be $1000.

   c. MNO, Ltd., bond with a 7 percent coupon and a 9 percent yield to maturity, which is ten years from today.

Solution

Step one   First ask yourself: "Should the price be above or below par?" Well, what do you think? Below par is right. The price must be below par because MNO pays only $70 interest per year, no more and no less. Thus, the only way to realize a higher return (9 percent) is to pay *less* than the par value.

Step two

$$\text{Price} = \$70 \times (P/A,\ 9\%,\ 10) + \$1000$$

$$\times (P/F,\ 9\%,\ 10)$$

$$= \$70 \times 6.4177 + \$1000 \times 0.4224$$

$$= \$871.64$$

Step three   If the coupon rate were higher than the yield to maturity, the bond would be priced above par.

Step four   Another observation needs emphasis: Be very careful to separate the coupon and yield rates in the present value calculations. The coupon indicates the *cash returns* in the form of interest payments. Yield to maturity is the interest rate used to compute present values of both coupon payments and the principal payment. It will be used twice in the calculations. Think of this point as you solve the next problem.

4. What will be the yield to maturity from PDQ, Inc., fifteen-year bonds that have 8 percent coupons and are selling today for $848? (Hint: First review problem 8 in Chapter 4 of the *Study Guide*.)

Solution

Step one

$$\text{Price} = \text{PV of interest} + \text{PV of principal}$$

$$\$848 = \$80 \times (P/A, i, 15) + \$1000(P/F, i, 15)$$

Step two   We don't know what the yield to maturity is (it's i percent), and so a trial-and-error solution is needed. Before guessing randomly, think whether the yield should be above or below 8 percent (the coupon rate). From step one in the solution to problem 3c, the answer is *above* 8 percent. Why? Because if the current bond price is below par value, buyers will earn a yield to maturity that is higher than the coupon rate. This happens for two reasons. The first is that the coupon return represents an interest payment based on par. If the bond is bought below par, the return will be higher. The other reason is that there will be a capital gain to bondholders who buy bonds at prices below par since the issuer redeems the bonds at maturity for par value.

Step three   Try 9 percent:

$$\$848 \overset{?}{=} \$80 \times (P/A, 9\%, 15) + \$1000 \times (P/F, 9\%, 15)$$

$$\overset{?}{=} \$80 \times 8.0607 + \$1000 \times 0.2745$$

$$\overset{?}{=} \$919.36$$

So 9 percent is not the yield. The present value of the benefits of $919 is too high; it can be reduced by using a higher discount rate.

Step four   Try 10 percent:

$$\$848 \overset{?}{=} \$80 \times 7.6061 + \$1000 \times 0.2394$$

$$\overset{?}{=} \$847.89$$

which is approximately correct, and so the yield to maturity is 10 percent.

5. Suppose investors require a return of 14 percent on Ronron common stock. It is currently selling for $50 per share, and dividends per share are expected to be $2. What is the anticipated growth rate?

Solution

Step one   Solve the constant dividend growth model for the growth rate.

$$g = k - \frac{D_1}{P} = .14 - \frac{2}{50} = .10 \text{ or } 10 \text{ percent}$$

6. Apply the constant rate of growth model to DEF, Inc., stock on which investors require a return of 15 percent. The dividend next year is expected to be $3 per share and is expected to grow at 5 percent per year thereafter.
   a. Determine the value of DEF shares.

Solution

Step one

$$P = \frac{D_1}{k - g} = \frac{3}{.15 - .05} = \$30 \text{ per share}$$

Step two   This is the "value" according to the model and specific assumptions about future performance. The actual market price may be quite different because other investors use different models and/or assumptions.

   b. What is the effect on price if investors expect the growth rate to double?

Solution

Step one This means the growth rate would increase to 10 percent.

Step two

$$P = \frac{3}{.15 - .10} = \$60$$

Thus the price would double if the expected growth rate doubled.

c. Suppose the return required by investors increased to 20 percent. What is the value of the stock, assuming the original growth rate still applies?

Solution

Step one

$$P = \frac{3}{.20 - .05} = \$20 \text{ per share}$$

Step two This is interesting; investors require more (a 20 percent return instead of 15 percent), but they are willing to pay less ($20 per share instead of $30). Is this logical? Of course, since the assumption is that nothing has changed within the company; its estimated dividend and growth rate is the same. The only way, then, for investors to receive a higher return is to pay a lower price. Notice the similarity to bond valuations; if interest rates (expected returns) rise, bond prices fall. Keep in mind, however, the critical difference between stock and bonds. Shareholders can receive higher or lower payments from the company, whereas bondholders receive a fixed amount (unless a disaster occurs).

d. Using the original data and supposing that DEF shares were selling in the market at $25 per share, what would be the expected return?

Solution

Step one

$$k = \frac{D_1}{P} + g = \frac{3}{25} + .05 = .17, \text{ or } 17\%$$

Step two This return is higher than the 15 percent return that investors require. What would happen? People, noticing an opportunity to earn a higher-than-required return, would buy DEF shares. This action would cause the price to increase toward the $30 estimated value. Another way of looking at this situation is to compare the valuation model price of $30 with the actual market price of $25. Investors, seeing an undervalued stock, would buy, causing the market price to rise—the same result as predicted before.

CHAPTER SIX

RISK AND RETURN

QUINTESSENCE

The value of an asset is determined by analyzing the amounts and timing of future cash flows *and* the risk (variation) of the expected returns. Risk is based on historical variations in the returns. It is measured with probability distributions and through the Capital Asset Pricing Model (CAPM), which relates returns to the riskfree rate plus a premium to compensate for risk. According to the CAPM, risk of a security depends on the degree to which its returns vary with the returns in the entire stock market. Diversification can be used to reduce portfolio risk.

OUTLINE

I. What
   A. The price or value of a security is determined by the amount and timing of cash flows and the risk (variability) of those cash flows.
   B. Risk also depends on the relationship between the cash flows of the particular asset and the cash flows from other assets in the portfolio.
   C. Values of securities can be computed using an objective measure of risk that is independent of how much a person dislikes risk.

II. Why
   A. Risk influences value or prices paid. Observe how risk affects returns in the following examples:
      1. Top-quality companies pay lower interest rates for loans, compared with those paid by individual borrowers.
      2. A football coach is paid more than a business professor.
      3. A structural steelworker earns more than a worker on the ground.
   B. The objective of financial management is to increase value. Since everything in the future is uncertain in varying degrees, it is necessary to know how to measure risk and how it affects the firm's value. This helps people make better decisions.

Statistical Measures of Risk

III. How
   A. Probability distributions are used to measure risk.
      1. A **discrete probability distribution** has a limited number of possible future values and corresponding probabilities that any particular value will occur.
      2. The **mean** or **expected value** of the distribution is computed by adding the products of each outcome and their respective probabilities.

73

Standard Deviation
Variance
	3. The **standard deviation** measures variability around the expected value. **Variance** is the square of the standard deviation.
	    a. If there is no risk, the standard deviation and variance will be zero.
	    b. The higher the standard deviation, the greater the risk or uncertainty of the expected value.
	    c. Outcomes with low probabilities of occurrence have less effect on the amount of risk.
	    d. The standard deviation is measured in the same units as the variable itself. So for stock prices both the outcome and risk will be reported in dollars, or they could be converted into rates of return in percentages.
	4. In **continuous probability distributions,** ranges are used for the variable instead of the single-figure outcomes.

Diversification	B. Investing in at least two different assets is **diversification,** which reduces the total portfolio risk. 1. The amount of risk reduction depends on the degree to which the returns from two securities are offsetting.

Correlation	a. Opposite moves (like a teeter-totter) have a -1.0 **correlation.** The variability of returns for a portfolio with equal amounts of these two stocks would be zero. This is a no-risk situation.
	    b. The correlation for moves in tandem is $+1.0$.
	    c. Most stocks tend to be positively correlated (between 0.5 and 0.6), so total risk can be lessened but not eliminated.
	    d. Returns in foreign company stocks may move in opposing directions although globalization of economies and stock markets reduces the independence. Also exchange rate movements add risk.
	2. The expected return on a portfolio is the weighted average of the anticipated returns for each individual security.
	3. Portfolio risk, or variation in the total return, can be further reduced by more diversification, e.g., by adding more securities.
	C. Risk and return theory

Market Risk	1. Even well-diversified portfolios will always have some risk because security returns tend to move up and down together. This minimum risk is the **market risk,** which cannot be diversified away.

Beta	2. The **beta** coefficient measures the degree to which a security's returns move with the market.
	    a. A beta above 1.0 is more risky than the market, below 1.0 is less risky, and a value of 1.0 means the stock moves exactly in step with the market.
	    b. Portfolio risk can be reduced most by adding stocks having low betas. It is increased when stocks with betas above 1.0 are added.
	    c. Beta coefficients are estimated by calculations using historical returns for the particular stock and for the market in general.

Major changes affecting the company will likely alter the estimates for betas.

CAPM

3. The **Capital Asset Pricing Model (CAPM)** says the expected return for a particular security (k_J) is equal to the riskfree rate (i) plus a premium for bearing risk.

   a. Part of the premium results from the difference between the expected rate of return for the market as a whole (k_M) and the riskfree rate.

   b. This premium is then modified by the historical pattern of variation between the returns to the individual stock and those experienced in the overall stock market. Remember, the responsiveness of a particular security's returns to the market is measured by its beta coefficient (beta$_J$). For example, a stock with a beta of 0.7 will, on average, experience only 70 percent of the rise or fall in the market.

   c. All this (CAPM) is put together in a formula:

   $$k_J = i + (k_M - i)\text{beta}_J \qquad (6\text{-}1)$$

Security Market Line

   d. The graph of this return and risk relationship forms the **security market line.** It indicates the going rate for risk bearing; how much return investors expect to compensate them for a given amount of risk. This trade-off is shown below:

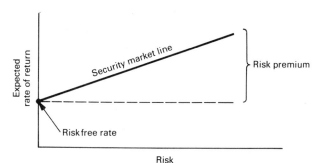

FIGURE 6-1

Calculating Stock Prices

   e. The model can be used to determine if a stock is under- or overvalued—after all, it is the Capital Asset *Pricing* Model.

   i. First the expected return is computed from Eq. (6-1).

   ii. This is used as the discount rate in the constant growth model presented as Eq. (5-5). (If you don't recall the concept of the price of a security's being the present value of future cash flows, this would be a good time to review.)

   iii. Compare the calculated price with the current price quote for the stock to determine if it is appropriate to buy or to sell.

CAPM and Changes over Time

f. The terms in the CAPM need to be further interpreted.
   i. The market premium $(k_M - i)$ is usually assumed to be constant over time.
   ii. The riskfree rate changes with shifts in the overall supply of and demand for money in the economy.
   iii. The risk of a particular company relative to the market (beta) will change as investor perceptions of the firm change.

Summary of CAPM

4. Implications of CAPM include:
   a. The required or expected return from every financial asset is directly related to the riskless rate of interest.
   b. The risk of investing can be reduced by diversifying.
   c. People expect to be compensated for investing in stocks in general as well as for choosing any particular stock.
   d. Return and risk are perceived to be commensurate; higher returns require increased risk taking.

Uses of CAPM

   e. CAPM can be used:
      i. In cost-benefit calculations for capital expenditures.
      ii. To show how increasing debt will increase the returns required by stockholders.
      iii. For measuring the performance of portfolio managers, e.g., managers of mutual funds.
   f. While CAPM is no panacea and has problems, it offers considerable value in analyzing risk and return—the title of this chapter—and an appropriate note on which to conclude.

Arbitrage Pricing Theory

5. **Arbitrage Pricing Theory** (APT) incorporates basic economic conditions into the pricing model.
   a. CAPM is too simple for more complex securities such as convertibles and options. It only uses the individual security returns in relation to market returns.
   b. APT recognizes the sensitivity of the security returns relative to such factors as changes in industrial production, inflation, and interest rates. More research needs to be done to make APT a useful tool.
   c. Other advanced pricing models are discussed in Chapter 22.

COMPLETION QUESTIONS

risk

cash flows

1. The (*risk/return*) from investing in a financial asset depends on the relationship between the (*cash flows/profits*) from that asset and the cash flows from other assets owned by the individual.

independent of

2. A good measure of risk is (*dependent on/independent of*) an individual's attitude toward risk.

continuous	3. A (*continuous/discrete*) probability distribution is one in which a variable can achieve any value.
Expected	4. (*Expected/Future*) value is the weighted average of possible returns.
standard deviation	5. A measure of uncertainty of returns is called the _____ _____.
no	6. A standard deviation of zero indicates _____ risk. The larger
larger	the standard deviation, the (*smaller/larger*) the risk.
	7. Risk measures do not attempt to identify the source of risk but instead
variability	indicate the (*level/variability*) of returns.
dollars, percentages	8. Returns can be expressed either in _____ or as _____.
diversification	9. The purpose of (*concentration/diversification*) is to reduce portfolio risk.
	10. Comparisons of historical patterns of returns from a security with those from
correlation coefficient	a portfolio are measured by the _____ _____. If this
+1.0	statistic is (*+1.0/−1.0*), the investment and the portfolio move up and
−1.0	down together. If it is _____, they move in equal proportions but in opposite directions.
	11. To achieve the greatest reduction in portfolio risk requires adding invest-
lowest	ments having the (*lowest/highest*) correlation coefficients and/or the (*low-
lowest	est/highest*) standard deviations.
	12. According to portfolio theory, risk has two major considerations: (*relia-
variability, diversification	bility/variability*) and _____.
	13. A particular investment will have different impacts on two different port-
correlation coefficient	folios because the _____ _____ with each portfolio
different	will be _____.
higher	14. People expect (*lower/higher*) returns from the riskier assets. The prices they
lower	are willing to pay for riskier assets are (*lower/higher*) because the returns
higher	are discounted at (*lower/higher*) rates.
positive	15. The (*positive/negative*) correlation of stock market returns is due to the dependence of returns of most stocks on general economic conditions.
	16. The returns from a well-diversified portfolio move up and down (*in an
together with	opposite direction to/together with*) the entire market.
	17. Beta measures how sharply and closely a security's price moves on average
with	(*with/against*) the market.
increases	18. Adding a high beta security to a diversified portfolio (*increases/decreases*) the portfolio's risk.

Capital Asset Pricing	19. The _____ _____ _____ Model is a theory about how prices and rates of return on risky securities are determined.
beta	20. According to the CAPM, a security's risk is measured by its _____ value.
take on	21. A premise of the CAPM states that the way to increase the expected rate of return from an investment is to (*avoid/take on*) additional risk.
U.S. Treasury bills	22. The interest rate on riskless securities is measured by the rate on (*U.S. Treasury bills/AAA corporate bonds*).
security	23. The (*bond/security*) market line shows the relationship between risk and return for an individual financial asset.
portfolio	24. In assessing the value of an individual security, investors should be concerned with how it affects the total risk and return of their _____.
correlation	25. The _____ between an individual security and the general market is an important factor in determining a security's risk.
measuring, evaluating	26. A difficulty with the CAPM involves _____ and _____ people's expectations.
arbitrage	27. An advanced asset pricing model is developed in _____ pricing theory.
	28. Crossword puzzle for terms in Chapters 5 and 6. (Look at the end of the problem section; answer at end of *Study Guide*.)

PROBLEMS

1. Suppose PDQ, Inc., has major products that are patented but these patents will expire over the next ten years. Estimates of return given bankruptcy and the probability that bankruptcy will occur are as follows:

Years	Rate of return, %	Probability
1–5	−30	0.05
6–10	−10	0.10
11–15	+ 4	0.15
Never	10	0.70

What would be the expected rate of return?

Solution

Step one

$$\text{Expected return} = \text{sum of each rate of return} \times \text{its probability of occurrence}$$

$$= -30 \times 0.05 + -10 \times 0.10 + 4 \times 0.15$$
$$+ 10 \times 0.70$$
$$= 5.1\%$$

2. The common stocks of ABC Co. and XYZ Corp. are estimated to offer returns over the next year according to the following table:

ABC		XYZ	
Return, %	Probability	Return, %	Probability
−20	0.05	−30	0.1
−10	0.05	0	0.2
5	0.1	10	0.5
10	0.3	50	0.2
20	0.5		

Compare risk and return for these two stocks.

Solution

Step one The expected returns are:

$$\text{ABC: } -20 \times 0.05 + -10 \times 0.05 + 5 \times 0.1 + 10$$
$$\times 0.3 + 20 \times 0.5 = 12.0\%$$
$$\text{XYZ: } -30 \times 0.1 + 0 \times 0.2 + 10$$
$$\times 0.5 + 50 \times 0.2 = 12.0\%$$

Step two Risks are measured by the standard deviations:

$$\sigma^2_{\text{ABC}} = 0.05 \times (-20 - 12)^2 + 0.05 \times (-10 - 12)^2$$
$$+ 0.1 \times (5 - 12)^2 + 0.3$$
$$\times (10 - 12)^2 + 0.5 \times (20 - 12)^2$$
$$= 51.2 + 24.2 + 4.9 + 1.2 + 32.0$$
$$= 113.5$$
$$\sigma_{\text{ABC}} = 10.7$$

$$\sigma^2_{XYZ} = 0.1 \times (-30 - 12)^2 + 0.2 \times (0 - 12)^2$$
$$+ 0.5 \times (10 - 12)^2 + 0.2 \times (50 - 12)^2$$
$$= 176.4 + 28.8 + 2.0 + 288.8$$
$$= 496.0$$
$$\sigma_{XYZ} = 22.3$$

Step three XYZ stock is considerably more risky, and yet it offers the same expected return; thus an investment in ABC would be preferred.

3. Walter, who is the investment manager for Vista Values Mutual Fund, estimates the following portfolio return and risks are available:

Portfolio	1	2	3	4
Expected return, %	11	14	18	21
Standard deviation, %	5	12	20	30

Which option should he choose if his cost of borrowing is 10 percent and riskless investments earn 10 percent?

Solution

Step one Data are supplied for a graphical solution, assuming the portfolios listed represent the efficient frontier of investment opportunities.

Step two Plot the risk and return data:

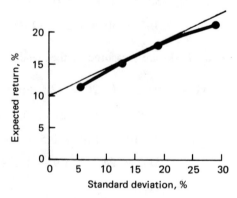

FIGURE 6-2

Step three Thus portfolio 3 is the best choice because it represents the highest return for a level of risk, given a borrowing and lending rate of 10 percent.

4. Use the Capital Asset Pricing Model to estimate the return expected by investors from a stock whose beta is 0.8 if the return from the market is estimated to be 16 percent when the riskfree interest rate is 9 percent.

Solution

Step one The CAPM equation is:

$$k_J = i + (k_M - i) \text{ beta}_J$$
$$= 9 + (16 - 9)(0.8)$$
$$= 14.6\%$$

Step two Note that the expected return on this stock is less than the market return. This is because the stock is less risky in the sense that when the market return moves up or down the stock itself is likely to change by only 80 percent of the amount of the market change.

Step three The expected return for the stock could have been solved graphically by plotting the security market line:

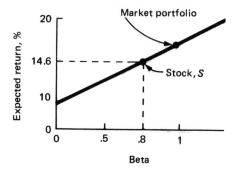

FIGURE 6-3

5. Given a riskfree return of 6 percent and investor requirements of a 15 percent return when the risk level is 8:
   a. Plot the security market line (SML).

Solution

Step one   In this text we assume that the SML is linear so that it can be plotted with two points. One observation is 15 percent return at 8 units of risk, and the other is 6 percent return at a zero risk.

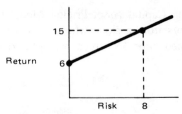

FIGURE 6-4

b. If the supply of and demand for money changed so that the riskfree return increased to 10 percent, what would be the return investors require from securities having a risk level of 8?

Solution

Step one   Required return = riskfree return + risk premium.

Step two   The risk premium from the security market line (in part *a*) was 15 − 6, or 9 percent, and so the required return now would be 10 + 9 = 19 percent.

Step three   Note that the required return can also change because of a change in investor attitudes toward risk (risk premium). This would cause the slope of the security market line to increase or decrease; a change in the riskfree rate results in an upward or downward parallel shift in the SML.

c. Given the original SML, what would happen if Gratebi shares offered an investor an expected return of 20 percent and a risk level of 8?

Solution

Step one   For the same risk, investors would be anticipating a 20 percent return on Gratebi compared with 15 percent for securities in general.

Step two   This situation would cause people to buy Gratebi shares, which would drive Gratebi's price up, thereby lowering its expected return. This action would continue until Gratebi was selling at a level that offered a return in line with the market.

ACROSS

1. This value is always less than the future value.
8. Interest rates on bonds are promised ____.
10. A way to reduce portfolio risk.
12. In a perfect world all assets would offer the same ____.
14. Investors compare this return with the one they require.
18. A lower grade bond rating.
20. Bonds will be redeemed at par value at this time.
21. The ____ coefficient is computed to assess the impact of adding a security to a portfolio.
22. ____ asset pricing model.
23. In addition to the amounts and timing of cash flows, their ____ must also be considered.

DOWN

2. A measure of risk is the ____ deviation.
3. A cash flow from a stock.
4. This value is more than its present value.
5. Top rating for bonds.
6. ____ markets hypothesis.
7. The likelihood of occurrence.
9. ____ walk hypothesis.
11. Risk is the ____ of returns.
13. Investors seek this in addition to the riskfree return.
15. A list of securities.
16. The security ____ line.
17. Stocks pay dividends; bonds pay ____.
18. Stock prices are a leading indicator of ____ trends.
24. Arbitrage pricing theory.

CHAPTER SEVEN

THE COST OF CAPITAL

QUINTESSENCE   In a most basic sense, a firm will be successful if it can earn returns on its investments that are greater than the cost of financing those investments. This chapter covers concepts and procedures for determining the minimum requirement for keeping everybody happy. The minimum rate is the cost of capital. It is the weighted average of capital costs and is equal to the sum of the products of each component cost and its relative importance or usage. Current capital market conditions, including investor attitudes and expectations, are used in determining costs and weighting factors. The cost of capital for foreign investments must incorporate different risks and costs of financing used abroad.

OUTLINE

I. What
   A. The cost of capital is the minimum acceptable rate of return on new investments being considered by a firm. It is calculated as the weighted average of the costs of the types of capital used to finance the acquisition of assets.
   B. This chapter presents the logic of alternative methods for computing component costs and for combining them into an overall cost. Special adjustments are necessary for foreign investments.

II. Why
   A. Firms have continually occurring investment opportunities, and they need to make choices from among these prospects. The value of the firm will be reduced if these investments do not earn at least the cost of capital.
   B. Knowing the costs of different sources of money makes it possible to use this information when deciding on methods to pay for assets.
   C. The cost of capital is used in setting rates that regulated companies (e.g., electric utilities) can charge their customers.
   D. Overseas projects are inherently riskier.

Average Cost of Capital

III. How
   A. The key concept involves the **average cost of capital** k_a.
      1. It is determined by adding the products of the cost of each financing component and its proportionate amount. For example, k_a = cost of debt × proportion of debt + cost of common stock × proportion

85

of common stock. The component costs are the returns investors require on the securities they own.

2. Assumptions
   a. New projects have the same risk to the firm as existing projects. This means the firm's risk characteristics will not be changed by the new investments being considered.
   b. General financing policies are not affected by the projects being undertaken. In other words, the financial risk of the firm will not be changed.

3. The cost of capital is a minimum requirement, a hurdle rate, which must be met by new investments. If the returns exceed this figure, the excess will accrue to the shareholders. This makes them very happy; you would smile too.

4. k_a reflects the average risk of the total company. In the context of the security market line as introduced in Chapter 6, k_a is typically in between the expected returns from debt and stock.

B. Determining the cost rates

Use Current Debt Costs

1. Keep in mind that this is basically a problem of computing the returns *currently* required by investors and that these rates are influenced by the business and financial risks of the firm.

2. **Cost of debt**
   a. Calculate the yield to maturity for each type of debt used by the firm, e.g., senior bonds and subordinated bonds.

Use Market Values

   b. Use the *market value* of each type of debt to compute the weighted average rate on the debt. Note the reliance on *current* data; historical figures are not relevant to current decisions.

Tax Adjustment

   c. Income taxes have the effect of reducing the firm's cost.
      i. Effective rate = interest rate $\times$ (1.0 − tax rate).
      ii. The cost of debt is really what the company pays net of taxes. Bondholders still get the full return they expect; indeed, the company writes them checks. Uncle Sam helps out by allowing the interest payments to be deducted as an expense for the business. The result is a reduction in taxes. For example, a firm in the 40 percent tax bracket whose bondholders expect a 10 percent return has a net cost of debt of 6 percent. The government, in effect, pays the other 4 percent since it collects that amount *less* in taxes.
      iii. Refer to Exhibit 7-1 in the text for further help in understanding the logic of the income tax adjustment.

Preferred Stock

3. **Cost of preferred stock**
   a. The preferred stock rate equals the annual dividend divided by the market price.
   b. If several preferred issues are outstanding, compute the weighted average rate as was done for debt.
   c. Since dividend payments are not a deductible expense (recall that this contrasts with interest), there is no adjustment for taxes.

Common Stock	4. **Cost of common stock**
	a. This is the most difficult rate (cost) to determine because there are no fixed payments to common shareholders, as is the case with debt and preferred stock.
	b. Alternative methods of calculating the cost of common stock include:
	i. Historical rate of return
	(a) Use actual data on stock prices and dividends from a recent period to compute the return.
	(b) One must be cautious in using this technique. Remember it is the *current* cost that is sought. The past may not be a good indicator because of changes in the company, investor expectations, risk attitudes, and so forth.
Estimate Dividends	ii. Estimate of future dividends
	(a) If past dividends were approximately constant and there is no indication of a change in this pattern, the rate of return k_s is readily computed as the dividend yield:

Zero Growth Rate

$$k_s = \frac{D_1}{P} \qquad (7\text{-}1)$$

        (b) In the more typical case, dividends are expected to grow. If the growth rate g is constant,

Constant Growth Rate

$$k_s = \frac{D_1}{P} + g \qquad (7\text{-}2)$$

        Problem 8d in Chapter 5 in the *Guide* provides an application of this equation.

CAPM

     iii. **Capital Asset Pricing Model**

        (a) This is a very different approach that can be applied to many situations, including those where dividends are expected to be erratic or are nonexistent.

Riskless Rate

        (b) Use the current rate on long-term U.S. government bonds.

Market Premium

        (c) The market risk premium is about 6 percent from Table 5-2 in the text.

Beta

        (d) The beta for a stock comes from published sources such as Value Line or Merrill Lynch.

$$k_s = \text{riskless rate} + (\text{risk premium} \times \text{beta}) \qquad (7\text{-}3)$$

THE COST OF CAPITAL   **87**

Debt plus Premium

    iv. When none of the above methods applies, use the yield to maturity on the firm's debt as a reference point.

        (a) k_s will be higher because of the inherently greater risk involved in owning common stock as opposed to owning bonds.

        (b) Add some allowance—say, 4 percent to 6 percent—to the *pretax* cost of debt.

No Tax Adjustments for Stock

  c. No tax adjustments are necessary because, as in the case of preferred stock, dividends are not deductible.

  d. It is often desirable to compute k_s using several of the methods outlined above. The task of coming up with a cost of common stock is indeed difficult, for it is not a scientific procedure. Rather, it involves a combination of sound concepts and applied judgment.

Weights

C. **Determining the proportions (weights)**

  1. Alternatives include using:

    a. The existing proportions on the firm's balance sheet.

    b. The proportions of financing planned to pay for scheduled new investments (next year's fundraising).

    c. The expected future financing proportions (pro forma balance sheet).

Use Market Values

    d. The current proportions of the *market values* of the firm's outstanding securities.

  2. Method *d* is recommended for these reasons:

    a. The chicken-or-the-egg dilemma.

      i. The future financing package can't be determined until the need for funds is known.

      ii. The need for funds (new investments) can't be planned until the cost of money is computed; a high cost makes some projects unprofitable, thereby reducing the amount needed for new investments.

      iii. Current market value proportions (alternative *d*) are known when investments are being screened.

    b. The fact that current market values match up with the current market data used to determine component costs makes the process consistent; both costs and proportions are derived from information that reflects currently prevailing investor expectations of future returns and attitudes toward risk.

Multiply Weights and Costs

D. **Computing the average cost of capital k_a**

  1. Multiply the cost of each type of financing by the proportion used (based on market values) and add these products. This is analogous to computing your grade point average: the "costs" are A = 4 points, etc., and the "proportions" are the number of credits for each course.

  2. Does this sound simple? It really is, *except* don't forget the role of reasoned judgment.

3. Review the calculation, in the text, of the average cost of capital for Basic Brands to get a better feel for the process.

E. The cost of capital for foreign investments:
1. Must be modified because:
   a. Overseas projects are riskier due to
      i. Exchange rates.
      ii. Political uncertainties such as expropriation and controls on repatriation of cash.
   b. Foreign investments typically use some local funds which have different costs because of host country
      i. Tax laws.
      ii. Accounting practices.
2. Use proportions (weights) and financing costs that are appropriate to the unique circumstances of each foreign investment.

COMPLETION QUESTIONS

minimum
new
1. The cost of capital is the (*minimum/maximum*) acceptable rate of return on (*new/old*) investments.

weighted
2. The average cost of capital is the (*arithmetic/weighted*) average of the costs of types of capital used.

proportions, weights
3. The (*costs/proportions*) of each type of capital are used as _____ to the costs of different sources of money.

investments
risk, unchanged
4. To use the average cost of capital to evaluate new _____, it is assumed that the _____ character of the firm remains _____.

financing
5. Another assumption is that the (*financing/personnel*) policies of the firm are unaffected by the new investments.

average
cash flow
interest, dividends
6. The _____ cost of capital can be shown to be the minimum acceptable rate of return by computing the (*retained earnings/cash flow*) necessary to pay (*interest/principal*) and (*taxes/dividends*).

currently
investor
7. In principle, the procedure for determining the cost rate of each source of capital is to calculate the return (*currently/historically*) required by each type of (*banker/investor*).

yield to maturity
8. The rate on debt is determined by first computing the (*prime interest rate/ yield to maturity*).

yield to maturity
9. If more than one form of debt is used, the average cost is computed by multiplying each _____ _____ _____ times the

proportion	(*proportion/amount*) of that type used, and then computing the sum of these products.
	10. The weights used in aggregating different costs of debt are derived from
market	the (*book/market*) values of the types of debt.
lower	11. The effect of income taxes is to (*lower/raise*) the cost of debt to the firm.
	12. With a tax rate of 40 percent and a yield to maturity of 9 percent, the
5.4	effective cost of debt is _____ percent.
	13. If Congress were to raise corporate income tax rates, firms would tend to
increase	(*increase/decrease*) the amounts of debt they use.
dividend	14. The cost of preferred stock is equal to the annual (*interest/dividend*) divided
preferred	by the current (*common/preferred*) stock price.
equal to	15. For preferred stock the before-tax cost is (*higher than/equal to*) the aftertax cost.
	16. If Congress were to allow dividend payments to be deductible, companies
increase	would tend to (*increase/decrease*) their usage of preferred and common stock.
common	17. The cost of (*common/preferred*) stock is very difficult to determine because
fixed	there are no (*cash/fixed*) payments, as there are for other securities.
historical	18. The (*historical/current*) rate of return method for computing the cost of common stock relies on the assumption that the past is a good indicator of the future.
	19. If investors currently require higher risk premiums, the historical rate of
low	return would be too (*low/high*).
	20. If a regular and constant amount of dividend payments in the past is likely
dividend	to continue, the return required by common stockholders is the _____
yield	_____.
common stock	21. If growth is expected in dividends, the cost of (*common stock/preferred*
dividend yield	*stock*) is equal to the _____ _____ plus the (*inter-*
growth	*est/growth*) rate.
	22. For firms not having paid any dividends, the return required on common
adding, to	stock can be estimated by (*adding/subtracting*) a risk allowance (*to/from*)
debt	the firm's cost of _____.
riskfree	23. When using the CAPM to estimate the cost of capital, the (*riskfree/interest*)
beta	rate is added to the product of the risk premium and the stock's _____.

24. Incorporating a risk allowance factor into the cost of common stock is logical
greater than   because investors expect returns on common stock to be (*greater than/less than*) returns on debt.

Current   25. (*Historical/Current*) market values are recommended for determining the
proportions   (*returns/proportions*) of each type of capital.

proportions   26. Basing _____ of capital sources on existing or pro forma (*in-*
balance sheet, current   *come statement/balance sheet*) figures ignores (*current/past*) market conditions.

27. Because interest rates and investor attitudes and expectations are continually
constant   changing, the cost of capital for firms will not be _____ over time.

judgment   28. The cost of capital determination requires a blend of concepts and _____.

29. The cost of capital for foreign investments is different because of different
financing   (*languages/financing*).

30. Funding overseas investments is different because of differences in host
risks   country (*money/risks*).

PROBLEMS

1. PDQ, Inc., has two forms of debt outstanding: a bank loan that was just negotiated and a twenty-year bond that was issued five years ago. The $10 million bond issue carries a provision that its claims are to be junior to any bank borrowing, including existing amounts and amounts undertaken in the future. Today this subordinated bond, having an 8 percent coupon, is selling for $848. The interest rate on the recent $5 million bank loan is 7 percent. The income tax rate for PDQ is 55 percent.
   a. What is the before-tax cost of each of the two types of debt?

Solution

Step one   Since the bank loan was just negotiated, it represents current conditions; thus its cost is 7 percent.

Step two   The bond, however, requires some calculations; the yield to maturity must be determined. Try to solve for this on your own; refer to the solution in problem 8 of Chapter 4 to check your method if you have trouble. The answer is 10 percent.

   b. What is the before-tax average rate on debt?

Solution

Step one The key point here is to use *current* market values in weighting the costs.

Step two For the bank loan this is $5 million.

Step three The $10 million bond issue has a current market value of

$$\frac{848}{1000} \times \$10 \text{ million} = \$8.48 \text{ million}$$

Step four

$$\text{Average debt rate} = 7 \times \frac{5}{5 + 8.48} + 10 \times \frac{8.48}{8.48 + 5}$$

$$= 7 \times 0.37 + 10 \times 0.63$$

$$= 8.9\%$$

c. What is the effective rate on the debt?

Solution

Step one

$$\text{Effective rate} = \text{average before-tax rate} \times (1 - \text{tax rate})$$

$$= 8.9 \times (1 - 0.55) = 4.0\%$$

End of Solution.

2. PDQ, Inc., also has a preferred stock issue that pays an annual dividend of $3.60 per share. The stock is currently quoted at $36 per share. What is the cost of preferred for PDQ?

Solution

Step one

$$\text{Cost of preferred} = \frac{\text{annual dividend}}{\text{current price}}$$

$$= \frac{3.60}{36} = 10\%$$

Step two Remember that no tax adjustment is necessary because dividends are not deductible.

3. Nostalgia, Inc., sells sentimental-type products. Its directors apparently feel the same way about dividends because the company has paid $2 per share each year over the past decade; everyone seems happy, however. What is the cost of common stock if it is now trading at $15?

Solution

Step one This is a no-growth situation, and so the current dividend yield is needed.

Step two

$$k_s = \frac{2}{15} = 13.3\%$$

4. Repetitions, Ltd., has also paid a constant annual dividend of $2 per share. Its stock was trading five years ago for $25 per share, compared with today's price of $28. There is no reason to believe that this experience will not be repeated in the future, and the historical rate of return is expected by current investors. What is the cost of common stock?

Solution

Step one The historical rate of return concept requires the calculation of the return based on past dividend and stock price movements—say, over the past five years.

Step two k_s is the return on a $25 investment figured from the following equation:

$$\$25 = \$2 \times (P/A, k_s, 5) + \$28 \times (P/F, k_s, 5)$$

This is a trial-and-error problem. Hint: Try 10 percent, but if you have trouble, refer to the solution of problem 7c in Chapter 4. (Repetitions, Inc., was then called XYZ Company.) Using a rate of 10 percent, you get the following:

$$\$25 \overset{?}{=} \$2 \times 3.7908 + \$28 \times 0.6209$$

$$\overset{?}{=} \$24.97$$

This means that k_s is approximately equal to 10 percent.

5. Lisa's Linens and Lingerie, Ltd., a publicly traded stock, has a beta of 1.4. What is the cost of LLL's common stock if the risk premium for the stock market is 6 percent and the riskfree rate is 10 percent?

Solution

Step one   Using CAPM:

$$k_s = \text{riskfree rate} + (\text{market premium} \times \text{beta})$$

$$= 10 + (6 \times 1.4)$$

$$= 18.4\%$$

6. PDQ, Inc., has completed a successful ten-year period of growth during which its dividends rose from $1.10 per share to $3.42 per share, paid in the recently completed year. Investors expect the past performance to continue indefinitely. The stock price today is $96 per share. What is the cost of common stock k_s to this firm?

Solution

Step one   The dividends have been growing and are expected to continue to grow. The growth rate g can be found as follows:

$$\$1.10 = \$3.42 \times (P/F, g, 10)$$

$$(P/F, g, 10) = 0.3216$$

Looking in the tables at the P/F factors in the ten-year row, the number closest to 0.3216 appears in the 12 percent table.

Step two   The past growth rate of 12 percent is expected to continue; thus

$$k_s = \frac{D_1}{P} + g$$

Step three Whoa! The $3.42 dividend was paid in the most recently completed year. The equation calls for D_1, the dividends expected *next* year. D_1 will be 12 percent more than the recent dividend of $3.42; $D_1 = \$3.42 \times 1.12 = \$3.83$.

Step four Now proceed.

$$k_s = \frac{3.83}{96} + 0.12 = 0.04 + 0.12 = 0.16, \text{ or } 16\%$$

Step five Take a minute to compare the last four problems. In problem 3, the firm was paying a constant dividend, and so the dividend yield was expected to provide the return to investors. In problem 4, a modest price appreciation was taken into account in addition to the dividend yield. The Capital Asset Pricing Model was used in problem 5. Problem 6 illustrates a more typical method of recognizing growth by computing the rate and adding it to the next year's dividend yield. In all cases we are trying to estimate what returns stockholders require in the future. As an indication, we look to the past and project those results forward. Sometimes the projections need to be modified; perhaps the previous growth rate has been above normal and a lower rate is more reasonable to use, or maybe a no-growth firm has merged with another and a new ball game begins. The idea is to recognize that the past is only a reference point; judgment is called for before accepting simple extrapolations.

7. Nancy has decided to open a telephone answering service. The cost of her lot, building, and equipment is $150,000. A bank will lend her two-thirds of this amount for 10 percent, and she has cash for the remainder.
   a. What is her before-tax cost of capital if she thinks a return of 15 percent on her own investment is minimal?

Solution

Step one The component costs are known: 10 percent for debt and 15 percent for equity. Taxes are ignored in this problem, but the adjustment to the debt cost would apply if a tax rate were given.

Step two The weights of debt and equity are two-thirds and one-third, respectively, and so the average cost of capital for Nancy is

$$0.10 \times 2/3 + 0.15 \times 1/3 = 0.117, \text{ or } 11.7\%$$

b. What is the minimum before-tax cash flow required to keep Nancy happy?

Solution

Step one   Cash flow is the amount needed to provide the returns required by those who put up the capital. The bank needs 10 percent of $100,000, or $10,000 (ignoring repayments of principal). Nancy wants at least 15 percent of $50,000, or $7500.

Step two   The total minimum requirement = $10,000 + $7500 = $17,500.

Step three   This is also the average cost of capital in dollar terms. As a check,

$$\frac{\$17,500}{\$150,000} = 0.117, \text{ or } 11.7\%$$

c. If Nancy expected a 40 percent tax rate, what would be her minimum required annual cash flow?

Solution

Step one   To allow for taxes, the additional cash needed to provide aftertax profits for her equity must be computed.

Step two   To earn 15 percent (after the 40 percent tax bite) on her $50,000 investment requires:

$$\frac{0.15 \times \$50,000}{(1 - 0.4)} = \$12,500$$

Step three   The cash flow requirement is $12,500 + $10,000, or $22,500.

Step four   A check of the figure is appropriate because the adjustment for taxes is often confusing. The income statement would appear as follows:

Revenues less cash expenses	$22,500
Interest, 10%	10,000
Taxable income	$12,500
Income tax, 40%	5,000
Net profit	$ 7,500

This provides the required return on equity, k_s, of

$$\frac{\$7500}{\$50,000} = 0.15, \text{ or } 15\%$$

and a cost of debt, k_d, of

$$\frac{\$10,000}{\$100,000} = 0.10, \text{ or } 10\%$$

8. Compute the average cost of capital for PDQ, Inc., given its recent balance sheet as listed below *and* other data as presented in problems 1, 2, and 6.

PDQ, Inc., balance sheet, December 31, 19xx
(In millions of dollars)

Assets		Liabilities and equity	
Current	.....$10	Bank loan	...............$ 5
Fixed	25	Bonds (8%)	 10
Total	........$35	Preferred stock (100,000	
		shares—$50 par)	 5
		Common stock (200,000	
		shares—$1 par)	 2
		Retained earnings	13
		Total	...................$35

Solution

Step one   PDQ has three sources of capital: debt, a preferred issue, and, of course, common stock. The previous solutions indicate costs of these components as 4, 10, and 16 percent, respectively.

Step two   Determine the proportions of each component. Remember that market values, *not* book values (total of $35 million), are used.

Step three   The market value of the debt is $5 million from the bank loan and $\frac{848}{1000} \times \$10$, or $8.48 million, from the bond.

Step four The market value of the preferred equals the number of shares times the current price:

$$100{,}000 \times \$36, \text{ or } \$3.6 \text{ million}$$

Step five In a similar manner the market value of the common stock is:

$$200{,}000 \times \$96, \text{ or } \$19.2 \text{ million}$$

Step six From this information the proportions or weights are:

Component	Market value	Proportion of total
Debt	$13.48	0.37
Preferred	3.6	0.10
Common	19.2	0.53
	$36.28	1.00

Step seven Using these proportions and the costs developed in problems 1, 2, and 6, the average cost of capital is:

Component	Cost	Weight	Weighted cost
Debt	4	0.37	1.48
Preferred	10	0.10	1.00
Common	16	0.53	8.48
			10.96 (say 11%)

Step eight If there had been no market for the common stock (a privately held firm), the cost of this component could have been estimated by adding an allowance for risk to the before-tax cost of debt. Another method of determining a cost of common would be to ask the owners (if there are only a few, as in a privately owned firm, this is possible). They should respond with a rate that they feel compensates them for the risk they are subject to. Remember that the cost of capital doesn't always involve simple and precise calculations; much judgment must be used in developing an estimate of what investors will require as adequate compensation for putting up the money.

CHAPTER EIGHT

FUNDAMENTALS OF CAPITAL BUDGETING

QUINTESSENCE   Capital expenditure decisions are of crucial importance because they involve large amounts of money and the impacts are felt for long periods. To make wise investment choices, it is necessary to know how to compute and evaluate costs and benefits of proposed projects. Successful investing consists of making commitments to projects which earn at least a return that covers the cost of financing the projects. Evaluation criteria are present value, internal rate of return, payback period, and accounting rate of return. Because money has a time value, present value and internal rate of return are the most desirable, with present value being the best choice.

OUTLINE   I. What
     A. Capital budgeting is the process of determining *how much* to spend and *which* long-lived assets to acquire for the purpose of producing goods and services. The central part of this effort involves calculations to determine whether the return from an investment exceeds the cost of financing that investment.
     B. Important to development of the capital budget are:
       1. Calculations for evaluating investment proposals.
       2. Management usage of the various techniques.

     II. Why
     A. Capital expenditures are very important because normally:
       1. The dollar amounts are large.
       2. The investments are in assets that have long lives. In other words, careful analysis is required because a mistake in this area will probably be an expensive error and take a long time to rectify.
     B. Incremental cash flows associated with an investment are used because this stream of changes in the firm's purchasing power is the best measure of an asset's productivity.

III. How

Capital Budgeting Process

A. Steps in the **capital budgeting process**
 1. Forecast sales and the plant and equipment needed to meet the expected sales.
 2. Compare proposed investments with the cost of capital and make accept-or-reject decisions.
    a. Senior management may originate proposals, but the majority of ideas usually come from lower management in a bottom-up approach.
    b. Even though the final budget approval is at the top, operating managers often have the authority to approve expenditures below a certain amount.
 3. Revise and review budgets to:
    a. Account for new data.
    b. Compare expected and actual results.
       i. This pinpoints areas to emphasize and those to deemphasize.
       ii. It facilitates learning of strengths and weaknesses in the process.

Computing Cash Flows

B. **Marginal,** or **incremental, cash flows** generated by an investment are the most widely used measures of costs and benefits. They represent actual outflows and inflows—the amounts of money paid out and received.

Exclude Depreciation Except for Computing Taxes

 1. Net cash flow = inflows − outflows = revenues − expenses *excluding* depreciation − capital expenditures − income taxes.
    a. Income taxes = tax rate × (revenues − expenses *including* depreciation but *excluding* interest). This is a bit tricky, so pay close attention to what is included or excluded. Two points that will help keep this straight are:
       i. Depreciation is a noncash expense, so don't subtract it from cash inflows. However, it is an allowable expense for tax purposes, so do subtract it when figuring the taxes.
       ii. Interest has to do with financing, which at this point is of no concern, so don't subtract interest anyplace. (These charges were considered via the cost of capital in Chapter 7.)
    b. Net cash inflow is computed every period, typically every year. Usually a project begins with a cash outflow (purchase cost), and so the net cash flow initially is negative.
    c. Remember:
       i. The emphasis is on cash and not accruals.

Use Marginal Cash Flows

       ii. The key in determining *marginal* cash flows is to compute *changes* in cash flows if the investment is made. Also the timing of the changes must be recorded, i.e., *how much* and *when*.
    d. **Cash flows** are used to help evaluate an investment's desirability, whereas **cash budgets** are used to plan operations and financing.

2. In this chapter, cash flows are assumed to be all of the same risk; treatment of varying risks is covered in Chapter 10.

Benefit-Cost Measures

C. **Evaluation techniques**
   1. After determining cash flows, the problem becomes one of deciding whether to make an investment; this involves computing some measure that will compare costs with benefits.
   2. **Present value**
      a. This tells what the project cash flows are worth in today's dollars.
      b. It incorporates the time-value-of-money principle by discounting future cash flows at the cost of capital.

Net Present Value

      c. The **net present value (NPV)** of an investment is computed as follows:

$$\text{NPV} = \text{present value of future cash flows} - \text{initial cost}$$

$$= \frac{CF_1}{1 + k} + \frac{CF_2}{(1 + k)^2} + \cdots + \frac{CF_n}{(1 + k)^n} - I$$

$$\boxed{\begin{aligned} &= CF_1 \times (P/F, k, 1) + CF_2 \times (P/F, k, 2) \\ &\quad + \cdots + CF_n \times (P/F, k, n) - I \end{aligned}} \qquad (8\text{-}1)$$

Or, if the cash flows are equal and occur at regular intervals (an annuity):

$$\boxed{\text{NPV} = CF_1 \times (P/A, k, n) - I} \qquad (8\text{-}2)$$

Accept/Reject Decision

      d. Interpreting NPV
         i. If NPV is positive, the rate of return is greater than the cost of capital, so accept the project.
         ii. If NPV is zero, the rate of return is equal to the cost of capital, and so the project is marginally acceptable.
         iii. If NPV is negative, the rate of return is less than the cost of capital, so reject the project.

Mutually Exclusive Investments

      e. **Mutually exclusive** investments exist if, when one alternative is accepted, the others will not be needed. Choose, from the group of mutually exclusive investments, the one which has the *highest positive* NPV.
      f. The rules in items *d* and *e* above apply when the firm can get all the money it wants at the cost of capital rate used in the computations. If it can't raise the funds needed according to the

Capital Rationing

acceptance criteria, a problem of **capital rationing** occurs. Stay

Internal Rate of Return

3. **Internal rate of return (IRR)**

   a. This is the *discount rate r* that gives an NPV of zero. It is the rate of return of a project, and it is the same as the yield to maturity on a bond.

   b. It can be found in the equation

$$NPV = 0 = \frac{CF_1}{1 + r} + \frac{CF_2}{(1 + r)^2} + \cdots + \frac{CF_n}{(1 + r)^n} - I$$

$$= CF_1 \times (P/F, r, 1) + CF_2 \times (P/F, r, 2)$$
$$+ \cdots + CF_n \times (P/F, r, n) - I \qquad (8\text{-}3)$$

   i. This is a tough equation to solve, especially if the project lasts for more than two years. A trial-and-error solution is needed. Remember the problems of determining return on common stock (problem 7c in Chapter 4) and calculating the yield to maturity (problem 8 in Chapter 4)? You don't? Then this would be a good time to go back and review the solutions, keeping in mind that these problems were really seeking the internal rate of return.

   ii. If the cash flow returns are an annuity, the problem is greatly simplified and can be readily solved according to the equation

$$NPV = 0 = CF \times (P/A, r, n) - I \qquad (8\text{-}4)$$

Accept-Reject Rules

   c. Decision rules. Compare r with the cost of capital k, and if:
   i. $r > k$, the project should be accepted.
   ii. $r = k$, the project is marginally acceptable.
   iii. $r < k$, the project should be rejected.

With NPV, *k* Is Known
For IRR, NPV Is Zero

   d. The relationship between NPV and IRR is quite straightforward:
   i. The NPV method uses the cost of capital as the discount rate to calculate the NPV; the IRR method uses an NPV of zero and then computes the discount rate.
   ii. The decisions arrived at by either method usually give the same acceptances or rejections. IRR can cause problems; see items *e, f,* and *g* below.
   iii. Graphic illustration is helpful. In Figure 8-1 the cost of capital is less than the internal rate of return, so the NPV is positive. Note that the NPV declines as the discount rate is increased. This is the typical case.

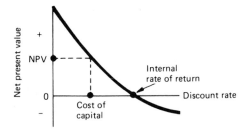

FIGURE 8-1

Mutually Exclusive Investments

e. For *mutually exclusive investments* compute the internal rate of return of *incremental* cash flows.

   i. First subtract the set of cash flows of one project from those of another.

  ii. Compute the r of these incremental cash flows.

 iii. If r is greater than $k,$ choose the project whose cash flows were being subtracted from; in the text example of D minus $E,$ D was chosen since the r on the incremental cash flows, $D - E,$ was 13.8 percent, which was greater than the cost of capital of 10 percent.

 iv. Using the "winner," subtract the cash flows of another of the mutually exclusive projects to compute a new set of incremental cash flows and then determine a new r.

  v. Test the reigning champion for acceptance by computing the project r and applying the decision rules in item 3c above.

 vi. (This is the last point.) Note that only at the end of the process is a project r computed. It would be tempting to compute r for each of the mutually exclusive projects and then choose the highest r. Resist this temptation! You might end up picking the second- or third-best choice, or worse. To apply the IRR method to mutually exclusive projects requires an incremental analysis procedure; there are no shortcuts.

Reinvestment Rate

f. The **reinvestment rate** assumption will influence the choice of investments.

   i. This has to do with the assumed rate of return on cash flows as they become available to the firm.

  ii. For mutually exclusive projects:

    (a) If the reinvestment rate is the same as the cost of capital, choose the highest NPV or the best project that emerges from the incremental analysis used with the IRR method.

    (b) In a special (and rare) case, r can be computed directly and the project with the highest r chosen when the cost of all projects is the same and when cash flows can be reinvested at the calculated r for a period that is the same for all projects.

g. Summary comparison of NPV and IRR

    i. IRR has an appeal because it gives a number that is easy to relate to, i.e., 20 percent. This is offset by the fact that the calculations required are usually more complex and in some cases require very difficult interpretations.

NPV Is the Best Criterion

    ii. NPV works better; it is recommended.

    iii. Additional support of NPV is offered in the text Appendixes 8A and 8B.

Payback

4. **Payback period** method

a. The payback period is the time to recover, via aftertax cash flows, the initial investment.

b. In this method the quicker the payback, the better; accept only those projects that have a shorter payback than the maximum time set by management.

Disadvantages

c. Disadvantages of this method

    i. It ignores cash flows after the payback period; no credit is given for these returns.

    ii. It ignores the timing of cash flows within the payback period; no extra credit is given for early returns.

d. "Advantages." (This word is in quotes because each of the alleged "pro"s can be effectively refuted.)

    i. Exposure to risk can be minimized by always asking how long it takes to get the money back or simply by accepting only short paybacks. (This still ignores most of the time-value-of-money criticism.)

    ii. Payback can be used as a rough screen in conjunction with another, more theoretically correct criterion, i.e., NPV. (Why mess around? Use the justifiable approach in the first place.)

    iii. Payback is simple. (More careful analysis is easily worth the trouble—in the case of NPV, the additional effort is insignificant.)

e. Payback is still widely used. (The Schall-Haley readers know better.)

Accounting Rate of Return

5. **Accounting rate of return (ARR)**

a. This is the average annual aftertax accounting *profit* divided by the average investment.

Disadvantages

b. Two problems here:

    i. Profits are *not* cash flow. Can you imagine some accountant trying to deposit profits in the bank?

    ii. The time value of money is ignored, just as in the payback method.

NPV and IRR Are Widely Used

D. Company usage of capital budgeting techniques

1. Increasing numbers of firms are using NPV or IRR.

Project Analysis

2. The larger, more capital intensive firms use NPV or IRR.
3. This popularity is due to the benefits that result from better project selection.
E. Typical investment projects (example problems are given at the end of the chapter):
   1. Cost reductions from adding additional assets: e.g., automate a process.
   2. Revenue increases from adding additional assets: e.g., build a new plant.
   3. Replacement of existing assets: e.g., buy a better machine.
      a. When a used asset is sold for more than its book value, the tax due on the gain is recorded as a cash outflow.
      b. A loss in book value reduces taxes due; the amount of the tax reduction is treated as a cash inflow.

COMPLETION QUESTIONS

Capital
1. *(Capital/Operating)* expenditures are made for the purpose of acquiring assets that are used for several years.

budgeting
invest, assets
2. Capital *(budgeting/rationing)* is the process of determining how much to *(sell/invest)* and which long-lived *(assets/liabilities)* to acquire.

returns
cost
3. The evaluation of projects involves comparison of the _____ from the investments with the _____ of acquiring and financing the assets.

expenditures
long
4. Capital budgeting is very important to firms because the _____ are large and the assets *(short/long)*-lived.

cash flow
5. The most widely used measure of returns from investments is *(profit/cash flow)*.

interest
depreciation
6. In computing cash flows, *(interest/dividends)* and cost recovery, which is equivalent to _____, are excluded from the expenses.

depreciation is
7. However, *(dividends are/depreciation is)* included when figuring income taxes.

cash flows, today's
8. Present value tells what the *(profits/cash flows)* are worth in _____ dollars.

time-value
discounting, cost
capital
9. Present value incorporates the _____-_____-of-money principle by *(compounding/discounting)* cash flows at the _____ of _____.

present value	10. The net present value (NPV) equals the _____ _____ of future cash flows minus the (*initial cost/salvage value*) of the project.
initial cost	
greater	11. If the NPV is positive, the rate of return is (*less/greater*) than the cost of capital. In this case the project should be (*accepted/rejected*).
accepted	
equals	12. When the NPV is zero, the rate of return (*exceeds/equals*) the cost of capital.
negative, rejected	13. Projects having a (*positive/negative*) NPV should be (*accepted/rejected*) because their returns are less than the financing costs.
	14. Two or more alternative investments that will do the same thing are known as _____ _____ investments.
mutually exclusive	
	15. The best of several mutually exclusive investments is the one having the (*highest/lowest*) NPV.
highest	
internal rate, return	16. The _____ _____ of _____ is the discount rate that gives an NPV of zero.
yield, maturity	17. The IRR is another name for the _____ to _____ on a bond.
easier	18. Solving for the IRR is made much (*easier/harder*) when the cash returns are an annuity.
cost, capital	19. If the IRR is greater than the _____ of _____, the project should be (*accepted/rejected*).
accepted	
less, cost	20. Reject projects whose IRR is (*greater/less*) than the _____ of _____.
capital	
NPV, discount	21. In the (*NPV/IRR*) method, the _____ rate is known; in the _____ method, the _____ rate is unknown.
IRR, discount	
zero	22. NPV is _____ in all IRR calculations.
exclusive	23. In applying IRR to evaluate mutually _____ investments, use _____ cash flows.
incremental	
greater	24. If the IRR on incremental cash flows is (*greater/less*) than the cost of capital, choose the project whose cash flows are being subtracted from.
	25. After the best of the mutually exclusive projects is identified, compute its (*cash flow/IRR*) to determine whether it should be accepted.
IRR	
NPV	26. According to the text, the best method for evaluating projects is _____.
time	27. The payback period is the (*return/time*) it takes to recover the (*initial investment/salvage value*).
initial investment	

rejected
28. If a target payback period, as set by management, was four years and a proposed project required five years, the project should be (*accepted*/*rejected*).

after

timing, during
29. The payback method ignores cash flows (*during*/*after*) the payback period and does not recognize the _____ of cash flows _____ the payback period.

is not

payback
30. The simplicity of calculation (*is*/*is not*) a valid reason for using (*IRR*/*payback*).

accounting

rate, return

profits
31. Of the project evaluation methods discussed, all except the _____ _____ of _____ use cash flows; this method instead uses (*profits*/*dividends*).

rate, return

value
32. The accounting _____ of _____ does not account for the time _____ of money.

PROBLEMS

For problems 1 through 9 use the situation as described immediately below. Make only the changes set forth in the specific problem and refer to the original information for all other data.

BCD, Inc., is considering constructing another plant, which would add capacity to increase its sales by 20 percent over this year's level of $20 million. With the new plant, which costs $7.5 million, the total cash expenses (excluding taxes) are expected to increase from $15 million to $17.5 million. Assuming that the tax rate is 40 percent, existing annual depreciation is $1.5 million, and straight-line depreciation applies to the new project, which has a life of fifteen years and no salvage value:

1. Compute the cash flows using the format of Exhibit 8-1 in the text.

Solution

Step one The secret to determining cash flows is to compare the firm on a with-and-without basis, looking for *changes* in cash flows. Sometimes these are quite readily determined, but they can involve rather complex calculations. To minimize confusion, it will be helpful to form a habit of following the format presented in the table below. While the added cash flows could be determined without using the "with" and "without" columns in the table, it is advisable to fill them in and get used to the procedures so that it will be easier to handle the more difficult situations.

Step two   Sales with the new plant are 120 percent of the existing level, or $20 \times 1.2 = \$24$ million.

Step three   The depreciation on the new plant is $\dfrac{\$7.5}{15}$, or $0.5 million, giving a total of $1.5 + $0.5, or $2.0 million.

Step four   Other entries in the table are:

| | Cash flows from a new investment, $ millions | | |
Item	Cash flows without the new plant	Cash flows including the new plant	Added cash flows from the new plant
Sales	20	24	4
Cash expenses	15	17.5	2.5
Taxes:			
Revenues less expense ... 5.0		6.5	1.5
Less depreciation 1.5		2.0	0.5
Taxable income 3.5		4.5	1.0
Income tax	1.4	1.8	0.4
Net cash flow	3.6	4.7	1.1

Step five   The cash flows are:

Period	Cash flow, $ millions
0	−7.5
1–15	1.1

Assumptions:		Summary of changes in cash flows:		
Asset life	15 years	Sales		4.0
Initial cost	$7.5 million	Less expenses:		
Tax rate	40%	Cash (excl. taxes)	2.5	
Salvage value	zero	Taxes	0.4	2.9
		Equals cash flow		1.1

2. Suppose the plant was estimated to be worth $1.5 million at the end of its life. How would this affect cash flows?

Solution

Step one   The impact of the $1.5 million salvage value would be as follows:
a. Depreciation (straight-line) is:

$$\frac{\text{Initial outlay} - \text{salvage value}}{\text{Project life}} = \frac{\$7.5 - \$1.5}{15} = \$0.4 \text{ million}$$

b. Taxable income then equals $1.5 − $0.4, or $1.1 million.
c. Taxes are $1.1 × 0.4 = $0.44 million.
d. Annual cash flow = $4 − ($2.5 + $0.44) = $1.06 million.
e. In year fifteen the salvage value would be added to the regular cash flow to provide a return of $1.06 + $1.5, or $2.56 million.
End of solution.

3. Compute the net present value (NPV) of BCD's proposed new plant assuming the cost of capital is 10 percent. Do not adjust for salvage value.

Solution

Step one   NPV = present value of cash inflows − initial outlay.

Step two   Since the cash inflows occur every year and are equal, an annuity factor can be used.

Step three

$$\text{NPV} = \$1.1 \times (P/A,\ 10\%,\ 15) - \$7.5$$
$$= \$1.1 \times 7.6061 - \$7.5$$
$$= \$0.867 \text{ million}$$

Step four   The NPV calculation is easier when the cash flows are the same each year because the annuity factor makes it possible to compute the present value of the entire stream of cash flow (note the poetic beauty of financial terminology here: "stream of . . . flows") in one step. When cash flows vary, the computations take a little longer. This is illustrated in problem 10.

4. Compute the NPV at discount rates of 0, 5, and 15 percent.

Solution

Step one At 0 percent,

$$NPV = \$1.1 \times (P/A, 0\%, 15) - \$7.5$$
$$= \$1.1 \times 15 - \$7.5$$
$$= \$9.9 \text{ million}$$

Note that there is no table of factors at 0 percent. It isn't needed because a discount rate of zero will not penalize future cash flows at all. It is just like saying that "a dollar received today is the same as a dollar received any time in the future." Thus if you were to receive $1 per year for fifteen years, this would have a present value of the sum of $1 payments every year for fifteen years. The factor is simply 1×15, or 15. This is all pretty silly, you say. Well, think of the implicit assumption in the payback and accounting rate of return methods, which ignore the time value of money. Doesn't that win the prize for silliness?

Step two At 5 percent,

$$NPV = \$1.1 \times (P/A, 5\%, 15) - \$7.5$$
$$= \$1.1 \times 10.3797 - \$7.5$$
$$= \$3.918 \text{ million}$$

Step three At 15 percent,

$$NPV = \$1.1 \times (P/A, 15\%, 15) - \$7.5$$
$$= \$1.1 \times 5.8474 - \$7.5$$
$$= -\$1.068 \text{ million}$$

Step four Wait a minute! The NPV is negative. This means the project should be rejected; in other words, if the cost of money is 15 percent, this is an unprofitable investment. The effect of cost of capital on NPV will be discussed again in problem 7.

5. What would be the effect on the NPV if a salvage value of $1.5 million were estimated as in problem 2?

Solution

Step one Salvage value *reduces* the depreciation, resulting in *more* taxes and *less* cash flow. The annuity becomes $1.06 million per year, and a single cash flow of $1.5 million occurs when the project ends, fifteen years hence.

Step two

$$NPV = \$1.06 \times (P/A, \ 10\%, \ 15) + \$1.5 \times (P/F, \ 10\%, \ 15) - \$7.5$$

$$= \$1.06 \times 7.6061 + \$1.5 \times 0.2394 - \$7.5$$

$$= \$8.422 - \$7.5$$

$$= \$0.922 \text{ million}$$

6. Compute the internal rate of return (IRR) on the plant, given the original data and conditions.

Solution

Step one The IRR is the discount rate r that gives an NPV of zero.

Step two NPV $= 0 =$ present value of inflows $-$ initial cost.

Step three This is an annuity, which makes the computations much simpler; thus

$$0 = \$1.1 \times (P/A, \ r, \ 15) - \$7.5$$

$$(P/A, \ r, \ 15) = \frac{7.5}{1.1} = 6.818$$

Step four From the appropriate table, we find r to be very close to 12 percent.

Step five Note that the problem would be much more difficult if the cash flows varied every year in the future. The trial-and-error method would have to be followed.

7. The original data were for the new plant built using the X process. Suppose that a competing process, Y, will produce the same product but that the NPVs, in millions of dollars, at discount rates of 0, 5, 10, and 15 percent are 7, 3, 0.867, and zero, respectively. Plot the NPVs for each of these plants at different discount rates. Interpret the graph.

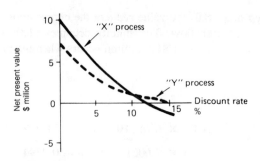

FIGURE 8-2

Solution

Step one   The X process is superior as long as the cost of capital is less than 10 percent, because the NPV is higher.

Step two   At 10 percent either process could be chosen.

Step three   Above 10 percent the Y process should be used because it has a higher NPV.

Step four   The IRR of X is 12 percent, and that of Y is 15 percent.

Step five   If the cost of capital is above 15 percent, no plant should be built because both alternatives will have negative NPVs.

8. Compute the payback period for BCD's proposed $7.5 million new plant.

Solution

Step one

$$\text{Payback period} = \frac{\text{investment}}{\text{annual cash flow}}$$

Step two   The cash flows are determined in problem 1 as $1.1 million per year:

$$\text{Payback period} = \frac{7.5}{1.1} = 6.8 \text{ years}$$

Step three This may seem like rather a long time to wait for the cash outlay to be recovered (almost seven years), especially if money has a high time value to the firm. Remember that the project life is fifteen years, and so considerable benefits will be reaped from this "late bloomer" after the payback period. The question is: Will there be enough benefits? Do you see why payback is such a weak tool for evaluating projects?

9. Compute the accounting rate of return on the new plant.

Solution

Step one This measure is equal to the average annual earnings divided by the average investment.

Step two From the solution to problem 1 we know that taxable income is $1.0 million and that taxes are $0.4 million.

Step three This means that the annual earnings will be $1.0 − $0.4, or $0.6 million.

Step four The average investment is one-half of $7.5, or $3.75 million. (If the project had a salvage value of $1.5 million, the average investment would be $\dfrac{\$7.5 - \$1.5}{2}$, or $3 million.)

Step five The accounting rate of return is

$$\frac{0.6}{3.75} = 0.16, \text{ or } 16\%$$

Step six How good is that? It's very hard to tell other than to say that the higher, the better, but because ARR uses profits and ignores the timing of the benefits, it is a rather poor indicator.

10. Purple Prune Packers, Inc., is considering the purchase of a $20,000 Perkins prune pitter, which will reduce costs, thereby increasing cash flows and earnings as follows:

Year	Cash flow	Earnings
1	$12,000	$4,000
2	8,000	3,000
3	5,000	2,000

Compute the payback period, the accounting rate of return, the internal rate of return, the NPV, and the profitability index assuming a cost of capital of 12 percent.

Solution

Step one This is a quickie. The only new wrinkle (pun intended) is the variation in the benefits every year.

Step two Payback period: This is the time required for the cash inflows to recover the initial outlay of $20,000. This occurs in *two years* ($12,000 + $8000 = $20,000).

Step three Accounting rate of return:

$$\text{Average annual profits} = \frac{\$12,000 + \$8000 + \$5000}{3} = \$8333$$

$$\text{Average investment} = \frac{\$20,000}{2} = \$10,000$$

$$\text{ARR} = \frac{\$8333}{\$10,000} = 0.833, \text{ or } 83\%$$

Step four IRR:

$$0 = \$12,000 \times (P/F, r, 1) + \$8000 \times (P/F, r, 2)$$
$$+ \$5000 \times (P/F, r, 3) - \$20,000$$

Try 10 percent:

$$0 \overset{?}{=} \$12,000 \times 0.9091 + \$8000 \times 0.8264$$
$$+ \$5000 \times 0.7513 - \$20,000$$
$$\overset{?}{=} \$1277$$

Thus, a higher discount rate is needed. Try 14 percent:

$$0 \overset{?}{=} \$12,000 \times 0.8772 + \$8000 \times 0.7695$$
$$+ \$5000 \times 0.6750 - \$20,000$$
$$= \$57$$

which is almost zero, and so the IRR is about 14 percent.

Step five   NPV:

$$NPV = \$12,000 \times (P/F, \ 12\%, \ 1)$$
$$+ \$8000 \times (P/F, \ 12\%, \ 2)$$
$$+ \$5000 \times (P/F, \ 12\%, \ 3) - \$20,000$$
$$= \$12,000 \times 0.8929 + \$8000 \times 0.7972$$
$$+ \$5000 \times 0.7118 - \$20,000$$
$$= \$651$$

Step six   The profitability index is the NPV divided by the investment:

$$\frac{\$651}{\$20,000} = 0.0326$$

11. Suppose that People's Manufacturing, Inc., also makes prune pitters but that their model is first-class, i.e., more expensive—in fact, double the Perkins price. The People's prune pitter will reduce costs even more: Net cash savings will come to $17,810 per year for the three years the machine lasts. Which machine should be purchased according to the IRR method?

Solution   **Step one**   These two investments are mutually exclusive, and so an incremental cash flow analysis must be performed.

	Cash flows, $ thousands		
Year	Perkins	People's	People's − Perkins
0	−20	−40.0	−20.0
1	12	17.8	5.8
2	8	17.8	9.8
3	5	17.8	12.8

Step two IRR for incremental cash flow:

$$0 = \$5.8 \times (P/F, r, 1)$$
$$+ \$9.8 \times (P/F, r, 2)$$
$$+ \$12.8 \times (P/F, r, 3) - \$20$$

Try 14 percent:

$$0 \stackrel{?}{=} \$5.8 \times 0.8772 + \$9.8 \times 0.7695$$
$$+ \$12.8 \times 0.6750 - \$20$$
$$\stackrel{?}{=} \$1.269$$

Thus a higher discount rate is needed.
Try 18 percent:

$$0 \stackrel{?}{=} \$5.8 \times 0.8475 + \$9.8 \times 0.7182$$
$$+ \$12.8 \times 0.6086 - \$20$$
$$\stackrel{?}{=} -\$0.256$$

This means that the IRR on the incremental cash flows is about 17 percent, which is above the cost of capital, and so the People's prune pitter is favored.

CAPITAL BUDGETING: SPECIAL TOPICS

QUINTESSENCE   Many times, alternative capital projects will have different lives, so the analyst must use multiples of one or the other in order to make the cost-benefit calculations on a comparable (equal-life) basis. Inflation expectations are incorporated into the cash flow estimates by the analyst and into the discount rate by current expectations of security market returns. For interrelated investments, the results of combinations are computed. Calculations for capital rationing are used to maximize the benefit for a given level of expenditure. Analysis for multinational corporations includes effects on cash flows of doing business internationally.

OUTLINE
I. What
  A. In practice, the analysis of capital investments requires the incorporation of many factors.
  B. Often there are several proposals for accomplishing the same benefit, but they will have unequal lives.
  C. All project costs and benefits are estimated at the time they are actually encountered.
  D. Cash flows from some projects are interdependent.
  E. Foreign investments take place in different circumstances which affect cash flows.
II. Why
  A. Capital budgeting must be complete to be realistic and helpful.
  B. Valid comparisons must be made to choose the best set of investments.
  C. Inflation affects cash flows.
  D. Acceptance of some projects affects cash flows in others being considered in the pool of potential projects.
  E. The most appropriate capital budget will maximize the benefit for a level of outlay.
  F. Good opportunities exist for doing business globally.
III. How

**Projects with
Different Lives**
  A. Comparing projects with *different lives*—ideally, they should be evaluated for equal time periods by assuming the consecutive purchase of

117

two or more of the shorter-life assets. In reality, an identical matching is not necessary; approximations are acceptable, especially if:
1. The project lives are not vastly different.
2. The projects are *long-lasting* and the differences are, say, between forty- and fifty-year lives.
3. The rate of return on *future* investments is close to the cost of capital.

Incorporating Inflation

B. **Inflation and capital budgeting**
1. Incorporate expected price rises into the estimates of future cash flows.
2. The cost of capital is based on market rates, which also take inflation expectations into account.

Interdependent Projects

C. **Interrelated investment opportunities**
1. Determine possible combinations of the interdependent projects.
2. Compute the cash flows and present value of each combination.
3. Choose the set having the highest positive NPV.
4. In theory, all investments are somewhat interrelated, but in practice most are approximately independent and don't require this procedure; follow it only when the interrelationships are significant.

Capital Rationing

D. **Capital rationing**—sort of like "too much month at the end of the money"
1. This is the case of not being able to accept all potentially profitable investments because of a limited availability of dollars for capital outlays.
2. The problem is not too unpleasant; it consists of picking the best from a group of acceptable projects.
3. Using the NPV method:
   a. Compute the total net present value for different groupings of acceptable projects that stay within the expenditure limit.
   b. Choose the set having the highest total NPV.
   c. This may take some time, especially if there is a large number of potentially acceptable projects. Use a special technique cited in the text footnote (dynamic programming), or, if the investments are independent:

Profitability Index

4. Use the **profitability index.**
   a. This is the NPV divided by the investment cost.
   b. Rank the projects according to decreasing profitability indexes.
   c. Go down the list, accepting all projects (they must be independent and not mutually exclusive) until all the available funds are committed.
      i. It will often not be possible to spend the entire capital budget, so be careful to check which of the last few projects should be chosen.
      ii. Keep in mind that the "limit" on capital spending is somewhat flexible; there may be compelling reasons to expand or reduce the total after analyzing the investment proposals.

E. Capital budgeting for the multinational corporation
  1. Cash flows from foreign projects may be hindered or enhanced by:
     a. **Blockages** (restrictions) of funds for repatriation (return to the parent firm).
     b. Setting transfer prices so as to maximize profits in the host country.
     c. Management fees and royalty charges paid to the parent.
  2. Use the incremental cash flow to the parent for NPV calculations.
  3. Include forecasts of exchange rate movements in the cash flow estimates.
  4. Additional exchange rate risks result from:

Economic Exposure

     a. **Economic exposure**—fluctuations in exchange rates cause changes in the NPVs in the home country currency.

Competitive Exposure

     b. **Competitive exposure**—fluctuations in exchange rates cause changes in product prices, e.g., they become more or less competitive. Some protection can be obtained through diversification by having supply sources in different countries.

Accounting Exposure

     c. **Accounting exposure**—fluctuations in exchange rates cause changes in the book value of the subsidiary which creates gains or losses and affects income taxes. This risk can be eliminated by keeping the book value (net equity position) at zero.
  5. Political risks include:
     a. Blocked funds—governmental regulations (which can change) that restrict repatriation.

Expropriation

     b. **Expropriation**—governmental seizure of assets with little or no compensation.

OPIC

  6. The **Overseas Private Investment Corporation** (OPIC) offers insurance against currency inconvertibility, expropriation, and war damage.

COMPLETION QUESTIONS

1. The general rule, when comparing projects of unequal life, is to make consecutive investments in the project with the (*shorter/longer*) life so as to approximately _____ the time period of the longer-lived investment.

   shorter
   match

2. The effects of inflation should be (*incorporated into/excluded from*) estimates of future cash flows.

   incorporated into

3. Interrelated investments are those whose _____ _____ are affected by the acceptance of the other interrelated investments. These projects are (*independent of/dependent upon*) one another.

   cash flows
   dependent upon

cash flows, NPV	4. First group interrelated investments into possible combinations. Then compute _____ _____ and (*NPV/IRR*) for the total of
highest positive	the investments in each combination. Choose the set having the (*highest positive/lowest negative*) NPV.
rationing	5. Capital (*budgeting/rationing*) is said to exist when a firm has more profitable investment opportunities than it can raise money to finance.
profitability	6. A method of picking the best investments from a list of acceptable ones involves the calculation of the _____ index. This measure is
NPV, investment cost	equal to the (*IRR/NPV*) divided by the _____ _____.
increasing	7. In practice, (*increasing/decreasing*) numbers of firms are using NPV or IRR
capital	for capital budgeting. Most of the larger (*capital/labor*) intensive firms use these techniques.
dollars	8. Cash flows from foreign subsidiaries should be translated into _____ for capital budgeting analysis.
economic, competitive	9. Exchange rate fluctuations cause impacts on _____, _____,
accounting	and _____ factors.
blockages	10. Political risks include fund (*balances/blockages*) and (*expropriation/capi-*
expropriation	*talization*).
transfer	11. Effects of restrictions on repatriation can be offset by adjusting _____
fees	prices and charging _____ for management assistance.
book value	12. Changes in exchange rates can change the (*book value/incorporation*) of the subsidiary.
	13. Subsidiaries having operations in natural resources may have substantial
expropriation	exposure to (*exploitation/expropriation*).
does not	14. The Overseas Private Investment Corporation (*does/does not*) make direct investments abroad.
wars	15. OPIC offers insurance against (*natural disasters/wars*).

PROBLEMS

1. Suppose the People's machine (as described in problems 10 and 11 of Chapter 8) because of a higher initial cost, also lasted longer—say, six years. Set up a table of cash flows showing how to evaluate these mutually exclusive investments which have different lives, but don't solve the cost-benefit analysis.

Solution

Step one The point of this problem is to compare the projects on as close to an equal-life basis as practical. In this case, the purchase of two Perkins pitters will do the job: the first one now and the second one in three years. Cash flows will then be:

	Cash flows, $ thousands	
Year	Perkins	People's
0	−20.0	−40.0
1	12.0	17.8
2	8.0	17.8
3	−15.0*	17.8
4	12.0	17.8
5	8.0	17.8
6	5.0	17.8

*This is the net cash flow comprised of the outlay for a new machine and an inflow from the last year of the old machine (−20 + 5 = −15).

Step two Now the cost-benefit part would be solved to compare these projects (NPV is the recommended technique).

Step three Any allowances for inflation should be included in the future cash flows; e.g., increase the cost of the pitter to be purchased three years hence or change the savings to reflect future costs.

2. Hare Oil Petroleum, Inc., is considering modernizing its refineries around the country. It can raise $10 million for new construction and wishes to choose the most profitable projects. They are each independent investments and vary according to the following table:

	$ Million	
Refinery	Investment	NPV
A	1.5	0.3
B	2.5	1.0
C	2.0	1.2
D	3.0	0.3
E	2.5	0.4
F	1.0	0.3
G	4.0	0.2

Solution

Step one The goal is to "get the most bang for the buck."

Step two To select the best set, one can try various combinations that stay within the $10 million limit, adding up the NPVs, and choosing the combination having the highest total NPV. However, this is a time-consuming process.

Step three Therefore, calculate the profitability indexes (NPV/investment) for each project and arrange them in decreasing order, thus:

Refinery	Profitability index	Cumulative investment, $ millions
C	0.6	2.0
B	0.4	4.5
F	0.3	5.5
A	0.2	7.0
D	0.1	10.0
E	0.08	12.5
G	0.05	16.5

Step four The $10 million is spent after accepting projects down through D. E and G, while acceptable, are not as relatively profitable and therefore should not be chosen unless more money is available.

Step five If the $10 million has not been totally exhausted (remember that it is often necessary to accept *all* or *none* of the project), then one should try substituting E or G for D to see whether a combination having a higher total NPV can be obtained.

3. Finance University guarantees that its students entering today will not have a tuition increase in real dollars during their four consecutive years of college. If inflation occurs at a 5 percent annual rate, what would be the fees at the beginning of the senior year if the current amount is $15,000?

Solution

Step one Finance U. is expecting to offer its education for a constant dollar amount. Adjustments to the fees are based on the preceding year's inflation.

Step two At the beginning of the senior year the fee level will have increased by the compounding of 5 percent for 3 years:

$$\$15,000 \times (1.05)^3 = \$17,364$$

4. Alphabet Chemicals, Inc., is considering introducing three new products: X, Y, and Z at investment outlays of $100, $150, and $50, respectively. They are each projected to have benefits, in present value terms, of $140, $180, and $70, respectively. However, they are interdependent because X inhibits sales of Y and Z, and Y and Z enhance each other's sales. The specific benefit present values of the combinations are X and Y = $300, X and Z = $160, Y and Z = $300, and all three offer $320. Which projects should be chosen?

Solution

Step one The rather confusing array of information can be ordered by listing the costs and benefits of each possible combination of projects and then computing the net present value (NPV).

Project	Cost	Benefit	NPV
X	100	140	40
Y	150	180	30
Z	50	70	20
X and Y	250	300	50
X and Z	150	160	10
Y and Z	200	300	100
X, Y, and Z	300	320	20

Step two The highest NPV is the combination of Y and Z. Note that all projects and all combinations are profitable; i.e., they have positive net present values. However, because of the negative impact of X on the other projects, the best decision is to choose only Y and Z.

CHAPTER TEN

RISK ANALYSIS AND CAPITAL BUDGETING

QUINTESSENCE   Good capital budgeting decisions require that differences in risks of proposed projects be reflected in the analysis. Most often this is done using judgment to adjust the discount rate or to raise the minimum acceptable rate of return for different risk categories of investments. Quantitative approaches to incorporating risk factors include sensitivity analysis, computer simulation, and decision tree analysis; these are used to help derive probability distributions that in turn are used to develop risk measures. The Capital Asset Pricing Model also provides a means for determining risk-adjusted discount rates. These rates can be estimated using betas for publicly owned stocks of companies in businesses that are similar to the projects being evaluated. For international projects, the cash flows and discount rates are to be adjusted to account for the risk impacts.

OUTLINE

I. What
   A. The problem of evaluating risky investments is discussed.
   B. Informal methods of incorporating risk into capital budgeting procedures are described.
   C. Quantitative approaches to risk analysis and investment decision making are presented, including probability distributions and the **Capital Asset Pricing Model (CAPM).**
II. Why
   A. Proposed investment projects have projected streams of cash flows that represent varying degrees of risk compared to each other.
   B. Risk does affect value, so there is a need to know how and how much. The most reasoned selection of capital investments requires a system for comparing the relative desirability of the projects. The method should include measures that account for:
   1. The amounts and timing of cash flows.
   2. The riskiness of those flows.
III. How
   A. Uncertainty of cash flows for every investment project must be analyzed to help minimize the potential for making wrong (costly) decisions. There are many ways to do this, but they all have the following in common:

125

1. A framework for analysis (most methods use the discounted cash flow approach).
2. An assessment of the project's risk.
3. An adjustment for that risk.

Judgment of Risk

B. There are three **informal methods of risk analysis.** Each of these nonquantitative techniques is based on *judgment*. As such, they have an accuracy problem because they do not consider how the firm's owners will value the risky cash flows from the projects proposed.

Conservative Estimates

1. Using **conservative estimates** of cash flows is the most common qualitative approach to risk evaluation.
   a. For example, one can reduce revenue projections and/or increase cost estimates.
   b. There are three major problems with this approach:
      i. With low-risk projects, the cash flow adjustments may overcompensate because the cost of capital used in discounting already includes a risk factor (remember the cost of capital is higher than the riskfree rate).
      ii. The conservative estimates method places total reliance on judgment for determining the *size* of the adjustments.
      iii. The people who originate the proposals may react to the adjusting process by making overly optimistic estimates of cash flows.

Raise Hurdle Rates

2. In the **judgmental risk evaluation** procedure, the calculated internal rate of return for projects must be *judged* to be sufficiently higher than the cost of capital in order for the proposal to be accepted. An experienced financial manager can use this method with some success.

Classify Projects

3. Large firms may use a **project classification** system for incorporating risk into capital budgeting decisions.
   a. The cost of capital is estimated for each division making a different product line.
   b. These divisional projects are classified according to their purpose so that "risk-reflecting" discount rates can be assigned to each group.
   c. The appropriate discount rates can be carefully estimated and well publicized in the firm. This latter factor inhibits game playing by the cash flow estimators.
   d. There is a problem in that the categories, by project types, may be too broad, resulting in the same discount rate for proposals with different risks.

Sensitivity Analysis

C. **Sensitivity analysis** is a systematic way to determine which factors affecting cash flows are most important.
   1. The procedure involves calculating NPVs of the project with "best estimates" of each factor and repeating the computations, changing the value of one variable at a time in the most conservative direction.

This isolates the sensitivity of NPV to different values of the influencing variables.

Cash Flow Variations

2. Additional effort can then be made to develop *better* estimates of the most crucial factors.
   a. Probability distributions of cash flows can be prepared, or
   b. Cash flows based on various scenarios using different combinations of the critical factors can be developed.

D. The most advanced technique of project risk analysis involves the preparation of probability distributions of the cash flows.
   1. The distribution can be **discrete** or **continuous** depending on the convenience and degree of accuracy needed.

Measuring Risk

   2. The complete distribution is usually not required; only the:
      a. **Expected value** (mean).
      b. **Standard deviation** (spread of values around the expected value).
      c. **Correlation coefficient** (degree to which two variables move together, $+1.0$, or in opposite directions, -1.0).

Coefficient of Variation

      d. The **coefficient of variation** is a *relative* measure of risk and is equal to the standard deviation divided by the expected value. It enables more valid comparisons of risk for projects with different-size cash flows.

   3. The standard deviation and correlation coefficient measure only part of the project's risk. The other part depends on the correlation of the project's cash flows with the U.S. economy.
      a. The higher this correlation, the higher the risk.
      b. Lower correlations mean the project behaves differently and therefore reduces the shareholders' risk. In other words, when the economy is down, this project is up (doing well). This helps even out the shareholders' returns, which means less risk.

Estimating Probability Distributions
Computer Simulation

   4. Two ways to estimate probability distributions are as follows:
      a. For large projects, a **computer simulation** using probability distributions of each influencing factor for each time period can be used to generate cash flow distributions.

Decision Trees

      b. **Decision tree analysis** is used to eliminate unfavorable alternatives in a sequential approach to developing probability distributions.

   5. Since investors can do their own diversifying, management should ignore correlations between investment projects.

Incorporating Risk

E. The final stage of project evaluation incorporates information gained in the analysis and measurement of risk according to one or more of the methods previously described.
   1. One procedure involves calculating the net present value using the appropriate discount rate(s).
      a. A different discount rate can be used for each time period,
      b. A single rate can be chosen that is based on the current rate on U.S. government securities plus a premium chosen by the financial manager,

c. A single rate that is based on projects with similar risk can be employed, or

d. A single rate can be used that is derived from a theoretical model of risk and return. [See section 3 below for a discussion of the Capital Asset Pricing Model (CAPM).]

2. Remember that the correlation of the project's cash flow with the U.S. economy is appropriate, not the correlation with the rest of the firm's cash flows, because:

a. Investors can diversify on their own.

b. Management should ignore correlation between project returns.

3. The CAPM provides a method for combining the riskfree rate i with a risk premium for a particular security, J. This term is computed as the product of beta and the difference between the return on the stock market portfolio k_M, and the riskfree rate. Thus,

$$k_J = i + (k_M - i)\text{beta}_J \tag{10-1}$$

Foreign Investments

F. Evaluating **foreign investments**

1. The foreign exchange risk and the political risk should be reflected in the cash flows and the discount rate.

2. If shareholders are not well diversified, the discount rate may be low because the cash flows are not highly correlated with the domestic economy.

3. For well-diversified owners (internationally) the discount rate will be higher because risks are not reduced as much, so the discount rates will depend on the correlation with the global economy.

COMPLETION QUESTIONS

uncertainty

1. The degree of _____ is different for each capital budgeting proposal and may also vary over time for a particular project.

2. Methods of analyzing a risky project have a framework for analysis, an

assessment, adjustment

(*assessment/allowance*) of the project's risk, and an (*arrangement/adjustment*) for the degree of risk.

judgment

3. Informal methods of risk analysis are all based on managerial _____ as to the project risk.

decreasing

4. Conservative estimates of cash flows would call for (*increasing/decreasing*)

increasing

revenue projections and/or (*increasing/decreasing*) costs.

optimistic	5. If senior management adjusts cash flows for risk, original estimates may be submitted on an overly (*optimistic/pessimistic*) basis to compensate.
increased	6. In judgmental risk evaluation, the minimum acceptable rate of return is (*increased/decreased*) to compensate for the perceived risk.
higher	7. In the project classification scheme of risk adjustments, a (*higher/lower*) discount rate would be used for evaluating a plant to be built for making a new product.
inhibit	8. The project classification system tends to (*inhibit/encourage*) game playing that may occur when more judgmental methods are used.
Sensitivity analysis	9. _____ _____ is a systematic way of determining which factors affecting project cash flow are most important.
does not	10. While sensitivity analysis provides useful information, it (*does/does not*) tell what decisions should be made.
probability distributions	11. The most advanced techniques of project risk analysis are based on estimated _____ _____ of the cash flows.
discrete, continuous	12. Probability distributions may be _____ or _____.
value, deviation *correlation*	13. Summary measures commonly used to describe a probability distribution are the expected _____, the standard _____, and the _____ coefficient.
simulation	14. Computer _____ of cash flows for each time period may be used to develop probability distributions for large-scale projects.
tree analysis	15. Decision _____ _____ is an efficient system for culling out undesirable alternatives when using probability distributions.
50	16. If the standard deviation of a probability distribution was $500,000 and the expected value was $10,000, the coefficient of variation would be _____.
relative	17. The coefficient of variation (CV) is a better measure of risk than the standard deviation because the CV is a(n) (*relative/absolute*) measure.
correlation	18. The part of a project's risk that cannot be diversified away depends on the (*correlation/standard deviation*) of the project's cash flow with the economy.
plus 1.0	19. Cash flows that move up and down in tandem with another variable will have a correlation coefficient of (*plus 1.0/minus 1.0*).
United States GNP	20. Most often, the correlation of a project's cash flows should be computed with (*United States GNP/General Motors' sales*).
probability distributions	21. Computer simulation and decision trees are used to generate _____ _____.

22. Project evaluation that incorporates risk can be done by computing NPV using a discount rate equal to the current return on U.S. government securities (*plus/minus*) a premium for risk.

plus

23. One method of incorporating risk into project analysis is to use an estimated rate of return on a stock that is publicly traded and that has (*profits/cash flows*) with risks that are similar to those of the project.

cash flows

24. According to the Capital Asset Pricing Model, a project's risk (beta) depends on the _____ of cash flows with the economy and the _____ of _____ of its cash flows.

correlation

coefficient, variation

25. All known methods of evaluating risky projects involve managerial (*judgment/financing*).

judgment

26. For overseas projects, foreign (*tax/exchange*) risk and _____ risk must be evaluated.

exchange

political

PROBLEMS

For problems 1 through 4, use the situation as described immediately below. Make only the changes set forth in the specific problem and refer to the original information for all other data.

Stor-It-Indoors, Inc. (SII), builds mini-warehouses, which last twenty years, and rents the space to small businesses and individuals. After a successful experience in one city, plans have been made for expansion into two other areas. City A has a large and diversified industrial, agricultural, and governmental employment base, while city B is much smaller and is dependent on one major employer—a forest products concern. This situation is reflected in the estimated correlations with the economy of 0.8 and 0.2 for the projects in city A and city B, respectively. Because of its size, city A already has several mini-warehouse operations, so SII is considering a relatively small facility costing $500,000. In an effort to be "firstest with the mostest" into city B, SII thinks a $1 million investment is justified. Other information regarding these two projects is as follows:

	City A		City B	
Forecast	Annual cash flow, $ thousands	Probability	Annual cash flow, $ thousands	Probability
Optimistic	80	0.3	200	0.3
Most likely	70	0.5	140	0.4
Pessimistic	50	0.2	70	0.3

1. Analyze the project cash flows. Specifically:
   a. Plot their probability distribution.

Solution

Step one

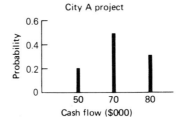
City A project

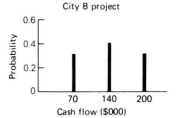
City B project

FIGURE 10-1

b. Compute the expected values.

Solution

Step one Expected value for the city A project = $80 × 0.3 + $70 × 0.5 + $50 × 0.2 = $69,000.

Step two Expected value for the city B project = $200 × 0.3 + $140 × 0.4 + $70 × 0.3 = $137,000.

c. Compute measures of risk for the two projects.

Solution

Step one Standard deviation is the square root of the sums of the products of the probability of each outcome times the square of the differences between the outcome and expected values. In this case,

$$\sigma_{city\ A} = \sqrt{0.3(80 - 69)^2 + 0.5(70 - 69)^2 + 0.2(50 - 69)^2}$$

$$= \sqrt{36.3 + 0.5 + 72.2}$$

$$= \sqrt{109}$$

$$= 10.4$$

$$\sigma_{city\ B} = \sqrt{0.3(200 - 137)^2 + 0.4(140 - 137)^2 + 0.3(70 - 137)^2}$$

$$= \sqrt{1190.7 + 3.6 + 1346.7}$$

$$= \sqrt{2541}$$

$$= 50.4$$

Step two Because the levels of the cash flows are quite different—expected values of $69,000 compared with $137,000—it is essential to adjust the uncertainty measure to allow for the effect of size. This is done by computing the coefficient of variation (CV):

$$CV_{city\ A} = \frac{10.4}{69} = 0.15$$

$$CV_{city\ B} = \frac{50.4}{137} = 0.37$$

Step three Now we can say, with confidence, that the *relative* uncertainty or variation in the cash flows of the project in city B is greater than that in the case of city A.

2. Which project is the most risky for Stor-It-Indoors?

Solution

Step one From the analysis of cash flows in problem 1, we know that the city B project has the highest degree of uncertainty.

Step two However, from the standpoint of diversification, the city A project is more risky since it has the highest correlation with the economy. This means that it offers the least help in ironing out the variations in the firm's performance. Projects that respond differently to economic fluctuations help the most in reducing risk, so city B is relatively better.

Step three This poses a problem of conflicting answers. The two risk considerations must be combined into one overall risk measure.

Step four Press on to the next problem to find out how to do this.

3. Assume that overall risk is the product of the two risk measures—the correlation with the economy times the coefficient of variation. Use this model to appraise the risk of the two projects.

Solution

Step one The overall risk measures are:

$$\text{Risk of city A} = 0.8 \times 0.15 = 0.120$$
$$\text{Risk of city B} = 0.2 \times 0.37 = 0.074$$

Step two These calculations indicate that the project in city A presents a higher risk to the firm when the variation and diversification elements are combined.

4. Suppose that Stor-It-Indoors examines locations in other cities and that the following table is developed:

Investment	Expected value of annual cash flows, $ thousands	Standard deviation, $ thousands	Correlation of cash flows with the economy
A	69	10.4	0.8
B	137	50.4	0.2
C	80	16.0	0.0
D	20	0.0	0.1
E	200	180.0	−0.2
F	8	4.0	−0.1

a. Rank the proposals according to risk associated with cash flow variation, variation with the economy, and overall risk.

Solution

Step one Compute the coefficients of variation (standard deviation ÷ expected value).

Investment	Standard deviation	Expected value	CV
A	10.4	69	0.15
B	50.4	137	0.37
C	16.0	80	0.20
D	0.0	20	0.0
E	180.0	200	0.90
F	4.0	8	0.50

End of solution.

b. Arrange the projects in decreasing order of CV values, assigning the highest risk to the highest CV. In a similar manner, rankings according to correlation with the economy are arranged in descending order:

Risk rankings (Highest to lowest)

By CV	By correlation with the economy	Overall risk
E	A	A
F	B	B
B	D	C or D
C	C	C or D
A	F	F
D	E	E

Step one The arrangement for overall risk, as shown above, is more difficult to establish. As a general rule, the ranking by correlation with the economy dominates the assessment of overall risk. However, there may be exceptions. When rankings of two projects are reversed, depending on the risk type, some method of combining the two measures must be used. Suppose that the overall risk is measured by the multiplication of the two risk factors. There are other possible ways to combine (addition or different weightings) these numbers, but for this problem assume that a simple multiplication is the way to do it. This gives overall risk measures as follows:

Project	Overall risk = CV × correlation
A	0.12
B	0.074
C	0.0
D	0.0
E	−0.18
F	−0.05

The rankings are then assigned according to decreasing order of the overall risk measure. Projects C and D cannot be distinguished in this example unless judgment calls for favoring C because it has a greater diversification impact (lower correlation with the economy). *End of solution.*

5. Bronco Burgers, Inc., has capital expenditure proposals which include:

Project	Cost, $ millions	Life, years	Annual net cash flow, $ millions	Target return, %
A. Increase production in home state	10	15	2	15
B. Build new plant in South America	15	10	4	20

Compute the net present value of each project.

Step one   BBI adjusts for risk by assigning different minimum rates of return to different risk categories of investment. Thus the foreign operation, which is subject to political and other unique risks, has a higher target, or hurdle, rate of return compared with the domestic project.

Step two   The net present value of project A is:

$$NPV_A = [(P/A, 15\%, 15) \times \$2] - \$10$$

$$= [5.8474 \times \$2] - \$10 = \$1.6948 \text{ million}$$

Step three   The net present value of project B is:

$$NPV_B = [(P/A, 20\%, 10) \times \$4] - \$15$$

$$= [4.1925 \times \$4] - \$15 = \$1.77 \text{ million}$$

Step four   Both projects have positive net present values and therefore both are acceptable.

6. Falcon Fish, Ltd., incorporates risk into its capital budgeting by assigning higher discount rates as cash flows are realized further and further into the future. Compute the net present value of a $10,000 investment that promises aftertax cash savings of $6000, $3000, and $5000 in years one, two, and three, respectively. The appropriate discount rates in those years are 12, 15, and 18 percent.

Solution

Step one Using the higher discount rates for more distant years reflects increasing uncertainty in the future.

Step two

$$NPV = \$6000 \times (P/F, 12\%, 1) + \$3000 \times (P/F, 15\%, 2) +$$
$$\$5000 \times (P/F, 18\%, 3) - \$10,000$$
$$= \$6000 \times 0.8929 + \$3000 \times 0.7651 + \$5000 \times 0.6086 - \$10,000$$
$$= \$10,668.70 - \$10,000$$
$$= \$668.70$$

7. Use the Capital Asset Pricing Model (CAPM) to determine the net present value of the investment described in problem 5. Assume the rate of return on the market portfolio is 14 percent and the beta is 1.5.

Solution

Step one

$$K_J = i + (K_M - i) \text{ beta}_J$$
$$= 6 + (14 - 6) 1.5$$
$$= 18\%$$

Step two Note that the market risk premium is $(K_M - i)$, or $(14 - 6) = 8$ percent. The discount rate is 18 percent.

Step three

$$NPV = \$4 \times (P/F, 18\%, 1) + \$8 \times (P/F, 18\%, 2)$$
$$+ \$10 \times (P/F, 18\%, 3) - \$10$$
$$= \$4 \times 0.8475 + \$8 \times 0.7182 + \$10 \times 0.6086$$
$$- \$10$$
$$= \$15.2216 - \$10$$
$$= \$5222$$

8. Capital Smudging, Ltd., is considering a $10,000 investment that is expected to return cash flows as listed in the following table. Management feels these estimates are uncertain and has reflected its feelings in a set of certainty-equivalent factors. The current rate of return on U.S. Treasury bills is 6 percent. Compute the NPV. (Note that certainty-equivalent factors are explained in Appendix 10A.)

Year	Expected cash flow, $ thousands	Certainty-equivalent factor
1	4	0.9
2	8	0.7
3	10	0.8

Solution

Step one This problem illustrates another method for incorporating risk into capital budgeting. The certainty-equivalent approach involves adjusting the cash flow estimates by a factor that compensates for risk. The resulting cash flows are then converted to present values using the riskfree discount rate. Thus:

Year	Expected cash flow	Certainty equivalent Factor	Certainty equivalent $000	Present value @ 6% Factor	Present value @ 6% $000
1	4	0.9	3.6	0.9424	3.4
2	8	0.7	5.6	0.8900	5.0
3	10	0.8	8.0	0.8396	6.7

$$\text{NPV} = \$3.4 + \$5.0 + \$6.7 - \$10.0$$
$$= \$15.1 - \$10.0$$
$$= \$5.1, \text{ or } \$5100$$

Step two Note the difference between this approach and the risk-adjusted discount rate method. In the latter procedure the adjustment applies to the discount rate; the adjustment in the certainty-equivalent method applies to the cash flows.

CHAPTER ELEVEN

RAISING INTERMEDIATE- AND LONG-TERM FUNDS

QUINTESSENCE   Companies finance their investments internally from retained earnings and externally by using debt and common and preferred stock. Fixed payments are made to debtholders and to preferred shareholders who also have priority of claims over the common stockholders. The bond indenture specifies promises the company makes which can be many because of the large variety of optional provisions such as callability, sinking funds, and even variable interest rates. Common stockholders control the company, have limited liability, and other unique rights. Publicly held firms choose to have their stock traded on an exchange or over the counter. New security offerings may be sold by the company directly to a few large investors or to investment bankers who either sell the securities privately to a small group or publicly to many investors. The investment bankers aid in pricing the issue and in meeting the regulations of the federal and state securities laws, the spirit of which is full disclosure of information necessary for investors to make informed judgments. Commercial banks, insurance companies, federal and local agencies, and others also provide intermediate and long-term funds to businesses. The international capital markets are a growing source of funds through foreign bonds and equities and Eurobonds.

OUTLINE

I. What
   A. This chapter covers intermediate- and long-term sources of funds and the environment in which the money is raised. Many new terms are introduced.
   B. Discussions center on characters of these sources, along with the pros and cons of alternative ways of raising the funds, such as public versus private offerings and international capital sources.

II. Why
   A. Debt and equity sources of capital are available in increasing variety, both at home and abroad.
   B. Knowledge of the environment of terms, customs, laws, and participants is vital to appropriately accessing these complex markets.

139

III. How

External Funds

A. Firms use **external funds** from issues of debt, preferred stock, and common stock in amounts limited by the proviso that an acceptable rate of return must be achieved.

Internal Funds

B. **Internal funds** come from retained earnings, which represent the major source of financing. These monies are limited by profits generated less dividends paid out.

Retained Earnings

1. Retained earnings and common stock are contributions from the owners.
2. Common and preferred stock are relatively minor sources of funds *on average*. The proportion of debt financing is considerably larger than the amount of new equity.

C. Characteristics of financing sources

Debt

1. **Debt** involves an arrangement whereby the borrower promises to repay principal plus interest.
   a. If these promises are broken, the providers of this financing source have priority of claims over other investors, including the power to close the firm down and take its assets.
   b. The claims on principal and interest are limited to certain amounts specified in the debt agreement; debtholders will not be happy with anything less, and they are not entitled to anything more. This type of investor is concerned mainly with the risk of a firm's failing to pay; judgment of this risk is reflected in the interest rate charged.
   c. Interest payments are tax deductible for the firm. (Recall from Chapter 7 how this results in a lower net cost of borrowing.)
2. As creditors, debtholders have priority over shareholders for claims on income and assets. Debtholders will be paid whether the firm earns a profit or not.

Bond Indenture

3. Long-term debt is usually evidenced by a promissory note called a **bond.** Its features are described in the **indenture,** which is a contract between the company and the lenders.

Coupon

   a. The company promises to pay interest (the **coupon rate**), usually semiannually.

Maturity Value

   b. At the end of the term of the debt the firm promises to pay the principal (also called **maturity value** or **face value**).

Market Value

4. The **market value** of a bond equals the present value of the interest and principal payments (this is a very important relationship—review Chapter 5 if you are unsure of how to use this bond valuation formula).

Protective Covenants

5. There are a number of general provisions in a bond indenture. More **protective covenants** for bondholders' protection mean greater constraints and obligations for the firm. This give-and-take is translated into interest rates—few restrictions mean higher rates, and vice versa. The decision concerning whether to include a provision depends on

how burdensome it is to that particular firm and on lender attitudes at the time of borrowing.

Trustee Role

    a. The **trustee,** usually a bank, represents the bondholders by making certain that all the provisions in the indenture are being met by the firm.

        i. If the company fails to live up to its promises—say, it misses a payment of interest—it is in **default** and the trustee will take prompt action to protect the bondholders.

        ii. The **Trust Indenture Act of 1939** covers the terms of the indenture and the role of trustees.

Call Terms

    b. The **call provision** enables a firm to redeem (pay off) its bonds early. In other words, they can be "called in" for a stipulated **call price** after they are issued, but before they mature.

        i. The call price, which usually begins at a **call premium** of one year's interest *above* the face value, declines over time to the face value.

        ii. The typical reason for calling a bond is to refinance at a lower interest rate.

        iii. Since the call provision is entirely for the company's benefit, the yield to maturity will be slightly higher (so as to compensate investors), compared with the yield for bonds having no call provision.

Sinking Fund

    c. A **sinking fund provision** requires the corporation to retire a certain portion of a debt issue before its maturity. This periodic retirement of some bonds, by calling them in or by buying them in the open market, reduces the risk of the remaining debt by reducing the amount of debt still outstanding.

Other Provisions

    d. Other examples of bond covenants include a limitation on dividends, the need to maintain a minimum amount of working capital, a limitation on further debt, and restrictions on the company's future investments or officer salaries.

Secured Debt
Mortgages

6. **Secured debt** has a priority claim on specific assets in the event of bankruptcy. Real property is pledged in a **mortgage;** personal property is pledged in a **chattel mortgage.**

    a. **First mortgage** bondholders have the senior claim on the property; **junior mortgage** debtholders have their claims subordinated to those of other creditors.

    b. A **blanket mortgage** covers all real property owned by the corporation.

Personal Property

    c. **Personal property** is pledged in **chattel mortgages** as security for:

        i. **Equipment trust certificates,** where equipment such as railroad cars are used.

        ii. **Collateral trust bonds,** for intangibles such as securities.

Debentures

7. **Unsecured bonds,** called **debentures,** are backed by the general

credit of the corporation. They are often issued by large, high-quality firms, particularly those with substantial amounts of liquid or tangible assets.

    a. A **negative pledge clause** is often used to specify that no new debt can be issued that has a priority over the debenture holders' claims on existing assets and, in some cases, on any assets acquired in the future.

Subordination

    b. **Subordinated debentures** have claims that are lower in priority compared with those of some form of senior debt such as bank loans or other short-term debt. In case of liquidation, senior debtholders must be paid in full before subordinated debtholders receive anything.

8. Riskiness concerns

    a. If inflation is high, the set amount of interest and principal payments may be insufficient so as to cause bondholders harm because the purchasing power they receive from those fixed payments has been substantially lowered.

    b. The trend to increased borrowing (more leverage) has resulted in higher default risk.

       i. Examples include leveraged buyouts and sales of parts of the company which weakens the position of existing bondholders because the assets being sold had been providing some bondholder protection.

       ii. This added riskiness has resulted in some debt becoming more like equity (common stock).

9. Less conventional forms of debt include:

Income Bonds

    a. **Income bonds,** which are unsecured debt that is entitled to interest payments only to the extent that they are earned by the firm.

       i. These bonds are used mainly by financially weak companies.

       ii. Income bond features *may* include sinking funds, the right to convert them into common stock, and a cumulative provision that specifies that interest not paid when due remains due and is payable when the earnings picture brightens.

Variable-Rate Bonds

    b. **Variable (floating) rate bonds** pay interest that is linked to something else such as Treasury bills, bonds, or the price of crude oil.

       i. These issues are somewhat equivalent to a series of short-term loans, each carrying the prevailing interest rate at the time the loans are made.

       ii. These bonds are more popular when interest rates are fluctuating considerably, causing investors to be hesitant to lend their money for long periods at fixed rates.

Low Coupon Bonds

    c. **Low coupon bonds,** also called **original discount bonds,** are issued with coupon rates that are substantially below the prevailing market rates (zero, which is very low, coupon bonds are also issued).

    i. Investors buy these bonds because they pay low prices and receive full face value at maturity. They lock in their return at the current rate and don't have to worry about reinvesting large amounts of interest at whatever returns they might obtain in the future. Also, these bonds are less likely to be called, because the issuers would have to pay considerably more than the original price they received.

    ii. From the company standpoint, a major attraction results from paying little or no interest, thereby enabling it to borrow more funds for a longer period of time.

    iii. Income taxes affect both sides. Investors must pay taxes on any interest and on the amortized portion of the discount. Companies can deduct each of these amounts.

Put Bonds

d. **Put bonds** allow bondholders to cash in their bonds at face value, sometime before scheduled maturity.

    i. This adds liquidity for investors.

    ii. Yields will be slightly less as a result. (Think of the trade-off here. When a "sweetener" is added to a bond, the company pays less interest.)

Project Financing

e. Sometimes large projects are financed with privately placed loans from commercial banks.

    i. This is called **project financing.**

    ii. The debt claims are limited to the project and as such are not tied to the company.

Junk Bonds

f. **Junk bonds** are *low-grade* (below BBB) and are also called "high-yield securities."

    i. About 1/5 of all publicly issued debt in the mid-80s was low grade and 1/2 of that was connected with mergers, leveraged buyouts, and other restructuring.

    ii. Many takeovers are initially financed with short-term debt, then long-term, low-grade bonds are issued.

    iii. Some issues are convertible into common stock, a few have warrants that are options to buy stock, and a number are variable-rate.

    iv. *So far*, the higher yields (4 to 5 percent above top-quality bonds) have more than compensated for the high risks. Default rates have averaged 3.3 percent each year. This frequency increased substantially in the latter 1980s causing many investors to avoid them.

Interest Rate Swaps

g. **Interest rate swaps** typically occur when a domestic company can borrow from a foreign bank at lower rates than would otherwise be available.

    i. For example, a company pays interest on a fixed rate loan from a foreign bank, and, in return, the bank pays that company interest on a floating rate loan of the same amount from the company.

ii. They are loans to each other, and each party benefits when the difference between the fixed rates in each country is greater than the difference between the floating rates in those two countries.

Preferred Stock Is a Hybrid

D. **Preferred stock** is an in-between type of security that has some properties of debt and some of common stock.

1. It resembles debt in that:

   a. It normally offers a fixed payment to investors. Preferred dividends are expressed as a percentage of par value or as a dollar amount paid annually on each share.

   b. The payments to preferred stock owners have priority over common stock payments.

      i. However, interest payments take precedence over *all* dividend payments.

Cumulative Dividend

      ii. Most preferred issues have a **cumulative dividend** provision which requires all past unpaid preferred dividends to be paid before any payments can be made to common shareholders.

   c. In a liquidation, preferred owners must be paid par value plus any unpaid dividends before the common stockholders receive anything. Debtholders' claims must be satisfied before any payments can be made on the preferred stock.

Call Feature

   d. Preferred stock has no maturity, but most issues are **callable** by paying a specified call premium.

Sinking Fund

   e. Preferred issues have **sinking fund** provisions less often than bonds do.

Participating

   f. In a few cases the issue may be **participating preferred.** This means preferred dividends must be increased along with any increases in the common stock dividends.

Adjustable Rate

   g. In the mid-1980s, **adjustable rate preferred** became popular. Dividends for this stock are' reset periodically, within some range, by being tied to the market rate on a debt security such as U.S. Treasury bonds.

Restrictions

   h. Other restrictions, similar to those imposed by a debt offering, may accompany a preferred issue.

      i. Sometimes a minimum amount of working capital must be maintained.

      ii. Limits may be placed on the issuance of new debt or preferred stock.

Convertible Warrants

   i. Preferred stock may be **convertible** into common stock. Sometimes preferred stock is issued with **warrants,** which are options to buy common stock.

Similarities to Common

2. Preferred stock is similar to common stock in that:

   a. Its claims on earnings and assets are subordinate to those of creditors.

b. It has voting privileges, although these are usually limited.

c. The issuance of preferred stock reduces the likelihood of bankruptcy by increasing the equity of the firm.

Advantages

3. The usage of preferred stock is influenced by its advantages and disadvantages from the standpoint of both investors and the firm.

For Investors

a. Corporate investors like preferred stock because:
   i. It offers a relatively safe and steady return.
   ii. When corporations receive either common or preferred dividends, they are allowed to exclude 70 percent of the amount received from their taxable income. (See Chapter 3 for more details.)

For Companies

b. Companies like to issue preferred stock because:
   i. It provides additional leverage for common stockholders since preferred dividends are usually fixed payments.
   ii. Preferred dividends can be omitted without placing the company in default or bankruptcy.
   iii. Voting control remains with the common stockholders.

Disadvantages

c. The two major disadvantages of preferred stock from the company's standpoint are:
   i. The increased risk to the stockholder of placing additional higher-priority claims on the firm's income and assets.
   ii. The non-tax deductibility feature of preferred dividends. Interest payments to bondholders result in more earnings left for the common stock than would be the case if preferred stock were used in place of debt and equal payments were made in the form of dividends.

Shareholder Rights
Residual Claim on
Income and Assets

E. Common stockholders' rights and privileges:

1. They have a **residual** right to *income* and *assets*.
   a. They receive what is left over after everyone else has been paid.
   b. The greater risk of the residual position is accompanied by a chance for greater reward; financial leverage magnifies the risks and potential rewards (or losses).
   c. Shareholders receive their benefits in the form of:
      i. Dividends as declared by the directors.
      ii. Capital gains due to reinvested earnings, which tend to increase the value of the shares.

Control

2. Stockholders **control** the firm through their right to elect the directors and vote on certain corporate actions such as mergers and changes in bylaws.
   a. The board of directors appoints the company's management.
   b. In practice, shareholder control is limited because management nominates the directors and most owners assign their voting rights over to management by a **proxy.**

Proxy

   i. Because of the inertia and apathy of many stockholders, effective control of a firm may be exercised by less than 50 percent of the stock outstanding.

        ii. Usually a company has to be mismanaged for a long time before the directors and management will be replaced.

        iii. A few firms have several classes of common stock, at least one of which may be nonvoting.

Preemptive Right

3. The **preemptive right** is the right provided by common law whereby existing stockholders may maintain their proportionate share of ownership.

   a. For example, a shareholder who has 1 percent of the outstanding shares has the first opportunity to buy 1 percent of the new stock issued.

   b. The intent of the preemptive right is to protect against:

        i. Involuntary loss of stockholders' proportionate share of ownership interest. This prevents management from arbitrarily issuing stock to friends.

        ii. Dilution of their financial interest in the firm. Any stock sold below the current market price will cause a drop in the total market values of the old stockholders' investment unless the preemptive right is in force.

   c. The preemptive right does not apply when common stock is issued:

        i. Unless it is so specified either in the state in which the company is incorporated or in the firm's charter.

        ii. As payment for property.

        iii. As payment for a merger acquisition.

Treasury Stock

        iv. As the result of the resale of **treasury stock** (these are shares the firm has previously bought back from shareholders).

        v. According to an employee stock option plan.

        vi. If shareholders, in a special election, have voted to waive the preemptive right.

Information

4. Stockholders with a just cause have the *right to inspect the firm's records to obtain information* about its operation.

Transfer Shares

5. An advantage of the corporate form of organization is the ease in which owners can exercise their *right to transfer shares* without restrictions.

Limited Liability

6. Stockholders have *limited liability*. They are not responsible for debt of their corporation. (A rare exception might occur if the stockholders used the company for illegal or morally reprehensible purposes.)

7. There are two types of **stockholder voting systems.**

Majority Rule Voting

   a. In **majority rule voting** a simple majority of the shares can elect *all* the directors. The minority of stockholders has *no* representation.

Cumulative Voting

   b. Under **cumulative voting** a significant minority of the shares can elect one or more directors if their votes are cast in a certain manner.

        i. In this system each stockholder receives votes equal to the number of shares held times the number of directors to be elected.

ii. The number of shares needed to elect a certain number of directors equals:

$$\frac{\text{Shares outstanding} \times \text{number of directors wanted elected}}{\text{Total number of directors to be elected} + 1} + 1$$

iii. An illustration of the calculation in cumulative voting elections is found in problem 4.

Accounting for Stock Issues

8. When recording a new stock issue, the cash and stockholders' equity accounts are increased by the amount of net proceeds.
   a. Two entries are involved in stockholders' equity.
      i. *Either* par value *or* stated value is credited with an amount equal to the par or stated value per share times the number of shares issued. The firm is prevented by law from making payments to stockholders from either of these capital accounts.
      ii. The remainder of the proceeds is credited to the paid-in surplus account.
   b. The market price per share, *not* the par or stated value, is used in financial decision making.

Listing Stock
Closely Held Firms

9. The listing of stock.
   a. **Closely held** firms may retain privacy and tight control by keeping their number of owners below a certain level.

Publicly Held Firms

   b. **Publicly held** companies have 500 shareholders or more *and* assets in excess of $1 million.
      i. These firms must publicly disclose their financial condition.
      ii. Their stock may be traded over the counter or on an organized stock exchange.
      iii. The advantages of greater publicity from a stock exchange listing and increased exposure to institutional investors have not been clearly supported by tests of stock prices that isolate the effect of listing.
      iv. The choice of whether to list is the company's, but listed firms must satisfy certain stock exchange and SEC requirements.

Retained Earnings

10. **Retained earnings** are profits remaining after dividends have been paid. They are the largest source of financing for businesses.
    a. Retained earnings are cumulated and used to finance new investments because earnings are limited and unpredictable.
    b. As a part of the equity, retained earnings are often a substitute for selling new stock because their use avoids control problems and fees associated with new stock sales.

F. Raising intermediate- and long-term funds

Private Placements

1. **Private security issues** (or private placements) are sold to a small number of investors such as pension funds and insurance companies. Most of these offerings are smaller and shorter-term debt issues.

Public Issues	2. **Public security issues** are sold to many investors.
	3. The matching principle of aligning the maturity of the debt with the time period in which the money is needed may not be appropriate for firms that will always have some debt outstanding.
Investment Bankers	4. **Investment bankers** aid in the sale of securities to individuals and institutions.
	a. By specializing, investment bankers:
	i. Can usually save firms money.
	ii. Know what investors want and how to contact them.
	b. Firms sell a few security issues (typically common stock) to investors without the involvement of investment bankers in a direct securities issue.
Negotiated Underwriting	5. Typically securities are issued through **negotiated underwriting.**
	a. The firm chooses an investment banker, and together they negotiate the price and terms of the offering.
	b. Underwriting occurs when investment bankers buy the issue for resale. They buy and resell the securities to investors for a profit— at least they hope to do this.
	c. The firm is thus *guaranteed a price for the issue;* the investment banker assumes the risk of selling for a profit, just like a grocery store or bicycle shop.
Competitive Bidding	6. Some firms, mainly railroads and public utilities, are required to sell their securities through **competitive bidding.**
Syndicates	a. Investment bankers group together to form a **syndicate** to enter a bid.
	b. The best bid is the lowest interest rate for bonds or the highest price for stock.
	c. Members of the winning syndicate are the underwriters. They share the risk of being able to sell the issue at a profit, just as in the negotiated offering.
Best Efforts/Agency	7. Very small firms and a few of the highest-quality large firms use investment bankers to sell their securities on a **best-efforts,** or **agency,** basis.
	a. In this procedure the investment bankers have no underwriting risk. They sell what they can, and they return any unsold securities to the issuing firm—just like the merchant who sells goods on consignment.
	b. This less frequently used method occurs mainly in common stock offerings.
Preliminary Discussions	8. In the preliminary underwriting discussions, one or more investment bankers tell the firm wishing to raise funds what they think investors will buy.
Originating House	a. The company selects an investment banker, who is called the **originating house.**
Underwriting Syndicate	b. The winner usually invites other investment bankers to join in forming the **underwriting syndicate.**

Fees

9. Fees are paid to investment bankers for their fund-raising assistance.
   a. These can be identified as:
      i. **Underwriting commissions** to compensate for the risk of being unable to sell the issue at a profit.
      ii. **Sales commissions** for actually selling the securities.
   b. The fees, as a percentage of the amount of funds being sought:

Lower for Larger Issues
Highest for Stock

      i. Decline as the issue size increases.
      ii. Are lowest for debt and highest for common stock, with preferred stock falling in between.

10. After being selected, the investment banker will use experts in engineering, accounting, etc., to assist in the investigation and evaluation of the firm.
    a. The resulting information is registered with state and federal regulatory bodies.
    b. These data are also made available to investors to provide them with a basis for making up their minds as to the value of the security being offered.

Pricing the Issue

11. Securities are priced, after the required registration is completed, on a general basis of meeting or beating what is offered by comparable issues.
    a. If the firm has other bonds outstanding, the interest rate must be slightly higher than the yield offered on those issues. If it has publicly traded stock, the new issue will be offered slightly below the current price.
    b. Another influence on interest rates for new bonds is the going rate being currently offered by bonds rated to be of similar quality.
    c. The pricing problem is more difficult for a firm selling its stock

Initial Public
Offering

    to the public for the first time. This is an **initial public offering.**
       i. These companies are **going public** to raise equity capital and/or to help the original owners sell part of their shares.
       ii. The price per share is set within a range (usually $2 to $15) considered appropriate by the investment banker. The key is in establishing the value of the business. An initial price is fixed and the number of shares is computed by dividing this figure into the total value.
    d. Recall from Chapter 5 that the value of common stock is the present value of the stream of future dividends.

Underwriting
Advantages

12. Advantages of underwriting include:
    a. Advice from an investment banker who is a pro regarding the type and terms of the offering.
    b. The activity of the investment banker to create a market for the stock after the initial sale. Investors like this because they can more readily sell stock they have purchased. (Recall the importance of a secondary market as an aid to the primary market described in Chapter 2.)

c. Less chance of the original owners' losing control, since the underwriter can sell the new stock to many investors with diverse interests—sort of a "divide and keep conquered" approach.

d. The knowledge that a definite amount of money will be raised at a specific cost. The underwriter guarantees this.

Securities Regulation Disclosure

13. The basic philosophy of securities regulation is to require complete and accurate *disclosure* of relevant information about the issuer and the securities being offered.

Blue Sky

a. State regulations are called **blue sky laws.**

Securities Act of 1933 Prospectus

b. The 1933 act required full disclosure of relevant information about the issue and issuer. This is accomplished by filing of the information for scrutiny by a federal agency and by the distribution of a **prospectus,** containing the facts, to potential investors. All issues being sold are subject to this regulation except the following:

Exemptions from Full Registration

   i. Issues sold to fewer than twenty-five investors.
   ii. Issues of $1.5 million or less during a single year.
   iii. Issues sold to residents of one state only.
   iv. Debt issues having maturities of 270 days or less.
   v. Issues by firms that are regulated by other federal agencies, for example, railroads.

SEC

c. The 1934 act established the **Securities and Exchange Commission** as the federal agency with responsibility for security issues and trading.

Purpose of Regulation

d. The purpose of regulation is not to prohibit trashy issues or even to prevent people from making bad investments. Regulations exist to help ensure that information will be available so that investors can make *informed judgments*.

Shelf Registrations

e. In 1983, the SEC authorized **Rule 415,** which streamlined the process for selling large amounts of debt securities to the public.

   i. This **shelf registration** provides firms with flexibility and convenience.
   ii. Firms seek SEC approval for a total figure but can then proceed directly with the sale of partial amounts at propitious times during a two-year period following the initial registration.

Private Placements

14. **Private placements** involve only a few investors who can have direct contact with the issuer.

a. Relatively little common stock is sold this way; relatively more preferred stock and substantial amounts of bonds are privately placed.

b. The necessity of registering the issue is avoided. This saves time, trouble, and expense and allows firms to keep their affairs more private.

c. If a company develops financial trouble, it can better negotiate with debtholders of a privately placed issue than it can with those who bought bonds in a public offering. (It's easier to talk to a few people than to a large group.)

    d. Disadvantages of private placements in the company's view are:

        i. A higher likelihood of loss of control to the new investor.

        ii. Higher financing costs, because a small group of investors has more bargaining power. They can usually demand and get higher interest rates and lower stock prices.

        iii. Relative difficulty in raising large amounts of capital.

Commercial Bank Lending
Mortgage Loans

15. Commercial banks make **mortgage** and **term loans.**

    a. **Residential mortgages** are used by individuals to buy homes over a period of 20 to 30 years. **Commercial mortgages** are made to businesses for less than 20 years in most instances. They finance plants, stores, and offices. Mortgage loans typically have equal payments composed of increasing proportions of principal and decreasing amounts of interest.

Term Loans

    b. **Term loans** may be *secured* or *unsecured.*

        i. They typically require quarterly, equal principal payments plus interest on the unpaid balance.

        ii. Term loans often contain *restrictions;* for example, dividends can be paid from retained earnings only and a minimum amount of working capital must be maintained.

Variable Rates

        iii. Most term loans are **variable-rate** loans tied to the prime rate. A **cap**, or ceiling, often applies that guarantees that the company will not have to pay more than a certain rate, no matter how high the prime rate goes.

Revolving Credit

        iv. **Revolving credit** arrangements are term loans that may last for three to five years. Typical provisions include compensating-balance requirements and variable interest rates that are tied to the prime rates.

16. **Insurance companies** make longer-term loans than banks do.

Insurance Loans

    a. Insurance loans are made at fixed rates and with a provision prohibiting early repayment. More recently many of these loans have been granted with variable interest rates, shorter maturities, and/or a feature requiring a share of the income from the project being financed **(equity kickers).**

Equity Kickers

    b. Banks and insurance companies sometimes cooperate to make long-term loans, with banks handling the early years and insurance companies handling the later periods.

Government Financing
SBA

17. The federal, state, and local governments offer several financing programs.

    a. The **Small Business Administration** (SBA) makes relatively low-cost loans to small businesses that cannot borrow from private sources at reasonable terms.

        i. It has special programs for low-income persons.

        ii. The SBA prefers to guarantee loans (up to 90 percent) made by banks and others.

iii. The maximum amount and maturity are $500,000 and twenty years.

Industrial Development Bonds

b. **Industrial development bonds,** for $1 million or less, are issued to build facilities that are then leased to a firm. Because the interest is tax exempt on these municipal bonds, they are a low-cost source of financing.

SBICs

c. **Small business investment companies** (SBICs) are privately owned firms that provide long-term debt and equity financing for small businesses only.

  i. The SBICs start with equity capital and raise more funds by borrowing from the SBA at low interest rates—a good deal.
  ii. They then lend or invest up to 20 percent of their equity in any one small business.
  iii. Dividends received are nontaxable—a good deal.
  iv. Losses on their investments are deductible from ordinary income—another good deal. This also applies to the SBIC owners, which is really a good deal.
  v. In spite of all the special privileges, SBICs haven't done very well (it's not too good a deal to be able to deduct losses from income if you have only losses).

Other Financing Sources

18. Leasing firms, business finance companies, equipment manufacturers, venture capital firms, and individuals also provide intermediate- and long-term financing.

International Sources

19. The integration of world capital markets has opened **international sources** of capital to businesses.

Foreign Bonds

a. **Foreign bonds** are sold in a country different from the home of the issuer.

Eurobonds

b. **Eurobonds** are also sold abroad, but they are denominated in the currency of the home country of the issuer.

Foreign Equity

c. **Foreign equity** involves selling shares in another country's stock market.

d. Advantages can be lower interest rates and the ability to raise more money in comparison with selling securities at home.

COMPLETION QUESTIONS

long-term debt
preferred stock

1. Firms rely more heavily on (*long-term debt/preferred stock*) than on (*long-term debt/preferred stock*) for financing.

lower
interest

2. Debt is a (*lower/higher*)-cost source of funds than equity because of the tax deductibility feature of _____.

leverage, greater

3. Financial (*leverage/stability*) is increased by using a (*lesser/greater*) amount of debt financing.

indenture	4. A(n) (*indenture/debenture*) is the bond contract.
coupon	5. The _____ is another name for the interest rate paid on bonds.
fixed	6. The bond interest is usually (*fixed/variable*) and is paid (*quarterly/
semiannually	semiannually*).
	7. The issuer of a bond makes two major promises to investors: to pay
interest, principal	_____ and to pay _____.
face	8. Bonds have a (*discount/face*) or par value, which is also the amount of
matures	principal payable when the bond _____.
market, present	9. The (*market/par*) value of a bond is the (*present/face*) value of the interest and principal payments.
yield	10. The discount rate applied to future bond payments is the _____
to maturity, return	_____ _____, which is the rate of (*dividends/return*).
	11. If market rates of interest rise after a bond is issued, the bond will sell at
discount	a (*premium/discount*).
higher	12. A bond selling at a premium offers a (*lower/higher*) coupon rate than the
yield to maturity	_____ _____ _____ available from similar bonds.
	13. The greater the number and significance of protective covenants, the
lower	(*lower/higher*) the interest rate on the bond.
	14. A provision requiring the issuer to gradually retire a portion of a bond before
sinking fund	it matures is called a (*sinking fund/call*) provision. It is advantageous to the
investor	(*firm/investor*).
trustee	15. The (*lessee/trustee*) is a third party acting in behalf of the bondholders.
	16. Bondholders may be forced to cash in their bonds before the maturity
call	date under the terms of a (*call/mortgage*) provision. They receive a pay-
above	ment (*above/below*) the face value of the bond, which is known as the
call price	_____ _____.
call premium	17. The amount of the _____ _____ usually begins at
coupon	one year's interest or _____ rate and declines to zero at the bond's
maturity	_____.
	18. A bond that is noncallable or that has some call protection will sell for a
lower	(*lower/higher*) interest rate than an otherwise identical but callable bond.
debentures	19. Unsecured bonds are known as _____.
negative pledge	20. A(n) _____ _____ clause prohibits the firm from is-

priority	suing an additional debt that has _____ over the outstanding debentures.
Subordinated, lower	21. _____ debentures have claims that are (*higher/lower*) in priority than those of senior debt.
Income	22. (*Mortgage/Income*) bondholders will receive interest payments only if they
preferred	are earned by the firm. These bonds are similar to (*preferred/common*) stock
are	except that the payments (*are/are not*) tax deductible.
personal	23. Two forms of debt secured by a pledge of (*personal/real*) property in a
equipment trust	chattel mortgage are _____ _____ certificates and
collateral trust	_____ _____ bonds.
closed-end	24. A (*first/closed-end*) mortgage prevents the company from issuing any more debt secured by the same property.
blanket	25. The most inclusive type of security pledge is a (*blanket/closed-end*) mortgage.
original discount	26. Low coupon or _____ _____ bonds offer interest
below	rates that are considerably (*above/below*) market rates.
Floating	27. _____ rate bonds offer interest rates that are linked to some rate such as that on Treasury bonds.
	28. An option that allows bondholders to cash in their bonds before maturity
put	would be a provision found in _____ bonds.
leveraged	29. Low-grade bonds that may be issued in a(n) _____ buyout are
junk	also known as high-yield securities, or _____ bonds.
swaps	30. Interest rate (*futures/swaps*) involve offsetting loans between a company and a foreign bank.
bonds, preferred	31. Fixed-income securities are _____ and _____
stock	_____.
cumulative, preferred	32. A(n) _____ dividend provision on (*preferred/common*) stock requires payment of all past-due dividends before any amount can be paid
common	to (*preferred/common*) stockholders. This provision is advantageous to the
investor	(*firm/investor*).
no	33. Preferred stock has (*no/a fixed*) maturity. It can sometimes be retired by a
call	(*call/voting*) provision.
common stock	34. Some preferred stock is convertible into the issuer's (*bonds/common stock*).
behind	35. The claims of preferred shareholders are (*ahead/behind*) those of debtholders.

does not	36. Most preferred stock (*does/does not*) have full voting privileges like those
common stockholders	of (*bondholders/common stockholders*).
increases	37. The use of preferred stock (*increases/decreases*) leverage, and it (*increases/*
decreases	*decreases*) the likelihood of bankruptcy.
participation	38. The (*participation/voting*) feature in a few preferred issues refers to the
	possibility of owners of these shares receiving higher dividends if the firm
	prospers.
are not	39. Preferred dividends (*are/are not*) tax deductible for the issuer; 70 percent
tax-free	or more of these dividends are (*tax-free/taxable*) to other companies who
	receive them.
is not	40. A firm (*is/is not*) in default when its preferred dividends are not paid.
	41. The incentive for refunding a debt or preferred stock issue is created by a
decline	(*rise/decline*) in the level of interest rates.
callable	42. A security must be _____ or maturing in order to be refunded
	at a lower interest or dividend rate.
rights	43. By knowing what (*rights/income*) investors expect, management can raise
	new funds without giving away too much.
residual, income	44. Stockholders have (*priority/residual*) claims on the firm's _____
assets	and _____.
directors	45. The right to control is exercised by electing (*directors/management*).
vote	46. Stockholders often assign their right to (*dividends/vote*) by giving their
proxy	(*proxy/dividends*) to management.
	47. If a shareholder owned 200 of a total outstanding 200,000 shares, the
preemptive right	_____ _____ would entitle the shareholder to pur-
100	chase (*100/1000*) shares in a new 100,000-share offering.
	48. If additional stock is sold below the price of outstanding shares, the market
decrease	price after the offering will (*increase/decrease*).
can	49. Stockholders with just cause (*can/cannot*) examine the company's books.
residual	50. In a bankruptcy proceeding the _____ claim of stockholders is
worthless	likely to be (*valuable/worthless*).
no say	51. The publicly owned company has (*no say/final say*) when any of its share-
	holders want to sell their stock.
are not	52. Stockholders (*are/are not*) responsible for debts of their company, and the
is not	company (*is/is not*) responsible for their debts.

53. While each of the stockholders' rights and privileges is important, the most significant thing management can do is to (*eliminate risk*/*earn a profit*).

earn a profit

54. Under a majority-rule voting system, all directors can be elected if a minimum of _____ shares vote for them when 100,000 shares are outstanding and 80,000 shares are voted.

40,001

55. Under (*cumulative*/*majority*) voting, a minority of shares can receive some representation.

cumulative

56. A stockholder owning 100 shares would be entitled to _____ votes when five directors were being elected in cumulative voting.

500

57. Dividends cannot be paid from either the _____ value or the _____ value account.

par

stated

58. When a firm receives $15 for each share and 100,000 shares are sold with a stated value of $12 each, (*$300,000*/*$1,200,000*) will be credited to the paid-in surplus account.

$300,000

59. Publicly held firms have at least _____ stockholders and assets of more than _____.

500

$1 million

60. It (*would*/*would not*) normally cause a firm's stock price to rise if its shares were to be listed on a stock exchange.

would not

61. Firms frequently receive aid in raising funds from the services of (*mortgage*/*investment*) bankers.

investment

62. Debt with a maturity of less than one year is referred to as (*short*/*long*)-term.

short

63. The process whereby a firm is guaranteed the receipt of a certain amount of money from an issue of its securities is called a(n) _____.

underwriting

64. A firm selects an investment banker, and the two parties come to an agreement over the price and other details of a security offering in a(n) _____ _____.

negotiated underwriting

65. Some railroads and some public utilities must sell their securities through _____ _____.

competitive bidding

66. The bid normally accepted on a bond issue will be the one with the (*lowest*/*highest*) interest rate or the (*lowest*/*highest*) price in the case of common stock.

lowest

highest

67. When investment bankers buy an issue for resale, they (*are*/*are not*) assured of realizing a profit.

are not

syndicates	68. Investment bankers may join together to form _____ to bid on and/or underwrite issues.
risks	69. Underwriting (*profits/risks*) may be so large with new issues of young firms that investment bankers may be willing to sell their securities only on a
best-efforts	_____-_____ basis.
originating house	70. The investment banker selected by the firm to underwrite an issue is referred to as the (*originating house/syndicate*).
underwriting	71. Fees for selling security issues are composed mainly of _____
sales	costs and _____ commissions.
decrease	72. The fees, as a percentage of the issue size, (*increase/decrease*) as the offerings grow bigger.
debt, common	73. Fees are lowest for (*debt/common stock*) offerings and highest for (*common/preferred*) stock issues.
more	74. Prices of securities being offered by a firm will usually be set so as to be slightly (*more/less*) attractive to investors than prices of similar issues outstanding.
initial public offering	75. Companies selling their stock to the public for the first time are said to be making an _____ _____ _____.
underwriter	76. If an initial public offering is priced too low, it will benefit the (*underwriter/issuer*).
broaden	77. Sale of new stock tends to (*broaden/concentrate*) the ownership.
develop	78. Investment bankers often (*develop/hinder*) a secondary market in securities that they underwrite.
information	79. The purpose of securities regulation is to provide investors with (*information/protection against loss*).
blue sky	80. State securities statutes are called _____ _____ laws.
prospectus	81. A(n) _____ containing facts about the issuer and the offering must be given to potential investors in a public offering.
1934	82. The SEC was established in the (*1933/1934*) act.
Private	83. (*Private/Public*) offerings are exempt from registration with the SEC, as are
commercial paper,	issues of (*long-term bonds/commercial paper*), (*interstate/intrastate*) offer-
intrastate, less	ings, and offerings of (*more/less*) than $1.5 million.
debt, shelf	84. Rule 415 enables large amounts of (*debt/equity*) to be sold under a (*shelf/full*) registration.

bonds, stock	85. More issues of (*bonds/stock*) than (*bonds/stock*) are privately placed.
greater	86. The potential for a loss of control is (*less/greater*) with a private offering.
lower	87. Financing costs are generally (*lower/higher*) with a public offering.
public	88. Greater amounts of funds can generally be raised in (*private/public*) offerings.
principal	89. Bank term loans usually have equal (*principal and interest/principal*) payments.
are not	90. Term loans usually (*are/are not*) fixed interest rate loans.
prime	91. Variable-rate loans are often tied to the _____ rate.
Insurance companies	92. (*Banks/Insurance companies*) prefer to make longer-term loans.
guarantee	93. The Small Business Administration (SBA) prefers to (*make/guarantee*) loans.
industrial development	94. Tax exempt financing for private businesses is available through (*variable-rate/industrial development*) bonds.
small business investment companies, debt and common stock	95. SBICs, _____ _____ _____ _____, invest in (*debt only/debt and common stock*) of certain other firms.
ordinary income	96. Losses to the SBIC and its owners are deductible from (*ordinary income/capital gains*).
does not	97. The federal government (*does/does not*) own SBICs.
have not	98. SBICs (*have/have not*) been highly successful for their owners.
Eurobonds	99. If a U.S. company sold dollar denominated bonds in the French capital market, they would be classified as _____.
	100. Crossword puzzle (see below).

ACROSS

1 _____ bonds are secured by the pledge of real property.

3 A bondholder is a _____ of the issuing company.

6 When interest or principal payments due are missed, the issuer is in _____.

8 A condition specified in the bond contract.

10 The provision that prevents a firm from pledging any more debt of the same priority on property. Hint: This is opposite to the open-end provision.

11 The maturity value of a bond.

13 A feature in a few issues of preferred stock that provides for increased dividends.

14 A provision allowing the issuer to redeem its bonds or preferred stock early.

15 Bond contract.

18 Claims that are junior to those of another creditor.

20 A mortgage provision covering all assets owned by the issuer.

21 Related to equipment financing.

24 A "sweetener" that may accompany bonds or preferred stock.

25 _____ trust certificate.

DOWN

2 Issuing new debts to retire outstanding debt.

4 An unsecured bond.

5 A person or company responsible to protect bondholder interests.

7 A senior security.

9 A type of bond that may not always pay interest when due.

10 Interest rate on a bond.

12 Assets may be pledged as _____.

14 A provision in preferred stock that benefits investors.

16 Costs paid by the issuer to have its securities sold.

17 A _____ fund allows for gradual retirement of senior securities.

19 Bond interest is paid as a percent of _____.

22 The interest rate is _____ for most bonds.

23 Pledge of personal property.

1. Billie's Bagels, Inc., has a bond that was issued five years ago with a coupon rate of 9 percent. If it matures twenty-five years from today and pays interest annually, what is the value of this bond ($1000 par) if similar bonds offer a yield to maturity of:

   a. 9 percent?

Solution

Step one The market value or present price is equal to the present value of the future payments of interest and principal, discounted at the yield to maturity.

Step two The coupon or interest payments are $90 per year, and $1000 will be paid as principal in twenty-five years.

Step three

$$\text{Value} = \$90 \times (P/A,\ 9\%,\ 25) + \$1000 \times (P/F,\ 9\%,\ 25)$$
$$= \$90 \times 9.8226 + \$1000 \times 0.1160$$
$$= \$1000.03$$

Step four This is essentially $1000, or par value, which is a confirmation of a point made in Chapter 5: When the coupon rate and yield to maturity are equal, the present value of the interest and principal will equal the par value.

   b. 7 percent?

Solution

Step one This bond will sell at a premium because its coupon rate is above the yield to maturity.

Step two

$$\text{Value} = \$90 \times (P/A, \ 7\%, \ 25) + \$1000 \times (P/F, \ 7\%, \ 25)$$
$$= \$90 \times 11.6536 + \$1000 \times 0.1842$$
$$= \$1233.02$$

c. 11 percent?

Step one   This bond will sell at a discount because the coupon rate is below the current going rate for this type of security.

Step two

$$\text{Value} = \$90 \times (P/A, \ 11\%, \ 25) + \$1000 \ (P/F, \ 11\%, \ 25)$$
$$= \$90 \times 8.4217 + \$1000 \times 0.0736$$
$$= \$831.55$$

Step three   Note the reaction of the market value to the change in market rates of return. When interest rates rise (yield to maturity is above the coupon rate), bond prices fall, and vice versa.

Step four   Also note that in each equation in problem 1a to c, the interest payment is the same $90, whereas the discount factors change to reflect the different yields to maturity.

2. What is the effect of semiannual interest payments? (Compute the value of a 9 percent bond with a fifteen-year maturity and a yield to maturity of 8 percent, assuming annual and then semiannual interest payments.)

Solution

Step one   With annual interest payments and annual compounding,

$$\text{Value} = \$90 \times (P/A, \; 8\%, \; 15) + \$1000 \times (P/F, \; 8\%, \; 15)$$
$$= \$90 \times 8.5595 + \$1000 \times 0.3152$$
$$= \$1085.56$$

Step two   A bond should be more valuable if interest is paid semiannually because investors receive half the interest payments six months earlier.

Step three   To compute this value, the interest payments are cut in half, but twice as many are received. The discount rate is also cut in half to reflect semiannual compounding, and the number of compounding periods is doubled.

Step four

$$\text{Value} = \$45 \times (P/A, \; 4\%, \; 30) + \$1000 \times (P/F, \; 4\%, \; 30)$$
$$= \$45 \times 17.2920 + \$1000 \times 0.3083$$
$$= \$1086.44$$

3. A portion of the balance sheet of Hopper Corporation is as follows:

Stockholders' equity	
Par value ($1 per share)	$ 1,000,000
Paid-in surplus	8,000,000
Retained earnings	16,000,000
	$25,000,000

a. What is the maximum amount of dividends that could be paid to current shareholders of Hopper?

Solution

Step one   Unless creditors have placed restrictions on dividend payments, the company could pay (assuming cash was available) the entire balance in the paid-in surplus and retained earnings accounts.

Step two The maximum amount of dividends is thus $8,000,000 + $16,000,000, or $24,000,000.

b. Suppose the company issues 500,000 new shares to the public for $12,500,000. If the flotation costs are 4 percent, what would be the entries on the shareholders' equity accounts to reflect the stock sale?

Solution

Step one The price per share paid by the public is $12,500,000/500,000 = $25.

Step two The flotation cost is 4 percent of $25, or $1 per share, and so the proceeds to the company are $24 per share, which is $24 × 500,000, or $12,000,000 in total.

Step three The entry to par value is $1 × 500,000, or $500,000.

Step four The remainder of the proceeds, or $11,500,000, is credited to paid-in surplus.

Step five After the stock sale, the shareholders' equity accounts will appear as follows:

Par value ($1 per share)	$ 1,500,000
Paid-in surplus	19,500,000
Retained earnings	16,000,000
	$37,000,000

4. Lydia's, Ltd., has 1 million shares outstanding and plans to sell 100,000 new shares for $40 per share. The current stock price is $50 per share. What would be the market price after the offering if nothing else happened to influence stock prices?

Solution

Step one The market value of the shares outstanding is 1 million × $50 = $50 million.

Step two The value of the new shares sold is 0.1 million × $40 = $4 million.

Step three The total value of the stock after the offering is $50 million + $4 million, or $54 million.

Step four The price per share would be $54 million/(1 million + 0.1 million) = $49.09.

5. Suppose that the investment banker chosen by R Company for the stock sale feels the offering price should be $10 per share and that a realistic value of the firm is $5,000,000. How many shares should be sold to the public if the current owners have 300,000 shares?

Solution

Step one The total stock outstanding after the sale will be $5,000,000/$10 = 500,000 shares.

Step two Since the current owners have 300,000 shares, the amount being sold to the public will be 200,000 shares.

Step three The total number of shares is arbitrary and is fixed when the price per share is set and vice versa. If a selling price of $5 per share was chosen, the firm would have 1 million shares outstanding. The key is the total value. Either the number of shares or the price per share will be chosen, and then the other is computed.

6. Potter, Inc., is a young company in need of more equity capital. It has not earned a profit before, but it will earn $200,000 this year if it can raise $1,000,000. Companies similar to Potter are selling at a P/E ratio of 10.
   a. What is the estimated value of Potter?

Solution

$$\text{Value} = \$200{,}000 \times 10$$
$$= \$2{,}000{,}000$$

b. The present owners are willing to sell 50 percent of the firm to raise the $1,000,000. What will the issue price of the stock be if the original owners have 25,000 shares?

Solution

Step one The present owners want to have 50 percent of the outstanding shares, and they own 25,000 shares; thus there must be 25,000 new shares sold, which will bring the total number outstanding after the offering to 50,000 shares.

Step two In order to raise $1,000,000 by selling 25,000 shares, the offering price must be $40 per share ($1,000,000 ÷ 25,000).

Step three As a check, the price-earnings ratio can be used. The earnings per share will be $200,000 ÷ 50,000, or $4 per share. The price per share is 10 × $4, or $40, which is the same value as computed in step two.

CHAPTER TWELVE

FINANCING DECISIONS AND CAPITAL STRUCTURE

QUINTESSENCE   To help maximize the value of the firm, the financial manager must minimize financing costs by choosing the appropriate types and proper amounts of fund sources. The capital structure is decided as a result of determining the costs and benefits of alternative financing plans; included in the analysis are attributes and restrictions accompanying each source, as well as their risk and earnings impact on the firm. Final choices are made after examining the relationships and trade-offs between investment opportunities and financing capacity. The main thrust of this chapter is to provide a framework for evaluating the potential gains or benefits compared with the costs or losses involved in deciding how to finance and how much to finance.

OUTLINE

I. What
  A. In this chapter attention turns from the question of *what investments* should be made to the decision concerning *how to finance* the proposed projects.
  B. Techniques are presented for analyzing the impact of each type of financing on the earnings and risk of the firm.
  C. The relationship of capital structure to the value of the firm, in theory and practice, is discussed in terms of the impact of financial risk on the cost of capital.
  D. The chapter concludes with an explanation of the tie-in between investment opportunities and financing capabilities.

II. Why
  A. To maximize growth in the value of the firm, financing costs must be minimized.
    1. Alternative financing sources have different costs and impacts on earnings.
    2. The optimal capital structure is determined from a knowledge of the relationship between risk and return.

167

B. To properly plan the capital budget requires an understanding of the relationship between investment opportunities and financing capabilities.

III. How

Compare Financing Costs

A. Analysis of external financing methods

1. Preparation of the company's financing plan begins with estimates of amounts needed.

FRICTO

2. The effects of alternative financing choices may be evaluated by **FRICTO.**

   a. **Flexibility, F,** refers to the impact that a financing choice today may have on the availability of future financing options, i.e., borrowing capacity and unexpected difficulties.

   b. **Risk, R,** considerations are unique to each type of financing.

   c. **Income, I,** effects are substantially different for each source of funds, as outlined in Section 3 below.

   d. **Control, C,** is of particular concern to smaller firms.

   e. **Timing, T,** is important because of the wide swings in the availability and cost of each financing form; i.e., changes in markets have become much larger in recent periods.

   f. **Other, O,** factors of interest include collateral requirements, flotation costs, speed in raising money, and the potential for broadening exposure to additional providers of funds.

3. The relative costs of the four financing sources are:

   a. Debt will be best if funds are profitably invested. It has the lowest cost because of less risk (lower interest rate) and the tax deductibility feature of the interest payments.

   b. Preferred is second best; it has the next lowest cost.

   c. Common stock has the highest cost. Retained earnings save time and money in comparison to common stock.

EBIT/EPS Analysis

4. The above generalizations are only the beginning of the financial planning process. Because the future is uncertain, the impacts of financing alternatives must be examined at *different earnings levels* by looking at **earnings before interest and taxes (EBIT)** and **earnings per share (EPS)** relationships.

   a. $\text{EPS} = \dfrac{(\text{EBIT} - \text{interest})(1 - \text{tax rate}) - \text{preferred dividends}}{\text{total number of shares outstanding}}$

      i. The key to interpreting the graph of these relationships shown in Figure 12-1 is to notice the level of EBIT where the common stock line crosses the debt line. Then estimates of the future levels of EBIT are made. If EBIT is unlikely to fall below the cross (break-even point), debt would be recommended; lower EBITs indicate that the choice should be common stock.

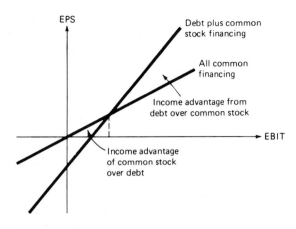

FIGURE 12-1 EPS impact from financing with debt vs. common stock.

Financial Leverage

ii. The graph also illustrates **financial leverage,** which is defined as the response in EPS to a change in EBIT.

    (a) It arises by using financing sources that require fixed payments; it's great if things (EBIT) go well, but it's bad news if EBIT falls below expectations.

    (b) If a firm uses no debt or preferred, the response of EPS to EBIT is 1 for 1; i.e., a 10 percent increase in EBIT results in a 10 percent rise in EPS.

    (c) With leverage, EPS shoots up (good) or down (bad) faster.

    (d) Another measure of financial leverage is the ratio, interest/EBIT.

For Additional Leverage Use Preferred Stock

    (e) The line for preferred stock falls below and parallel to the debt line. This means that the cross (break-even point) with common stock is higher compared with the debt case. See Figure 12-1 in the text for further details.

Leverage and Risk

5. In addition to the impacts on earnings, **risk** must be considered.

    a. In general, the advantage of higher expected returns from using leverage is accompanied by greater risks.

      i. For debt, the principal and interest payments are contractual; dire results (bankruptcy) occur if the promises to pay are broken.

      ii. Preferred stock involves less risk, but then the leverage advantages from it are also less.

Business Risk

    b. **Business risk** is a function of uncertainty of EBIT. It is related to the nature of the firm's revenues, production costs, liquidity, and management capability. If there were no business risk, a firm could finance in any manner it wished.

Financial Risk

     c. The probability of different levels of EBIT can be used to estimate **financial risk.** This risk is dependent on the method of financing. Using only common stock means zero financial leverage.

     d. The impact of leverage is to increase the variability in EPS, which increases the likelihood of loss, which in turn increases the interest rates on debt.

     e. According to the CAPM as discussed in Chapter 6, **beta** for a stock will increase as a result of the firm's using more leverage (debt and/or preferred stock). This in turn increases the firm's required rate of return.

Leverage Affects Value

B. **Financial leverage** and **value**

    1. The preceding discussion leaves us with a problem (would you believe a dilemma?): Since leverage introduces a risk-and-return trade-off, what is the optimal amount of leverage to incur? The answer lies in recalling how the cost of capital and value are related and then seeing how value is affected by capital structure. Knowledge of these interrelationships and judgment are used to decide how much to invest and how to pay for the investments.

    2. In perfect capital markets with no taxes, the total market value of the firm is not affected by the choice of financing method. The cost of capital remains the same because when debt, which is the lowest-cost funding source, is added, the firm becomes more risky, which causes higher expected returns on equity. In other words, increased cost of equity offsets the advantage of using lower-cost debt, so the average cost of capital remains unchanged.

Corporate Taxes Favor Debt

    3. *With corporate taxes* debt financing is superior to preferred and common because the tax deductible interest results in lower tax payments, which means that more funds are available to pay security holders.

Personal Taxes

    4. The effect of personal taxes is complex.

     a. Retained earnings are favored for financing because personal taxes are postponed until the stock is sold, whereas taxes must be paid on dividends as they are received.

Personal Taxes Favor Debt for Lower-Income People

     b. Debt financing is better for people in low tax brackets because the tax they pay on interest received is more than offset by the savings to the company from the interest deductibility feature.

     c. On balance, the Tax Reform Act of 1986 probably favors debt relative to equity.

     d. Remember that total returns to all investors are being considered. Since some people are better off with a particular type of financing than others, we have one explanation as to why a mixture of debt and equity is used.

    5. In practice, firms believe leverage is desirable up to a point. Factors influencing financing decisions are:

Changes in Capital Markets

a. Capital market imperfections such as varying conditions that cause changes in the costs of one form of financing relative to another.

Issue Costs

b. Expenses incurred in issuing common stock are greater than for issuing preferred stock, which in turn are higher than those for debt.

Bankruptcy Risk

c. Using more debt causes the probability of bankruptcy to increase. Bankers, customers, and others become nervous and reluctant to deal with the company. As the amount of borrowing increases, lenders raise their rates, thereby reducing the advantage of debt. At some point lenders refuse to grant further loans at any price.

Optimal Capital Mix
Maximizes Value

6. The **optimal capital structure** is the combination of debt and equity that provides:
   a. The highest total value of the firm since this also provides the highest return for the owners.

Minimizes Cost of Capital

   b. The lowest average cost of capital.

7. Guidelines for the optimal range, which cannot be determined precisely, come from the professional investment community, including institutional lenders, investment bankers, and rating agencies.

Bond Ratings

   a. High **bond ratings** are important to companies because:
      i. It is easier for high-rated firms to borrow money.
      ii. Interest rates are lower.
   b. Bond ratings are mainly determined by:
      i. The amount of pretax earnings available to pay interest (the more the better).
      ii. The ratio of debt to total capital (the smaller the better).

Retained Earnings Are Often Best

C. **Retained earnings** are often the best financing alternative.
   1. This source does not involve any dealings between investors (savers) and the company (user). On the other hand, negotiations always occur when any of the external sources are tapped.
   2. When money is needed for promising expansion plans:
      a. It could be borrowed, but debt-capacity considerations may not allow it.
      b. Investments could be cut back, but this might mean foregoing profitable opportunities.
      c. Common stock could be sold, but this involves substantial issuing and selling expenses, and this route could lead to control problems since the number of owners may be increased.
      d. Relying on retained earnings, even to the point of not paying any dividends, is favored because:
         i. This usually means growth in share values that is not taxable to investors until the shares are sold. Recall that shareholders receive returns from dividends and stock price appreciation.

ii. Retention of earnings provides temporary increases in liquidity and maintains financing flexibility.

New Stock

3. *In practice,* many firms still choose to sell new stock because:

a. Shareholders become discontented when dividends are reduced. They interpret this action as a sign of weakness; many stockholders count on receiving dividends regularly. It's hard to convince them that it is better to give than to receive.

b. The amount of retained earnings after dividend cuts may not be sufficient to finance all the expansion plans.

International Financing Policies

D. **International financing policies** must take into account the variations in banking, tax laws, and traditions in different countries.

1. These influences cause more debt to be used in Japan and West Germany.

2. In financing subsidiaries the multinational corporations should consider:

a. Obtaining capital from the cheapest market around the world.

b. Using foreign currency denominated debt to minimize exchange rate risk.

c. Having an amount of host country ownership so as to reduce the likelihood of political expropriation.

Financing Ties In with Investment

E. Relationship between financial structure and investment

1. The tie-in is via the cost of capital (k_a); the lower k_a is, the more projects will be acceptable.

2. If a *change* in capital structure is called for, the shift to the new optimal mix should be gradual and should be achieved by increased usage of one source over another. The planned *future* proportions are announced and used in weighting current costs to arrive at k_a.

3. The cost of capital will increase at some point as the capital budget gets larger, because:

a. Financing is needed from new investors who perceive greater risks and therefore require higher returns.

b. Investors also become concerned about the firm's overoptimism and its ability to accomplish an ambitious expansion program.

c. Costs of raising money increase as more reliance is placed on external sources.

Supply of and Demand for Funds

4. At this point we have recognized that the amount of potential investment is inversely related to k_a and that k_a is related directly to the amount of funds being raised; the lower the k_a, the more a firm wants to spend, but the more it spends, the higher the k_a. The question is: How do we get off this merry-go-round? The answer is found by using a basic economic concept—the supply and demand curves. The intersection of these curves indicates the optimal capital budget as shown in Figure 12-2. See problem 6 for an example of this process.

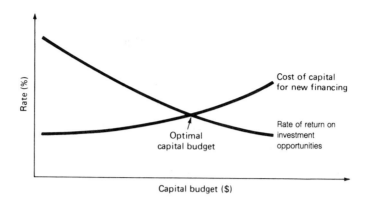

FIGURE 12-2 Rates of return and costs of capital for various investment and financing programs.

> 5. *In practice,* the capital budget is usually determined by first evaluating how easy it is to finance the proposed expansion programs. Then these are revised to incorporate any financing difficulties. Finally a group of projects is selected that has expected returns sufficient to justify financing costs.

Flotation Costs
    F. Issue fees cover legal, printing, and underwriting costs.
      1. Flotation costs are more for stock than for bonds, with bank loans being the cheapest.
      2. As the issue size increases, the charges, expressed as a percentage of the amount raised, decline.

Effects on Cost of Capital
      3. Incorporate the issue costs into the cost of capital:
        a. For debt, the tax saving from the amortized issue cost is deducted from aftertax interest cost. The adjusted cost is the discount rate that equates the net amount received from the issue to the present value of the interest and principal payments.
        b. For stock, the adjusted cost is equal to the estimated market rate multiplied by the ratio of gross to the net amount actually received by the issuer.

No Effect on Retained Earnings
        c. There is no adjustment necessary for the cost of retained earnings.

COMPLETION QUESTIONS

FRICTO
1. The acronym for a framework used in analyzing alternative financing choices is (*EXACTO/FRICTO*).

speed
2. In addition to flexibility, risk, income, control, and timing, the financing choices are influenced by the (*speed/accuracy*) of raising funds.

3. External financing methods can best be analyzed by examining the relationship of (*EPS/risk*) to (*EBIT/return*).

EPS, EBIT

4. Fluctuations in earnings before interest and (*dividends/taxes*) are due to (*business/financial*) risk.

taxes

business

5. Given a level of EBIT, _____ or common stock will be favored, depending on which type of financing results in the highest (*EPS/risk*).

debt

EPS

6. (*Operating/Financial*) leverage is the response of (*revenues/EPS*) to changes in EBIT.

Financial, EPS

7. A firm having a (*low/high*) business risk should generally have lower proportions of debt financing.

high

8. Companies using (*low/high*) proportions of debt financing have a high degree of financial (*leverage/returns*).

high

leverage

9. The ratio of interest payments to (*EPS/EBIT*) is also a measure of (*operating/financial*) leverage.

EBIT

financial

10. A high degree of financial leverage works best in situations where EBIT is (*increasing/decreasing*).

increasing

11. If the corporate income tax were (*increased/decreased*), debt would be more advantageous.

increased

12. If (*dividends/interest*) were to be allowed as tax deductions, more _____ _____ and _____ _____ would be used for financing.

dividends

preferred stock,

common stock

13. (*Preferred/Common*) stock offers less risk to the firm compared with debt, but then the potential benefits of leverage are (*more/less*).

Preferred

less

14. The relationships of value to the _____ of capital and to _____ structure are used to determine the (*optimal/minimal*) amount of leverage.

cost

capital, optimal

15. In perfect capital markets, with no _____, it makes (*considerable/no*) difference which types and amounts of financing are used.

taxes

no

16. In this situation, the average cost of capital is (*higher/unchanged*) because the cost of common stock (*decreases/increases*) to offset the use of (*lower/higher*)-cost debt.

unchanged

increases

lower

17. When corporate _____ are introduced, the favored source of financing is (*debt/common stock*).

taxes

debt

retained earnings	18. When personal income taxes are considered, shareholders prefer (*debt/retained earnings*) for financing.
bankruptcy	19. In practice, the usage of debt is limited by concerns about _____ .
debt	20. In practice, the advantages of adding _____ are eventually more
rise	than offset by default costs, which then cause the cost of capital to (*fall/rise*).
lowest, highest	21. The financial mix at the (*lowest/highest*) cost of capital or (*lowest/highest*)
optimal	total value is called the firm's _____ financial structure.
Retained earnings	22. (*Bank loans/Retained earnings*), as a source of financing, do not require
investors	any negotiation between the firm and (*investors/creditors*).
shareholders	23. Retained earnings have an advantage to (*creditors/shareholders*) because they are not taxed until the stock is actually sold.
dividend, disfavor	24. Investors tend to view (*dividend/price*) cuts with (*favor/disfavor*).
more	25. Companies in Japan and West Germany tend to use (*more/less*) debt compared to American firms.
	26. To minimize exchange rate risk, foreign subsidiaries should use (*little/con-*
considerable	*siderable*) host country denominated debt.
lower	27. Investment is encouraged by a (*lower/higher*) cost of capital.
capital	28. If a different _____ structure is desired, the shift to it should
gradual	be (*rapid/gradual*).
capital	29. As the (*operating/capital*) budget increases, the cost of capital (*de-*
increases	*creases/increases*).
	30. In theory, the amount of investment is determined by the intersection of
supply, demand capital	the _____ and _____ curves for (*revenue/capital*) to the firm.
cost of	31. The supply curve is a schedule showing the _____ _____
capital	_____ at different amounts.
cumulative, rates	32. The _____ total of investment outlays at different _____
return	of _____ is the demand-for-funds curve.
flotation	33. Another name for issue fees is (*equity/flotation*) costs.
lower	34. Issue fees are (*higher/lower*) for bonds than for stock.
higher	35. Flotation costs are a (*higher/lower*) percentage of small issues compared with larger ones.
debt	36. Issue costs are amortized for (*debt/stock*).
raise	37. The adjustments for issue costs (*raise/lower*) the cost of capital.

38. There is no adjustment to the cost of capital for flotation costs of (*common*

retained earnings   *stock/retained earnings*).

PROBLEMS

1. ABC Corporation expects that earnings before interest and taxes will increase next year to $6 million. The capital structure of the firm includes 100,000 shares of $1.20 preferred stock, a $10-million 8 percent bond issue, and 2 million shares of common stock. Assuming that ABC has an effective tax rate of 40 percent, compute the expected earnings per share.

Solution

Step one As a preliminary step, interest and preferred dividends must be calculated:

$$\text{Interest} = \$10 \text{ million} \times 0.08$$
$$= \$0.8 \text{ million}$$

$$\text{Preferred dividends} = 100{,}000 \times \$1.20$$
$$= \$0.12 \text{ million}$$

Step two

$$\text{EPS} = \frac{(\text{EBIT} - \text{interest}) \times (1 - \text{tax rate}) - \text{preferred dividends}}{\text{number of common shares}}$$

$$= \frac{(\$6 - \$0.8) \times (1 - 0.4) - \$0.12}{2}$$

$$= \$1.50 \text{ per share}$$

2. Suppose instead that EBIT for ABC reaches only 50 percent of the expected level. What would EPS be then?

Solution

Step one

$$\text{EPS} = \frac{(\$3 - \$0.8) \times (1 - 0.4) - \$0.12}{2}$$

$$= \$0.60 \text{ per share}$$

Step two   The *effects of leverage* are illustrated by a quick comparison of the changes in EBIT and EPS. EPS is only two-fifths of its former level when EBIT declines by one-half. Using the lower figures, EPS increases 2.5 times when EBIT doubles.

3. XYZ, Ltd., is planning a $10 million expansion and is considering raising the funds either by selling new stock at $50 a share or by borrowing at 10 percent. If the economy picks up, sales next year are expected to be $40 million. If conditions remain sluggish, sales will amount to only $25 million. The firm currently has 1 million shares of common stock outstanding and no debt or preferred stock. Estimated operating expenses next year are $30 million for the optimistic sales forecast and $22 million at the lower sales level. Taxes are 60 percent. Calculate EPS corresponding to each sales forecast and to each possible financing choice.

Solution

Step one   It is helpful first to determine several figures: Interest = $1 million if borrowing occurs. Selling stock will require $\dfrac{\$10 \text{ million}}{\$50 \text{ per share}}$, or 0.2 million new shares. The total shares under this plan will be 1 + 0.2, or 1.2 million.

Step two   Complete the following table (all figures are in millions of dollars):

	Stock financing		Debt financing	
	Pessimistic	Optimistic	Pessimistic	Optimistic
Sales	$25	$40	$25	$40
Operating expenses	22	30	22	30
Operating profit (EBIT)	3	10	3	10
Interest	—	—	1	1
Taxable income	3	10	2	9
Taxes (60%)	1.8	6	1.2	5.4
Profits	$ 1.2	$ 4	$ 0.8	$ 3.6
EPS: 1.2 million shares for stock	$1.00	$3.33		
1 million shares for debt			$0.8	$3.6

Step three   Given a level of EBIT, EPS can be computed from the equation used in problem 1 or from an income statement format as presented above—the result is the same.

Step four   Note that debt financing increases the fluctuation in EPS compared with stock financing. With leverage, EPS varied from $0.80 per share to $3.60 per share, while the range with stock financing was narrower—between $1 and $3.33 per share.

Step five   This problem illustrates the importance of accurate forecasts of the economy and of sales. In choosing between alternative financing methods, it is most helpful to have a good idea as to the likelihood of different outcomes. A strong belief in a healthy economy adds support to use of debt in this case.

4. Fli-Bi-Nite Airways, a company offering a charter service as well as more imagination than the ABC or XYZ firms, is considering buying a $20 million airplane. Depending on the frequency of usage, the plane is estimated to generate an annual EBIT of between $2 million and $4 million. Three financing plans are to be considered: 100 percent stock; 60 percent stock and 40 percent debt; and 20 percent stock and 80 percent debt. The firm currently has 100,000 shares outstanding and no debt or preferred stock. Assuming that new stock could be sold for $25 per share, that debt could carry a 9 percent interest rate, and that taxes are 50 percent, determine which financing proposal should be chosen.

Solution

Step one   Calculation of new shares to be sold:

$$100\% \text{ stock: } \frac{\$20 \text{ million}}{\$25 \text{ per share}} = 0.8 \text{ million shares}$$

$$60\% \text{ stock: } \frac{\$20 \times 0.60}{\$25} = 0.48 \text{ million shares}$$

$$20\% \text{ stock: } \frac{\$20 \times 0.20}{\$25} = 0.16 \text{ million shares}$$

Step two   These amounts will be added to the existing 0.1 million shares to equal 0.9, 0.58, and 0.26 million shares, respectively.

Step three Calculation of interest:

$$40\% \text{ debt: } \$20 \text{ million} \times 0.4 \times 0.09$$

$$= \$0.72 \text{ million}$$

$$80\% \text{ debt: } \$20 \times 0.8 \times 0.09$$

$$= \$1.44 \text{ million}$$

Step four Compute EPS as follows:

	100% stock		60% stock		20% stock	
	Low	High	Low	High	Low	High
EBIT	$2	$4	$2	$4	$2	$4
Interest	—	—	0.72	0.72	1.44	1.44
Taxable income	2	4	1.28	3.28	0.56	2.56
Tax (50%)	1	2	0.64	1.64	0.28	1.28
Profit	$1	$2	$0.64	$1.64	$0.28	$1.28
EPS	$1.11	$2.22	$1.10	$2.83	$1.08	$4.92

Step five Plot EBIT versus EPS.

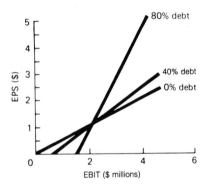

FIGURE 12-3

Step six The indifference point is at an EBIT of approximately $2 million. If management feels strongly that the company can easily earn at least this amount, the 80 percent debt financing alternative should be chosen since this leverage produces the most favorable results for shareholders.

Step seven Again note that the effects of leverage result in a wider fluctuation in EPS, which can be favorable *if* EBIT stays above the point of indifference. With 80 percent debt, a 100 percent increase in EBIT (from $2 million to $4 million) results in a 356 percent increase in EPS (from $1.08 per share to $4.92 per share).

5. P.O., Inc., builds post offices and leases them on long-term contracts to the U.S. Postal Service. A newly proposed $10 million facility offers annual profits to the company of $1.5 million. Stockholders in P.O. expect a 15 percent return. Existing earnings for this debt-free firm are $7.5 million per year. Apply the financial structure theory of Modigliani and Miller assuming perfect capital markets, no taxes, and no default costs to compute the value of P.O. if the new building were financed with all common stock *or* with an 8 percent debt issue. Also determine what the shareholder return would be under each financing plan.

Solution

Step one According to Modigliani and Miller, if the assumptions stated above are made, the financial structure makes no difference in the firm's value or in its average cost of capital.

Step two Since this business is long-term in nature,

$$\text{Value} = \frac{\text{earnings}}{\text{shareholder rate of return}}$$

$$= \frac{\$7.5 + \$1.5}{0.15} = \$60, \text{ or } \$60 \text{ million}$$

Step three This value is the same, according to Modigliani and Miller, no matter how the company is financed.

Step four The stockholder return doesn't vary either and would still be 15 percent using either stock or debt. (An implied assumption in this problem is that the new facility has the same risk as the existing assets of the firm.)

Step five If debt is used, stockholders become somewhat more nervous because a disgruntled debtholder can close the company down if debt payments aren't made when due. As a result of this added risk, stockholders "up the ante"; they raise their expectations of a return. Remember that k_a will be unchanged because the higher k_s will be offset by the use of lower-cost debt.

$$k_a = \text{stock rate} \times \text{proportion of stock} + \text{debt rate}$$
$$\times \text{proportion of debt}$$

With debt financing the value of the stock is 7.5/0.15, or $50 million; thus

$$k_a = 0.15 = k_s \times \frac{50}{60} + 0.08 \times \frac{10}{60}$$

$$k_s = \frac{0.82}{5} = 0.164, \text{ or } 16.4\%$$

Thus k_s has increased from 15 to 16.4 percent to compensate shareholders for the added risk of debt financing.

6. ZZZ Corporation, a sleep products concern, has the following potential capital budget:

Project	Cost, $ millions	Rate of return, %
A	1.2	16
B	0.5	11
C	0.9	25
D	5.6	28
E	0.2	12
F	3.2	15
G	0.4	35

From discussions with financing sources, it is estimated that $5 million could be raised at an average cost of 10 percent, the next $2.5 million at a cost of 13 percent, and the last $2 million at an average cost of 18 percent. What is the optimal capital budget?

Solution

Step one This problem requires a supply and demand funds analysis.

Step two The demand curve can be derived from rearranging the project data as follows:

Project	Rate of return, %	Cost, $ millions Project	Cost, $ millions Cumulative total
G	35	0.4	0.4
D	28	5.6	6.0
C	25	0.9	6.9
A	16	1.2	8.1
F	15	3.2	11.3
E	12	0.2	11.5
B	11	0.5	12.0

Step three The supply of funds curve is developed from the sources of financing amounts and cost data as follows:

Amount ($ millions) Incremental	Amount ($ millions) Cumulative	Cost, %
5.0	5.0	10
2.5	7.5	13
2.0	9.5	18

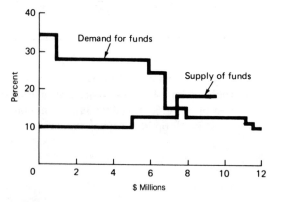

FIGURE 12-4

Step four The plot of these two curves indicates that the optimal capital budget should be $7.5 million. However, this would not be sufficient to finance project A, and so the budget would be $6.9 million unless an additional $0.6 million ($8.1 − $7.5) could be found at a cost of 16 percent or lower. The alert reader may wonder whether the capital rationing discussions could be applied here. They can and should be, but let's go to the next chapter after one more problem.

7. What is the cost of common stock that is sold to investors who expect a return of 14 percent? Assume the new shares are sold for $20 each and the issue costs are 5 percent.

Solution

Step one   This problem requires a flotation cost adjustment to the cost of capital. The adjusted cost equals:

$$14 \times \frac{20}{20(1 - .05)} = 14.7\%$$

End of solution.

CHAPTER THIRTEEN

DIVIDEND POLICY AND RETAINED EARNINGS

QUINTESSENCE   Profits from the firm's activities can be retained to finance new investments or to pay off debts, or they can be paid out as dividends to shareholders. Retained earnings are an important source of financing because the company can raise money internally without incurring the costs of issuing new securities. The decision to retain profits as retained earnings or to pay dividends is based on the investment opportunities available and the income taxes paid by the shareholders. If the potential for high returns from new investments exists, then earnings can be retained to take advantage of them and raise the net worth of the firm. Dividend payments to shareholders are taxable as personal income. Many investors prefer to have the firm retain earnings, resulting in an increased potential for capital gains which postpones taxes. Legal factors restrict dividend-paying ability, as can liquidity needs and the costs to the company and its shareholders associated with dividend payments. Most firms strive to achieve a steady growth pattern of cash dividends with major emphasis placed on stability. Stock dividends and splits do not affect shareowners' wealth.

OUTLINE
I. What
   A. Specific procedures are followed to make certain that the correct list of shareholders is paid the dividends they are entitled to receive.
   B. To establish a dividend policy, one must know about factors that are influential, including:
      1. Profitability of the firm's investment opportunities.
      2. Shareholder and corporate tax matters.
      3. Legal commitments and requirements.
      4. Liquidity and debt needs of the company.
      5. Cost considerations to the firm and its shareholders.
   C. A review of theory and actual practice indicates that companies base their dividends on some form of a fixed or variable relationship to earnings.
   D. A discussion of dividend reinvestment plans and an evaluation of stock dividends, stock splits, and share repurchases complete this chapter.

185

II. Why

    A. Firms are owned by, and run for, stockholders. Their long-run interest is the key in deciding the appropriate amounts to retain and to pay out in dividends.

    B. Dividend policy needs to be established in the light of investment and financing decisions.

III. How

Paying Dividends

    A. The dividend payment procedure.

        1. Dividends are normally set at a level that can be sustained even in bad times. They are typically paid quarterly in approximately equal amounts. Some firms pay an extra dividend at year-end in addition to the regular payments; all distributions are planned with long-run company investment needs and earnings in mind.

        2. Steps in the process include:

Announcement

            a. The board of directors decides on and announces a dividend that is to be paid to shareholders of record on some future date.

Record Date

            b. Payments will be made to persons owning the stock up to *but not including* four business days before this **record date.**

Ex-Dividend Date

            c. On the fourth day before the record date, the stock trades **ex-dividend** since anyone purchasing these shares that day, or thereafter, won't get the previously declared dividend.

Influences on Dividends

            d. On the ex-dividend day the stock price will fall by approximately the amount of the dividend.

    B. Factors affecting the dividend decision.

Profits on New Investments

        1. **Profitability of investment opportunities** encourages or discourages dividends; the higher the returns on new projects, the more demand for new funds and the greater incentive to finance internally by retaining earnings.

            a. This also saves flotation costs and defers taxes for owners.

            b. Young, rapid-growth firms usually don't pay dividends.

Taxes Favor Retention of Earnings

        2. **Tax considerations.**

            a. The Tax Reform Act of 1986 that eliminated lower tax rates to individuals on capital gains clearly changed the incentive for retaining earnings. However,

                i. Retained earnings are invested to earn money, which raises the value of the firm and its shares.

               ii. If shareholders need cash, they can sell a few shares to raise the funds. The taxes they will pay are based only on the portion that is a capital gain. Remember, individuals must pay tax on *all* the dividends. This means that in raising cash an individual will pay more taxes if the source is dividends than if the money needed had instead come from capital gains.

              iii. If cash isn't needed by shareholders, the higher-value shares can be held, and there will be no tax until the stock is actually sold. This postpones taxes, which is not possible if dividends are paid.

    iv. The above comments apply if the shareholder is a person. When the shareholder is another corporation, the company receiving the dividends pays corporate taxes up to 30 percent of the dividend payments, depending on the percentage of the paying corporation's stock that is held by the receiving firm.

Corporate Taxes

  b. The tax on excessive firm retentions of earnings places a limit on the ability of a company to retain earnings in the form of liquid assets. In other words, the IRS can penalize a business that does not pay dividends just so that its owners can postpone income taxes.

  c. The corporate tax code, which allows interest as a deduction but not dividends, encourages usage of debt and discourages dividend payments.

Laws and Contracts Restrict Dividends

3. **Legal requirements.**

  a. Terms of borrowing often restrict the ability to pay dividends.

  b. Preferred stock with a cumulative provision prohibits dividends on common stock *if* payments to preferred shareholders are behind schedule.

Capital Impairment

  c. There are constraints on **capital impairment.**

    i. This is a restriction in most state laws specifying that dividends may not exceed the amounts in retained earnings and paid-in surplus.

    ii. Dividends normally can't be paid by an insolvent firm (one whose liabilities exceed its assets).

Liquidity Needs

4. A firm's liquid assets position, requirements to repay debt, and unexpected cash demands influence the dividend-paying ability.

Costs to Firm and to Shareholders

5. Company and stockholder cost and preference considerations:

  a. Corporations incur greater fees and costs when they raise money externally compared with costs of distributing dividends. These higher charges are an incentive for retaining earnings because retained earnings have *no* transaction costs.

  b. Transaction costs to shareholders when receiving cash dividends are almost nil compared with costs of obtaining cash by selling shares. On the other hand, personal taxes encourage retained earnings—see 2a above.

Clientele Effect

  c. Different individual situations result in investors' being attracted to firms whose dividend policies match their own preferences. This is the **clientele effect.** It encourages companies to maintain predictable (stable) dividend policy, because shareholders don't like surprises in this area.

C. **Dividend policy** has two major dimensions:

Dividend Stability Payout Ratios

1. The degree of *stability* from year to year.

  a. Only a few firms have **stable payout ratios** (dividends divided by earnings). In this policy, dividends fluctuate with earnings.

Dollar Level	b. Most firms strive for a **stable dollar dividend,** where the cash amount of payments per share is relatively constant until there is considerable evidence that an upward adjustment in the level can be supported (sometimes a reduction is necessary).
Extras	c. A few corporations pay a stable dollar dividend as a regular amount and then add an **extra** payment at the end of a highly profitable year.
Stability Because	d. The stable dollar dividend plans, with or without extras, tend to provide dividends that fluctuate less than earnings; most firms are especially hesitant to cut dividends when earnings decline.
Investors Like It	i. Some investors plan on dividends as a regular source of income for living expenses.
Dividends Are Forecasts of Future	ii. Dividends are an indicator of management's belief in long-run future earning power; a cut implies poor expectations, and an increase reflects optimism.
Institutions Need It	iii. Many institutional investors are permitted to buy only stocks offering stable or growing dividends.
Long-Run Payout	2. **Long-run dividend payout ratio.** a. Most firms have relatively stable year-to-year dividend payments, but there is considerable variation among companies in the level of the average payout ratio.
Large, Old Firms Pay Out More	i. Large, mature companies tend to have high dividend payout ratios. ii. Smaller, rapidly growing firms usually have low payouts.
Imperfect Markets Theory **Best to Retain Earnings vs. High Payouts**	b. The **imperfect markets** school argues that dividend policy really makes a difference. i. One branch feels firms should favor maximum use of internal financing because of tax considerations (capital gains postpone tax payments in comparison to dividend income), costs of raising new funds, expenses of paying dividends, and flotation costs for selling new shares. These market "imperfections" lower the cost of equity from retained earnings. This encourages low dividend payments, thus making more funds available for the company to invest. ii. Another group contends that firms should pay dividends even if new shares must be sold to replenish the cash position. They feel shareholders are better off receiving their income in the form of dividends because corporations are smarter when it comes to timing the sale of stock (this is debatable). The group also believes dividend payments reduce shareholder risk (this is an invalid argument).
Perfect Markets Theory **Dividends Don't Matter**	c. According to the **perfect markets** theory, the advantage of internal financing over external equity financing is nil. These adherents contend that a stock's price doesn't depend on dividend policy, because some investors want high dividends while others

prefer low amounts. This means there is a market for any stock, regardless of its dividend payments.

d. So much for theory. What about practice?

    i. Evidence can be cited to support both theories.

    ii. Shareholders want stable (predictable) dividends.

    iii. Companies should sell new shares when more cash is needed and buy back shares when they have excess cash.

    iv. Most people believe dividends do matter.

Payout Residual Amounts

e. **Residual dividend policy** is the most popular and is based on the premise that internal financing is cheaper than external sources. Dividends are paid from amounts left over *after* equity investment needs are met. (Equity investment is investment funded by retained earnings and new stock sales.) Three approaches to this policy differ in terms of dividend stability:

Pure Residual

    i. **Pure residual dividend policy** pays dividends D_t that are the amounts left over after equity investment I_t^e has been deducted from earnings E_t. Thus

$$D_t = E_t - I_t^e \qquad (13\text{-}1)$$

This policy produces the most volatile dividend pattern.

Fixed Payout

    ii. The **fixed dividend payout ratio** plan determines dividends from a constant proportion q_t of earnings. Thus

$$D_t = q_t \times E_t \qquad (13\text{-}2)$$

where q_t is set so that, in the long run, $D = E - I^e$. In this approach, earnings and dividends fluctuate together.

Smoothed Residual

    iii. The **smoothed residual dividend policy** offers dividends at a constant dollar value so as again to have dividends, in the long run, equal the difference between earnings and equity investment needs. This plan typically produces the *most stable dividend* pattern.

Dividend Reinvestment

D. Many firms offer their stockholders an option to have their dividends used to buy more shares in the company. These automatic reinvestment plans reduce commission costs for investors, although shareholders still must pay ordinary income taxes on the dividends declared. All these offers are intended to make a company's stock more attractive.

1. Some firms have recently offered their shareholders an option to reinvest dividends in *new* shares to be purchased at a discount from the existing market price.

**Stock Dividends
and Splits**

2. A few companies offer their stockholders another type of dividend in the form of special purchase deals on the firm's products.

E. **Stock dividends** (20 percent or less) and **stock splits** (25 percent or more—between 20 and 25 percent can be labeled as either one) involve distributing more shares to existing stockholders.
   1. There is *no change* in the firm's assets or liabilities.
   2. The fall in the per share figures for earnings, book value, and stock price is approximately offset by a rise in the number of shares held by each stockholder.
   3. Empirical evidence indicates that the total market value of the equity increases roughly 2 to 6 percent when a firm distributes more shares. This is caused by more demand for the stock because:
      a. More people can buy lower-priced shares.
      b. Investors believe management has sent them a signal of better times ahead.
   4. In a **reverse split** the rises and falls are opposite, but again the real change that occurs after the dust settles is very small.

**Repurchased
Shares**

F. Companies sometimes buy back their shares. In the late 1980s the funds used for this purpose exceeded the total monies paid out in dividends.
   1. The repurchased shares are called **treasury stock,** which has no rights for:
      a. Dividends.
      b. Voting.
   2. The shares are not assets for the firm.
   3. Reasons for repurchase include:
      a. Tax savings for stockholders—if the company used the cash to pay dividends, the stockholders would be taxed on all the dividends but they pay taxes only on capital gains that may result if they sell their shares;
      b. A way to get around government controls limiting dividends (this situation is quite rare);
      c. As a technique to block a takeover attempt; and
      d. Special uses such as for stock option plans or for acquiring other firms.

COMPLETION QUESTIONS

quarterly   1. Normally dividends are paid (*quarterly/annuaity*).

board, directors   2. Dividends are declared by the _____ of _____.

ex-dividend   3. The _____ date occurs four business days before the date of
record   (*record/payment*).

ex-dividend   4. On the day a stock goes _____, its price will usually (*in-*
decrease   *crease/decrease*) by the amount of the dividend.

reduce	5. Dividend reinvestment plans (*increase/reduce*) commission costs for investors.
greater	6. The more profitable investment opportunities a firm has, the (*greater/less*)
retain	will be its incentive to (*pay out/retain*) earnings.
capital gains	7. The individual income tax rate on _____ _____ is
the same as	(*the same as/lower than*) the tax rate on dividends. However, because taxes
retain earnings	can be postponed, investors prefer companies to (*pay dividends/retain earnings*).
dividends	8. If a firm pays little or no _____, stockholders can still get a
capital gain	return by selling some shares at a(n) _____ _____.
	9. When the preferential tax treatment of capital gains was abolished in 1986,
increase	companies were encouraged to (*increase/decrease*) dividend payments.
	10. A penalty tax may be levied on a company that does not pay dividends
owners	so that its (*creditors/owners*) can avoid paying any taxes. This tax on excessive firm retentions (*does/does not*) apply to firms that have a proper use
does not	
retained earnings	for _____ _____.
interest	11. The corporate tax code, which allows (*dividends/interest*) as a deduction
dividends, encourage	but not (*dividends/interest*), tends to (*encourage/discourage*) usage of debt
retained earnings	and (*preferred stock/retained earnings*) as sources of financing.
restrict	12. Terms set in borrowing arrangements often (*restrict/enhance*) the firm's
dividend	_____-paying ability.
cumulative	13. If a firm has a (*nonvoting/cumulative*) preferred stock issue outstanding and it is behind on those dividends, common stockholders cannot receive any
preferred	dividends until all the _____ dividends past-due have been paid.
capital impairment	14. Prohibitions against (*booze/capital impairment*) refer to state laws that limit
retained earnings	firms to paying dividends from only _____ _____ and paid-in surplus.
insolvent	15. Firms that are _____ are precluded from paying dividends. These
liabilities	companies' assets are exceeded by their _____.
low	16. A firm that is often illiquid would tend to pay (*low/high*) dividends.
external	17. Charges incurred to raise (*internal/external*) funds and costs of paying dividends are an incentive to _____ _____.
retain earnings	
	18. Some investors seek companies paying high dividends, while others avoid
clientele effect	them. This is known as the _____ _____. It encourages firms to have _____ dividend policies.
stable	

19. The two major characteristics of a desirable dividend policy are (*stability/volatility*) from year to year and long-run target _____ _____.

stability

payout ratios

20. Dividends fluctuate with (*interest/earnings*) for firms choosing stable (*liquidity/payout*) ratios.

earnings

payout

21. The majority of companies strive to pay a stable (*dollar/percentage*) dividend.

dollar

22. Firms with fluctuating earnings can achieve stability by paying a (*stock/regular*) dividend plus a(n) _____ dividend at the end of each exceptionally (*profitable/unprofitable*) year.

regular

extra

profitable

23. A company can indicate optimism concerning its future by (*raising/lowering*) its dividends.

raising

24. A firm having a high long-run payout ratio probably has (*few/many*) profitable investment opportunities.

few

25. The market imperfections dividend theory says that firms should favor (*internal/external*) financing.

internal

26. The (*stable/residual*) dividend policy is based on internal financing's being the (*cheapest/costliest*) source of funds.

residual

cheapest

27. The most stable pattern of dividends is associated with the _____ _____ dividend policy.

smoothed

residual

28. Some firms offer their shareholders the opportunity to reinvest dividends to purchase (*new/old*) shares at a (*premium/discount*) compared with the existing market price.

new, discount

29. When a 10 percent stock dividend is paid, the stock price will (*fall/rise*) by about _____ percent.

fall

10

30. In a one-for-two _____ split, the stock price will (*increase/decrease*) by a factor of 2.

reverse, increase

31. Stock dividends and stock splits result in (*substantial/very little*) change in the total value of each investor's shares held.

very little

32. Shares repurchased by a company are called _____ _____.

treasury stock

33. (Extra credit for German speakers!) According to the perfect markets theory of dividend policy, _____ _____ _____ regarding the payout effect on capital costs or the levels of investment outlays.

Das Macht Nichts

PROBLEMS

1. Waterford Park, Inc. (WPI), paid $2.40 per share in dividends last year, which amounted to a 60 percent payout ratio. The firm had 1 million shares outstanding.

   a. What were WPI's earnings per share?

Solution

Step one

$$\text{Payout ratio} = \frac{\text{dividends per share}}{\text{earnings per share}}$$

$$\text{Earnings per share} = \frac{\$2.40}{0.60}, \text{ or } \$4$$

End of solution.

   b. How much was retained in the firm?

Solution

Step one

$$\text{Retained earnings} = \text{earnings} - \text{dividends}$$

$$= \$4 - \$2.40, \text{ or } \$1.60 \text{ per share}$$

Step two   In total dollars this is

$$\$1.60 \times 1 \text{ million, or } \$1.6 \text{ million}$$

2. Jeff and Peter decide to sell their stock and use the proceeds to open a business. Each one had purchased stock in a different company several years ago. Jeff received dividends of $3 per share on each of his 1000 shares. Today's price of $30 per share is the same as when he bought the stock. Peter paid $50 each for his 500 shares, which are now selling at $65 per share. His stock does not pay any dividends. Both men are in the 30 percent tax bracket. If they sell their stock now and pay the taxes due, who has the most money?

Solution

Step one Jeff will receive 1000 × $30, or $30,000. The taxes he will pay on the dividends received are $3000 × 0.30, or $900. Assuming he still has the cash from the dividends, he should have $30,000 + $3000 − $900 = $32,100.

Step two Peter will pay taxes on the capital gains as follows:

$$\text{Selling proceeds: } 500 \times \$65 = \$32{,}500$$
$$\text{Cost: } 500 \times \$50 = \underline{\$25{,}000}$$
$$\text{Capital gains: } = \$\ 7{,}500$$

The taxes due are $7500 × 0.30, or $2250. Peter's net proceeds will be $32,500 − $2250, or $30,250.

Step three The purpose of this problem was to show that even though the tax rate on income from dividends and capital gains is the same, the amount of taxes due is based on all dividends received but only the capital gains portion of the proceeds from the stock sales.

3. Zee Corp. has experienced a steady growth pattern with earnings per share rising at an average rate of 7 percent per year to a level of $3.60 per share two years ago. A strike last year resulted in a drop in earnings to $2.80 per share. The firm has 1 million shares outstanding and plans to spend $10 million for expansion of facilities in the year just started. What would have been the dividend payments during the strike year if the company had used one of the following policies:

a. A **stable long-run dividend-payout ratio** of 30 percent

Solution

Step one In this policy, dividends fluctuate with earnings.

Step two Dividends equal 0.30 × $2.80, or $0.84 per share.

b. A **stable dollar dividend** policy

Solution

Step one Cash payments will be relatively constant until there is considerable evidence that an adjustment can be supported or is necessary.

Step two   Companies are hesitant to cut dividends, and because the cause of the drop was temporary, it is reasonable to assume that the firm's growth will resume at the long-run average. Therefore dividends would probably be kept at the level of the last "normal" year of $1.08 per share (30 percent of $3.60).

Step three   If the temporary disruption in the long-run pattern had been *favorable*, i.e., yielded above-normal earnings, this policy would dictate a dividend of 7 percent more than the last normal year's dividend.

c. A **stable dollar dividend plus an extra**

Solution

Step one   Without knowing what the stable dollar dividend has been, we cannot tell exactly what the dividend would be except to say that there would probably be no extra dividend paid in the bad year.

Step two   Most firms using this policy have ups and downs and set the stable dollar amount at a level they expect to earn, as a minimum, in *every* year. The extra dividend, which is paid at year-end, is set to share above-normal profits; it is reduced or eliminated in bad years. The idea is to pay a minimum amount that stockholders can usually count on; they may get more in good years.

d. A **pure residual dividend** policy, assuming the firm plans to borrow $8 million to help finance its $10 million investment program

Solution

Step one   This policy sets dividends at the difference between what is earned and what is needed at "home" (earnings retained for equity investment).

Step two   Earnings last year were $2.8 million ($2.80 per share × 1 million shares). Equity needs are $2 million ($10 − $8).

Step three   Dividends will total $0.8 million ($2.8 − $2), or $\frac{\$800,000}{1,000,000} = \$0.80$ per share.

Step four Dividends set by this policy will vary considerably because they are dependent on (a) the amount of earnings, (b) the amount of capital spending, and (c) the amount of debt financing. Each of the items can change from year to year, causing a volatile dividend pattern.

4. A five-year history of earnings and dividends for two firms is shown below. One company is an automobile manufacturer, and the other is an electric utility. Identify which firm belongs to each record and state your reasoning based on the pattern of dividend payments.

Dollar per share data for Company A and Company B

Year	Company A		Company B	
	Earnings	Dividends	Earnings	Dividends
1 (most recent)	4.32	2.40	2.78	1.70
2	3.27	3.40	2.73	1.59
3	8.34	5.25	2.64	1.56
4	7.51	4.45	2.47	1.47
5	6.72	3.40	2.21	1.44

Solution

Step one A quick look at the earnings data gives an indication that company A is the automaker because of the ups and downs, compared with steady, modest growth in company B, which fits the utility industry pattern. But wait! This is cheating because we were asked to analyze the *dividend* data.

Step two The dividend history tells a similar story—wide fluctuation versus regular improvement.

Step three The payout ratio (dividends ÷ earnings) sheds some light:

	Payout ratio, %	
Year	Company A	Company B
1	56	61
2	104	58
3	63	59
4	59	60
5	51	65

Step four Both firms pay over half of their earnings out in dividends, but company *A* has a much wider range. One might wonder why *A*'s payout doesn't fluctuate even more. The reason is that the firm in a cyclical business is probably paying a regular dividend of $0.85 ($3.40 ÷ 4) per quarter in years 2 to 5 plus a year-end extra *if* earnings justify it. In the most recent year the regular dividend was cut to $0.60 ($2.40 ÷ 4) per quarter. Company *B* has inched its dividends along with an apparent target payout ratio of 60 percent.

Step five The analysis of dividends indicates that company *A* is the automaker and that company *B* is the electric utility.

5. Bell Company has 100,000 shares outstanding and declares a 20 percent stock dividend. If the total market value of the shares was $1 million, what would be the price per share after the dividend is paid, assuming nothing else happens to influence the stock price?

Solution

Step one The firm will be sending new shares to its stockholders, but that is *all* that happens. The company has not received any money, nor has its earning power increased as a result of the transaction.

Step two The value of the firm remains unchanged, as does the value of each stockholder's *total* shares. After the 20 percent stock dividend there will be 120,000 shares outstanding (100,000 × 1.2). The share price before was $10 ($1,000,000 ÷ 100,000). It will fall to $8.33 ($1,000,000 ÷ 120,000), but each owner will have 20 percent more shares to exactly offset the price decline. Someone who owned 100 shares before had an investment of $1000 (100 × $10). When the dust settles, the value will still be $1000 (120 × $8.33).

Step three This answer needs to be modified slightly. Recall that empirical evidence developed from companies that have stock splits indicates that the resulting value of each shareowner's position will normally increase by 2 to 6 percent as a result of the splitting action. This is because of increased demand for the stock. It means that the postsplit shares will be around $8.50 each (approximately a 2 percent gain in value).

6. On Thursday, July 29, the Fair Life Insurance Company directors met and declared a cash dividend of $0.50 per share payable on Tuesday, August 31, to stockholders of record on Wednesday, August 18.

a. When does the stock go ex-dividend?

Solution

Step one The ex-dividend date is four business days prior to the date of record.

Step two The record date is Wednesday, August 18, and so four *business* days before would be Thursday, August 12. On this day and thereafter purchasers of the stock will not be entitled to receive the dividend declared in July.

b. What is the last day on which you could buy the stock and receive the dividend just declared?

Solution

Step one This would be the trading day just before the ex-dividend date—in this case, Wednesday, August 11. *End of solution.*

c. What would be likely to happen to the stock price on the ex-dividend date if nothing else happened to influence the stock price?

Solution

Step one Anyone buying the stock on the ex-dividend date will *not* receive the dividend, whereas if the stock were purchased just one day sooner, the new owner would get the dividend. Since this change occurs literally overnight (now you get it, now you don't), the stock is worth less on the ex-dividend date. The price would fall, all things being the same, by the amount of the dividend, which is $0.50 per share.

Step two If a stock dividend instead of a cash dividend had been involved, the stock price would have reacted in a similar manner; a 10 percent stock dividend would cause the price to fall about 10 percent on the ex-dividend date.

d. What information is conveyed to investors when dividends are declared?

Solution

Step one Dividends are a *rough* indicator of the directors' feelings about the firm's future prospects. An increase in the cash payment is a healthy sign; a reduction is an indicator of troubled times. *End of solution.*

7. L, LTD., reported earnings of $20 million and dividends of $12 million in its most recent year. The firm has 5 million shares outstanding but has just announced plans for a two-for-one stock split. Assuming a current (pre-split) stock price of $80 per share, complete the following table:

	Earnings per share	Dividends per share	Price per share	Market value of the firm
Before the split				
After the split				

Solution

Step one The two-for-one split will double the number of outstanding shares to 10 million.

Step two This will have the effect of cutting each of the statistics, expressed on a per share basis, by half.

Step three Calculations are as follows:

	Before	After
Earnings per share, $	$\dfrac{20}{5} = 4$	$\dfrac{20}{10} = 2$
Dividends per share, $	$\dfrac{12}{5} = 2.40$	$\dfrac{12}{10} = 1.20$
Price per share, $	80	$\dfrac{80}{2} = 40$

Step four The value of the firm remains the same; nothing has really changed. Each stockholder has twice as many shares, but the price per share is about half the presplit price. The firm's value before was 5 million shares times $80 per share, or $400 million; after the split the value will be 10 million shares times $40 per share, or $400 million. Actually, it is expected to be 2 to 6 percent higher, which means the stock price will be about $41.50.

CHAPTER FOURTEEN

FINANCIAL STATEMENT ANALYSIS

QUINTESSENCE

Techniques and a framework for appraising the financial strengths and weaknesses of a firm are vital requirements for better understanding of that business. The tools used are ratios and funds flows, calculated from the balance sheets and income statements. The ratios are compared with industry norms, and the deviations from these standards help identify trouble spots or strong points. Areas of performance examined are liquidity (ability to generate cash), leverage (use of borrowed funds), activity (how hard the assets are working), and profitability (relative returns). The analysis relies on judgment for the interpretation of the relatively easy-to-calculate ratios. The process is much like that used by a skilled artist who creates a masterpiece out of ordinary paints and brushes or by a clever detective who sifts through many facts to uncover clues leading to the solution of a crime. Management, creditors, and shareholders all want to know about the financial condition of the company, what it has done with its resources, and where it may be going. Financial statement analysis helps to provide the information they need.

OUTLINE

I. What
   A. This chapter covers the logic, derivations, and use of ratios and funds flows computed from financial statements.
   B. Relative strengths and weaknesses of a company can be identified by comparing its ratios with industry norms.

II. Why
   A. Managers, debtholders, and stockholders need an organized framework to better analyze a firm's well-being.
   B. Corrective actions for strengthening a business can be suggested by the financial analysis.

Financial Statements

III. How
   A. A company's financial operations are accounted for in a series of reports:
      1. The **balance sheet** presents a firm's financial condition (assets, liabilities, and net worth) *at* a particular point in time (like a snapshot).

201

2. The **income statement** shows performance *over* a particular period of time (like a movie).
3. The **statement of retained earnings** indicates the amount of earnings retained up to the beginning of the time period covered and any increases or decreases due to the profits retained or losses during the period.
4. The **sources and uses of funds (cash) statement** shows where the firm obtained funds during the period and how they were spent.

Financial Ratios

B. **Financial analysis** begins by computing ratios from data in the financial statements. Users (e.g., bankers, managers, and stockholders) find some ratios more helpful than others.
1. Ratios are categorized into four basic types to better reveal particular aspects of a company's financial condition.

Liquidity Ratios

a. **Liquidity ratios** measure the firm's ability to meet its short-term obligations from its current assets.

Current

i. A **current ratio** (current assets ÷ current liabilities) that is too low may indicate difficulty in paying creditors as their claims come due. Too high a ratio means that the level of current assets may be excessive. Because the numerator and denominator of the ratio are composites of several individual accounts, the specific accounts must be examined to see where the trouble spot is when a flag of caution is raised.

Quick

ii. The **quick,** or **acid test, ratio** (the difference between current assets and inventories ÷ current liabilities) excludes inventories because they are the least liquid of the current assets.

Leverage Ratios

b. **Leverage ratios** indicate the firm's ability to meet its short- and long-term debt obligations from its total assets and from its earning power. The underlying logic stems from the basic promises of borrowers to pay back principal and interest. Leverage ratios help determine whether the amounts of borrowing and interest charges are excessive. The capacity for debt is influenced by the predictability of company income; the more reliable this inflow, the more debt can be supported.

Debt/Assets

i. Creditors prefer a low **debt to total assets ratio** (total liabilities ÷ total assets) since this means greater protection of their position.

Debt/Equity

ii. The **debt to equity ratio** (long-term debt ÷ stockholders' equity) indicates the debt portion of *long-term* financing. Equity represents a "cushion" for debtholders.

Times Interest Earned

iii. The **times interest earned ratio** (earnings before interest and taxes ÷ interest) measures the firm's ability to pay interest from its earnings. The higher the ratio, the more assurance for creditors that interest will be paid. Earnings before interest and taxes is used because this measures the amount generated and available to pay interest.

Fixed-Charges Coverage	iv. The **fixed-charges coverage ratio** (income available for meeting fixed charges ÷ fixed charges) measures the firm's ability to pay all fixed charges. These amounts include debt interest, sinking fund contributions, and lease payments.
Activity Ratios	c. **Activity ratios** measure how hard a company uses its assets. The objective is to have enough assets but not too many. Averages of the asset accounts at the beginning and ending of the period are used, especially if the levels vary significantly.
Inventory Turnover	i. A low **inventory turnover** (cost of goods sold ÷ average inventory) may indicate an excessive investment in inventories; a high ratio often means that the firm is running out of stock, resulting in poor service to customers.
Collection Period	ii. The **average collection period** (accounts receivable ÷ average daily sales) measures how long it takes after a sale to collect the cash. A short period may mean a very stringent credit policy *and* reduced sales; a long collection period may be the result of a lax credit policy and/or weaknesses in collection procedures.
Fixed-Assets Turnover	iii. A low **fixed-assets turnover** (sales ÷ fixed assets) is an indicator of idle or unproductive plant and equipment, i.e., too much investment in fixed assets. A high ratio is a signal that plant and equipment may be overworked, a condition of inefficient production.
Total-Assets Turnover	iv. The **total-assets turnover** (sales ÷ total assets) reflects how well assets are being used to generate sales. Low and high ratios are interpreted like the fixed-assets turnover ratios.
Profitability Ratios	d. **Profitability ratios** measure the firm's degree of success in earning a return on sales or on investment.
Gross Profit Margin	i. The **gross profit margin** (sales less cost of goods sold ÷ sales) reflects pricing policy and production efficiency.
Net Operating Margin	ii. The **net operating margin** (operating income ÷ sales) measures the effectiveness of production and sales in generating pretax profits. Operating income equals sales less the total of the cost of goods sold and operating expenses. All nonoperating items are excluded so as to give an indicator of performance in the firm's basic business operations. Also note that costs associated with financing sources are not included in this measure of efficiency.
Profit Margin	iii. The **profit margin on sales** (net income ÷ sales) may be low if it is offset by high turnover. (See the discussion of the Du Pont system below for an explanation.)
Return on Assets	iv. The **return on total assets** (net income including interest ÷ total assets) is the rate of return earned by the firm for all its investors, including debtholders.
Return on Equity	v. The key ratio for judging the firm's success in earning a

profit for its owners is the **return on equity** (net income available to common stockholders ÷ common shareholders' equity).

The above fifteen ratios are representative of literally hundreds of possible combinations of data from the balance sheet and income statements. They are the basic tools in the financial analyst's kit. The real key is to *use* them and others skillfully, i.e., to interpret them.

2. Summary of the ratios

Type	Title	Formula
Liquidity	Current	Current assets ÷ current liabilities
	Quick or acid test	(Current assets − inventories) ÷ current liabilities
Leverage	Debt to total assets	Total liabilities ÷ total assets
	Debt to equity	Long-term debt ÷ stockholders' equity
	Times interest earned	Earnings before interest and taxes ÷ interest
	Fixed-charges coverage	Income available for meeting fixed charges ÷ fixed charges
Activity	Inventory turnover	Cost of goods sold ÷ average inventory
	Average collection period	Accounts receivable ÷ average daily sales
	Fixed-assets turnover	Sales ÷ fixed assets
	Total-assets turnover	Sales ÷ total assets
	Gross profit margin	(Sales − cost of goods sold) ÷ sales
Profitability	Net operating margin	Operating income ÷ sales
	Profit margin on sales	Net profit ÷ sales
	Return on total assets	(Net profits + interest) ÷ total assets
	Return on equity	Net profit ÷ shareholders' equity

Industry Norms

3. Ratios for a firm are compared with industry averages, with the following points in mind:

Interpretations

    a. When the industry itself is subpar or sick, the individual company must be *above* average to be considered healthy.

    b. Some firms, especially larger ones, operate in several completely different industries. Their data must be broken down and their performance judged according to the norms in each line of business.

    c. Firms within an industry are different with respect to size, products, risk, operating conditions, etc. This means that the standard for a ratio may appropriately be somewhat different for some companies within the same industry.

    d. Ideally each firm will set levels for ratios that enable it to generate the best stream of earnings per share appropriate for its risk exposure.

       i. Liquidity and leverage ratios should be at or above some minimum safe level.

      ii. Activity and profitability ratios should be such that the company can maintain and expand sales at minimal cost in line with the quality of output desired. Profits should provide a return to adequately compensate for the risks the company has undertaken.

    e. All these factors mean that the industry averages will be a *general* guide that must be carefully adapted to each firm's particular situation. The analyst should also know about the company's production, marketing, and financing plans.

Interrelationships

4. Ratio analysis is a complex process. Each ratio reveals a different aspect of a company's condition; at the same time it must be remembered that these "parts" are *interrelated*. Knowing the interrelationships helps to better develop the entire picture.

    a. By examining several ratios together, it is possible to trace ways in which different policies affect overall performance.

Return on Equity

    b. For example, return on equity is the combined result of the net income to operating income ratio, the net operating margin, asset turnover, and the asset to equity ratio. This equation shows how a low profit margin can be offset by a high turnover, resulting in a desirable situation for the owners. This is the premise used in "discount" operations (low markup and high volume).

Time Trends

5. It is important not only to learn about a firm's condition at a *point in time* but also to know in which direction the ratios may be moving—*trends over time*.

    a. A weak but improving situation may not call for new remedies. (Leave the quarterback in—the last three passes, although intercepted, were to the right spot, but the receivers tripped and fell.)

    b. Results of past changes can be traced over time as an aid to formulating future policies.

Discriminant Analysis

c. Close monitoring of trends is necessary, because they may not continue, which can be good *or* bad.

d. **Discriminant analysis** is used to examine several ratios *simultaneously* from an *historical* perspective.

Caveats

6. In using ratios developed from financial statement data recognize:

a. The entries for assets and liabilities are *book values,* which may be different from the actual market values.

b. The income statement is based on allocations made according to generally accepted accounting principles and as such does not reflect cash flows or changes in shareholder wealth.

c. This means ratios using long-term assets should be adjusted to reflect market values and funds flow statements should be used for further evaluations.

Du Pont System

7. The **Du Pont system** of financial analysis is a measure of performance in terms of return on investment (ROI).

a. ROI based on *total assets* is

$$\boxed{\text{ROI} = \frac{\text{sales}}{\text{total assets}} \times \frac{\text{net income}}{\text{sales}} = \frac{\text{net income}}{\text{total assets}}} \qquad (14\text{-}1)$$

i. The end result, ROI, is the product of a turnover and a profitability ratio. An acceptable ROI can be achieved by high volume and low markup, or vice versa. Think how this relates to selling gasoline at the self-service versus the full-service pumps.

ii. The trouble with this version of ROI is that net income is not the proper measure of return associated with total assets. Net income is the return to those providing equity capital, the common stockholders. Assets are usually financed by stockholders *and* debtholders. The appropriate return on assets should include returns to both of these sources of funds—net income for stockholders and interest for debtholders. This would make the numerator in Eq. (14-1) net income plus interest. (It might also make the Du Pont people unhappy.) Anyway, another version of ROI has been developed.

A Better ROI Measure

b. ROI based on *equity* is

$$\boxed{\text{ROI} = \frac{\text{sales}}{\text{total assets}} \times \frac{\text{total assets}}{\text{stockholders' equity}} \times \frac{\text{net income}}{\text{sales}} = \frac{\text{net income}}{\text{stockholders' equity}}}$$

$$(14\text{-}2)$$

Improving ROI

       i. This measure introduces a ratio to account for how the assets are financed, i.e., total assets ÷ stockholders' equity.

      ii. The result is a logical consistency in the numerator and denominator; net income goes to the shareholders, and shareholders' equity is the measure of their investment.

  c. ROI can be improved by:

       i. Making more efficient use of existing assets and/or eliminating excess capacity, which will increase asset turnover.

      ii. Cutting costs and/or changing prices so as to increase sales revenue, which will raise the profit margin on sales. This ratio typically varies more within a given industry than asset turnover does; the latter ratio is influenced mainly by the line of business.

  d. All measures of ROI are rough because accounting depreciation instead of actual depreciation is used to compute profits and balance sheet figures. This distorts both the return and the investment figures.

Sources of Ratios

8. Sources of information for computing ratios for firms and industries include:

  a. Company reports.

  b. Investment advisory services such as Moody's, Standard & Poor's, and Value Line.

  c. Brokerage houses.

  d. Credit reporting agencies such as Dun and Bradstreet and Robert Morris Associates.

  e. Trade associations such as the National Hardware Association.

  f. Government agencies such as the Securities and Exchange Commission, the Department of Commerce, and the Small Business Administration.

Purpose of Ratio Analysis

9. The *purpose* of ratio analysis is to provide a shortcut method for revealing certain crucial facts about a firm's operations and its financial condition. The ratios are the tools used by different groups of analysts to appraise a business from their viewpoint.

  a. Creditors want to know the company's capacity to repay its debt.

       i. Short-term creditors are interested primarily in liquidity ratios. Long-run financial strength and future outlook are also important, because a healthy firm can raise long-term funds to repay short-term debt and because current assets of a firm can deteriorate rapidly.

      ii. Long-term lenders look (a) at leverage ratios to see how much debt the company has, (b) at profitability ratios to appraise the operating effectiveness, and (c) at liquidity ratios to evaluate the firm's policy and ability to meet its short-term obligations.

  b. Security analysts examine ratios to help indicate the desirability of investing in a company's stock and bonds.

c. Governmental regulatory agencies use the ratios as an aid in setting rates for utilities and railroads.

d. The management of the firm itself computes ratios to measure the ability to pay creditors, to minimize costs, and to tell how the company is doing in providing returns to its owners.

Funds Flow Analysis

C. **Funds flow analysis** is the determination of the sources and uses of cash—a view of a firm's receipts and outlays.

1. It is helpful in checking on plans versus actual results.

Sources of Funds

2. **Sources of funds** and examples are:

a. Decreases in assets—selling inventory. (The depreciation allowance, which is an offset against fixed assets, is treated as a source because it is a *noncash* charge used in computing net income. In arriving at changes in *cash* this allowance must be added back.)

b. Increases in liabilities—borrowing money.

c. Increases in owners' equity—retaining earnings. (Note that net income and dividends have been combined first, to arrive at retained earnings.)

Uses of Funds

3. **Uses of funds** and examples are:

a. Increases in assets—buying equipment.

b. Decreases in liabilities—paying off bills.

c. Decreases in owners' equity—losses.

Comparative Balance Sheets

4. A statement of sources and uses of funds is prepared by computing changes in balance sheet accounts from one period to another in the **comparative balance sheet approach.** A *pro forma* statement can be developed, from forecasts of financial transactions, to show expected cash inflows and outflows.

5. Sometimes "funds" are defined as working capital.

a. Then changes in nonworking capital accounts are classed as sources and uses of working capital.

Changes in Financial Position

b. This approach provides a **statement of changes in financial position.** It divides fund sources and uses into groups associated with operations (net income and depreciation), with investment (assets), and with capital transactions (financing).

6. Remember that depreciation is called a source of funds because of the way net income is defined. Since depreciation is subtracted from revenues it must be added to net income to arrive at cash flow.

COMPLETION QUESTIONS

1. Financial statement analysis involves the calculation and interpretation of

ratios, strengths   _____ and funds flows for the purpose of indicating _____

weaknesses   and _____ in a firm.

balance sheet	2. The _____ _____ shows the magnitudes of assets, liabilities, and shareholders' equity (*at/during*) a (*point/period*) in time.
at, point	
income statement	3. The _____ _____ measures inflows and outflows over a span of time.
loss, more	4. If a firm has a (*profit/loss*) in a period or if it pays out (*more/less*) in dividends than it earns, its retained earnings will decline.
cash	5. In the text, funds are normally considered to be the same as (*cash/profit*).
short	6. Liquidity ratios measure the firm's ability to meet its (*short/long*)-term obligations from funds invested in its (*current/fixed*) assets.
current	
quick	7. Because inventories may not be salable at values shown on the books, the _____ ratio is computed as another measure of liquidity.
Leverage	8. _____ ratios indicate a firm's ability to meet all debt obligations from its (*assets/liabilities*) and its (*net worth/earning power*).
assets, earning power	
less	9. The (*more/less*) variable the income stream, the greater the capacity for debt.
low, high	10. Creditors prefer a (*low/high*) debt to total assets ratio and a (*low/high*) times interest earned ratio.
Income, fixed	11. (*Property/Income*) taxes are added back to profits and other (*fixed/variable*) charges to compute coverage ratios because interest and certain other charges will be paid before a company will have any taxes due.
Activity	12. Firms want enough assets but not too many. _____ ratios help indicate proper asset levels.
accounts receivable	13. A short collection period is good in the sense that a firm is collecting its _____ _____ efficiently, but it may be missing sales opportunities because its credit and collection policies are too (*lax/stringent*).
stringent	
low	14. A (*low/high*) fixed-assets turnover probably means that a firm has excess capacity.
sales, assets	15. Profitability ratios measure returns on _____, on _____, and on _____.
equity	
assets	16. The return on total (*assets/net worth*) uses net income plus (*dividends/interest*) in the numerator.
interest	
Industry	17. _____ averages are used as a guide in determining whether a particular firm's ratios are relatively high or low.
depressed	18. When an industry is (*depressed/thriving*), an individual firm's performance must be stronger than average for it to be considered healthy.

19. Ratios for companies in the same industry may be different as a result of variations in individual firms' _____, _____, or _____.

size products
risk

20. Companies in service industries usually have very little inventory, which means that their current ratios will be (*low/high*).

low

21. A situation in which a highly profitable company does not have enough cash to pay its current liabilities illustrates the importance of knowing the (*independence/interrelationships*) of the ratios.

interrelationships

22. Computing ratios for several different years allows the analyst to check for _____ over time.

trends

23. The (*Du Pont/General Motors*) system of financial analysis measures performance in terms of _____ on _____, which is equal to the product of two types of ratios, namely, _____ and _____.

Du Pont
return, investment
activity
profitability

24. The trouble with the ratio of net income to total assets is that these factors are not consistent with each other. A better matching of terms is net income plus _____ compared with total assets or net income used alone with _____ _____.

interest
shareholders' equity

25. ROI can be quite similar for two firms in the same line of business even though they operate very differently. One company may rely on a (*low/high*) _____ margin to generate a high asset _____. The other firm may offset a (*low/high*) asset turnover with a high profit margin. The first type of operation is often called a (*discount/full-service*) business.

low
profit, turnover
low
discount

26. ROI is not a highly accurate measure of performance, because it relies on accounting _____ instead of _____ _____.

profit, cash flow

27. Of the four different types of ratios, creditors are least interested in _____ ratios.

activity

28. A(n) _____ _____ analysis helps tell where a firm raised its money and where it was spent.

funds flow

29. If a company's inventory rose during a period, the increase would be a (*source/use*) of funds.

use

30. Dividend payments are (*sources/uses*) of funds.

uses

PROBLEMS

1. Financial Statements for Jeff's Jai Alai and Jicama Corporation are listed in the following table.

Balance sheet, December 31, 1991
(Millions of dollars)

Assets:	
Cash	$ 2
Accounts receivable	14
Inventory	21
Plant and equipment	63
Accumulated depreciation	(10)
Total	$90
Liabilities and shareholders' equity:	
Accounts payable	$14
Notes payable	10
Other current liabilities	4
Bonds payable	5
Preferred stock (10 percent)	4
Common stock	20
Retained earnings	33
Total	$90

Statement of income, year ended December 31, 1991
(Millions of dollars)

Sales		$100
Cost of goods sold		44
Gross margin		$ 56
Operating expenses:		
Administrative expenses	$20	
Selling and advertising expense	16	
Lease payments	9	
Total operating expenses		$ 45
Net operating income		$ 11
Interest expense		1
Earnings before taxes		$ 10
Taxes (50 percent)		5
Earnings after taxes		$ 5

Compute the following financial ratios and group them into the four basic types for presentation: times interest earned, fixed-assets turnover, acid test, net operating margin, debt to total assets, return on equity, debt to equity, fixed-charges coverage, gross profit margin, average collection period, profit margin on sales, inventory turnover, current ratio, return on total assets, and total assets turnover.

Solution

Step one

a. Liquidity

$$\text{Current} = \frac{\text{current assets}}{\text{current liabilities}} = \frac{\$37}{\$28} = 1.32$$

$$\text{Quick or acid test} = \frac{(\text{current assets} - \text{inventories})}{\text{current liabilities}}$$

$$= \frac{(\$37 - \$21)}{\$28} = 0.57$$

b. Leverage

$$\text{Debt to total assets} = \frac{\text{total liabilities}}{\text{total assets}} = \frac{\$33}{\$90} = 0.37$$

$$\text{Debt to equity} = \frac{\text{long-term debt}}{\text{shareholders' equity}} = \frac{\$5}{\$57} = 0.09$$

$$\text{Times interest earned} = \frac{\text{earnings before interest and taxes}}{\text{interest}}$$

$$= \frac{\$10 + \$1}{\$1} = 11.0$$

$$\text{Fixed-charges coverage} = \frac{\text{income available for meeting fixed charges}}{\text{fixed charges}}$$

$$= \frac{\text{operating income} + \text{lease payments} + \text{interest expense}}{\text{lease payments} + \text{interest expense}}$$

$$= \frac{\$11 + \$9 + \$1}{\$9 + \$1} = 2.1$$

c. Activity

$$\text{Inventory turnover} = \frac{\text{cost of goods sold}}{\text{average inventory}} = \frac{\$44}{\$21} = 2.1$$

$$\text{Average collection period} = \frac{\text{accounts receivable}}{\text{average daily credit sales}} = \frac{\$14}{\$100 \div 360} = 50.4 \text{ days}$$

$$\text{Fixed-assets turnover} = \frac{\text{sales}}{\text{fixed assets}} = \frac{\$100}{\$53} = 1.9$$

$$\text{Total-assets turnover} = \frac{\text{sales}}{\text{total assets}} = \frac{\$100}{\$90} = 1.1$$

d. Profitability

$$\text{Gross profit margin} = \frac{\text{sales} - \text{cost of goods sold}}{\text{sales}} = \frac{\$100 - \$44}{\$100} = 56.0\%$$

$$\text{Net operating margin} = \frac{\text{operating income}}{\text{sales}} = \frac{\$11}{\$100} = 11.0\%$$

$$\text{Profit margin on sales} = \frac{\text{net income}}{\text{sales}} = \frac{\$5}{\$100} = 5.0\%$$

$$\text{Return on total sales} = \frac{\text{net profits} + \text{interest}}{\text{total assets}}$$

$$= \frac{\$5 + \$1}{\$90} = 6.7\%$$

$$\text{Return on equity} = \frac{\text{net income available for common}}{\text{common shareholders' equity}}$$

$$= \frac{\$5 - \$0.4}{\$57 - \$4} = 8.7\%$$

(Note that preferred dividends are 10% of $4 million, or $0.4 million. This must be subtracted from net income.) *End of solution.*

2. On the basis of the answers to problem 1 and the average ratios for the jai alai and jicama industry listed below, discuss the strengths and weaknesses of this firm.

Financial ratio	Jeff's Jai Alai and Jicama	Industry standard
Current	1.32	1.1
Quick	0.57	0.6
Debt to total assets	0.37	0.2
Debt to equity	0.09	0.2
Times interest earned	11.0	4
Fixed-charges coverage	2.1	2
Inventory turnover	2.1	6
Average collection period	50.4 days	55 days
Fixed-assets turnover	1.9	1.5
Total-assets turnover	1.1	2
Gross operating margin	56.0%	53%
Net operating margin	11.0%	10%
Profit margin on sales	5.0%	5%
Return on total assets	6.7%	10%
Return on equity	8.7%	11%

Step one Liquidity: Jeff's has a slightly higher current ratio. Since its quick ratio is in line, the slight edge in liquidity must be due to a relatively high inventory.

Step two Leverage: Jeff's uses more total debt (considerably more short-term but less long-term). However, it has the earning power to handle it since the coverage ratios are both higher than the norms.

Step three Activity: The company should look at its inventory levels, which, as pointed out in step one, may be too high. The fixed assets are supporting higher levels of sales than the industry norm, but the large inventories drag the firm down to below the standard for total-assets turnover.

Step four Profitability: Jeff's Jai Alai and Jicama appears to be quite successful compared with similar firms according to the operating and profit margin ratios. However, the company lags behind the average when return on investment is considered. The key reason is probably the excessive inventories.

3. Paul Thomas Corporation has experienced a steady expansion of manufacturing capacity and sales over the past three years. Its financial condition has not improved. Using 1989 as the standard of comparison, discuss which ratios have appeared to deteriorate by 1991 and what action might be undertaken to restore the firm's financial health.

Paul Thomas Corporation financial analysis

	1989	1990	1991
Current ratio	3.0	2.8	1.6
Quick ratio	1.1	0.9	0.5
Debt ratio	0.3	0.4	0.5
Times interest earned	6.0	6.2	5.9
Fixed-charges coverage	4.0	2.9	1.7
Inventory turnover	4.0	3.5	4.1
Average collection period	30	28	31
Fixed-assets turnover	3.0	3.5	4.2
Total-assets turnover	2.1	2.3	2.4
Net operating margin	15%	14%	10%
Profit margin on sales	8%	7%	5%
Return on total assets	6%	4%	3%
Return on equity	12%	9%	7%

Solution

Step one   The firm has experienced a persistent decline in liquidity. The fact that both measures (current and quick ratios) have fallen indicates that the problem must be due to lower cash and/or accounts receivable balances. To identify which account is the culprit, we check the average collection period. Since it has remained about the same, the drop in liquidity is probably due to a reduction in cash.

Step two   The fixed-charges coverage has declined significantly. Notice that the times interest earned ratio has remained about the same, which means that other fixed charges have increased. Since the debt ratio increased, the asset expansion has probably been through leasing. The fixed- and total-assets turnovers increased, which means sales expanded faster than assets. The result has been to work the assets harder but not more profitably.

Step three   All the profitability measures have deteriorated. This is probably in part because of the apparent leasing program. If leasing were a net benefit, the result should be rising return on investment ratios. The company should try to reduce the leasing costs by buying those facilities, by subleasing them and constructing other plants, etc. In addition, the firm needs to increase its cash position.

4. A partial analysis of the financial condition of Matthew Tyler Meats, Inc., yields the following ratios:

Current	2.5
Quick	2.0
Inventory turnover	4.0
Net operating margin	10%

If its current liabilities are $6 million and its operating expenses are $15 million, what must have been its sales for the most recent year? Use your knowledge of ratio analysis to solve this problem.

Solution

Step one   The key to this problem is to write the formula for each ratio, fill in known values, and then solve for the unknown amounts.

Step two

$$\text{Current ratio} = \frac{\text{current assets}}{\text{current liabilities}}$$

$$2.5 = \frac{\text{current assets}}{\$6}$$

$$\text{Current assets} = \$6 \times 2.5 = \$15 \text{ million}$$

Step three

$$\text{Quick ratio} = \frac{\text{current assets} - \text{inventory}}{\text{current liabilities}}$$

$$2.0 = \frac{\$15 - \text{inventory}}{\$6}$$

$$\text{Inventory} = \$15 - (\$6 \times 2)$$

$$= \$3 \text{ million}$$

Step four

$$\text{Inventory turnover} = \frac{\text{cost of goods sold}}{\text{inventory}}$$

$$4 = \frac{\text{cost of goods sold}}{\$3}$$

$$\text{Cost of goods sold} = 4 \times \$3 = \$12 \text{ million}$$

Step five

$$\text{Net operating margin} = \frac{\text{operating income}}{\text{sales}}$$

$$0.10 = \frac{\text{operating income}}{\text{sales}}$$

Here we are stymied. We have one equation and two unknowns, which means that there is an infinite number of solutions. However, there is a way out! Operating income equals sales less the total cost of goods sold plus operating expenses—both of which are now known. Thus

$$\text{Net operating margin} = 0.10 = \frac{\text{sales} - (\$12 + \$15)}{\text{sales}}$$

$$\text{Sales} - 0.1 \text{ sales} = \$27$$

$$\text{Sales} = \frac{\$27}{0.9} = \$30 \text{ million}$$

5. Prepare a sources and uses of funds statement for Jeff's Jai Alai and Jicama Corporation on the basis of the data below:

Comparative balance sheets
(Millions of dollars)

	12-31-90	12-31-91
Assets:		
Cash	$ 6	$ 2
Accounts receivable	12	14
Inventory	17	21
Plant and equipment	48	63
Accumulated depreciation	(8)	(10)
Total	$75	$90
Liabilities and shareholders' equity:		
Accounts payable	$ 9	$14
Notes payable	6	10
Other current liabilities	2	4
Bonds	2	5
Preferred stock	4	4
Common stock	14	20
Retained earnings	38	33
Total	$75	$90

Solution

Statement of sources and uses of funds for 1991
(Millions of dollars)

Sources of funds:	
Decrease in cash	$ 4
Increase in accumulated depreciation	2
Increase in accounts payable	5
Increase in notes payable	4
Increase in other current liabilities	2
Increase in bonds	3
Increase in common stock	6
Total	$26
Uses of funds:	
Increase in accounts receivable	$ 2
Increase in inventory	4
Increase in plant and equipment	15
Decrease in retained earnings	5
Total	$26

Step two   Note that retained earnings decreased, making this item a use of funds. This decline is due either to a loss in 1991 or to the fact that dividend payments exceeded profits in 1991.

6. Heidi plans to open a women's clothing store and expects first-year sales of $200,000. Her banker, whom she hopes will be friendly, has asked her to prepare a pro forma balance sheet and other financial statements. Norms for retail clothing businesses are listed below:

Account	% of sales
Cash	5
Accounts receivable	10
Inventory	20
Fixed assets	45
Accounts payable	15
Net profits	5

Complete the balance sheet at the end of the first year of operation if she initially invests $50,000 in her business, retains all earnings, and borrows the necessary financing from her bank.

Heidi's Exclusives
Balance sheet, December 31, 19xx

Assets:	Liabilities and equity:
Cash	Accounts payable
Accounts receivable	Bank loan
Inventory	Equity:
Fixed assets	Common stock
	Retained earnings
Total	Total

Solution

Step one Multiplying the percentage of sales represented by each of the accounts will yield an estimate for Heidi's situation. For cash this is 0.05 × $200,000, or $10,000. In a similar manner the amounts for accounts receivable, inventory, fixed assets, and accounts payable will be $20,000, $40,000, $90,000, and $30,000, respectively.

Step two The common stock account will be $50,000, which is her original investment.

Step three Retained earnings begins with a zero balance and grows by the entire amount of her profits, which will be 0.05 × $200,000, or $10,000 (recall that she does not plan to pay any dividends).

Step four The total projected assets, from step one, will be $160,000. Adding the equity accounts of $50,000 and $10,000 to the accounts payable of $30,000 provides financing of $90,000. Thus Heidi will need a loan from her banker of $160,000 − $90,000, or $70,000.

Step five The pro forma balance sheet will be (000s omitted):

Assets		Liabilities and equity	
Cash	$ 10	Accounts payable	$ 30
Accounts receivable	20	Bank loan	70
Inventory	40	Equity:	
Fixed assets	90	Common stock	50
		Retained earnings	10
Total	$160	Total	$160

CHAPTER FIFTEEN

BREAK-EVEN ANALYSIS AND THE MEASUREMENT OF LEVERAGE

QUINTESSENCE

Break-even analysis is a technique for determining how income is affected by *changes* in sales volume and/or *changes* in cost and price structure. The response of profits to these factors can be magnified by leverage, which exists when some of the costs do not change when output varies. These are the fixed costs; those that vary at different production levels are variable costs. Fixed costs are further separated into (1) those associated with the operating needs, leading to operating leverage, and (2) those connected with debt (interest charges), which lead to financial leverage. With an understanding of break-even analysis and leverage it is possible to see how the size of *and* variation in income are affected by the way the operation is run and financed. Understanding this relationship is important because the value of the firm is determined by the amount of earnings and the variability of those earnings.

OUTLINE

I. What

    A. **Break-even analysis** is the study of the relationship between the volume of production, the costs, and profits.

       1. Costs that vary with output are called **variable costs.**

       2. Costs that do not vary are called **fixed costs.**

    B. The existence of fixed costs leads to **leverage.**

       1. **Operating leverage** results from fixed production costs.

       2. **Financial leverage** is associated with fixed financing costs.

II. Why

    A. The value of the firm is determined by the *amount* and *riskiness* of income (see Chapters 5 and 6). In this chapter we "step behind" these factors to analyze a major influence on the amounts and variability of earnings—the use of leverage.

    B. Knowledge of the tie-in between leverage, income, and value enables the financial manager to help specify production methods, product pricing, and output volumes so as to maximize the value of the company.

III. How

Break-Even Analysis

A. Break-even analysis is used to learn how profits respond to changes in production costs, sales volume, and product prices.

1. Costs are classed as fixed or variable.

Fixed Costs

a. Fixed costs do not vary as output changes. For example, depreciation expense, property taxes, interest on debt, management salaries, and rent on a building are the same whether 2000 or 20,000 units are produced.

Variable Costs

b. Variable costs vary with the level of output. In other words, the more you make, the more it takes. Variable costs include materials, direct labor, and sales commissions.

c. Three factors must be considered when classifying costs:

i. Costs may be fixed over a certain range of output, but outside that range they may change; for example, more airplanes are needed after the existing fleet is filled to capacity, which will then cause fixed costs to rise.

ii. Costs may be fixed in the short run but variable in the long run. As an illustration, take the case of a firm needing to expand its production. A new facility typically takes several years to design and build. In the meantime, plant costs are fixed until the new operation is completed.

iii. Some costs remain fixed until there is evidence that a rise or fall in output is going to be permanent. For example, layoffs of management or the sale of facilities may be delayed pending the confirmation of a reduced level of activity.

Combining Costs

2. Fixed and variable costs are combined, and the total is subtracted from sales output to compute pretax income. If this calculation is repeated at different output levels, Figure 15-1 can be drawn.

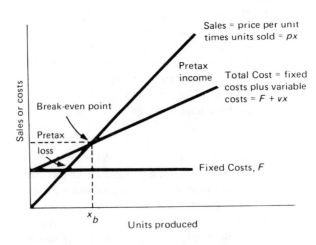

FIGURE 15-1 Break-even chart.

3. The break-even volume x_b can be found in the graph in Figure 15-1, from a table that was used to develop the data for the graph, or by means of an algebraic solution of Eq. 15-1 (see problem 1):

Break-Even Point

$$x_b = \frac{F}{p - v} \qquad (15\text{-}1)$$

    a. The break-even point in terms of dollars of sales is equal to x_b times the sales price.

Contribution Margin

    b. The denominator in Eq. (15-1) is the spread between the selling price and its variable cost. This is the dollar increase in pretax income per unit of sales. It is called the **contribution margin.**

Effects of Changing Revenues or Costs

4. The impacts of different policies that affect sales and/or costs can be studied using break-even analysis. Examples are:

    a. If a product price is lowered to stimulate sales, the break-even point will increase. However, net income may also increase—it depends on how much sales rise.

    b. Sales may be increased by advertising or spending money on research for product improvement. This adds fixed costs, which raises the break-even point *and,* it is hoped, income. Again, it depends on how responsive sales are to the efforts and expenditures made to increase them.

Nonlinear Break-Even Analysis

5. **Nonlinear break-even analysis** is used when costs are nonlinear and/or the product price varies.

    a. In these situations variable costs and/or sales price per unit are different at different levels of output. The preceding discussion assumed that both these elements were constant per unit. To illustrate the point of varying variable costs, suppose an experienced widget assembler can put 100 widgets together every day. A new employee can be added to the work force but can produce only 75 units in a shift. If both workers are paid the same wage, the labor cost per unit is lower for 100 units of production than for 175 units.

    b. A graph similar to Figure 15-1 can be prepared to illustrate the varying variable-cost situation. The optimum level of production is at the point where the difference between the sales and total cost is maximized; at lower or higher output, income will be less. This result is quite logical, because a firm needs *enough* production to reach efficient operation. Beyond that point, efficiency falls and costs rise faster than revenues, causing income to decline.

6. Break-even analysis, while being a very useful tool for financial planning, has limitations.

Limitations to
Break-Even
Analysis

a. The output range and time period over which the assumptions about fixed costs and variable costs hold may be too restrictive. In other words, watch out when break-even analysis is applied at output levels that are outside the range where the cost data are accurate.

b. Even within the range where the numbers are assumed to be accurate, uncertainty as to the costs and prices at different output levels still exists.

c. This means that break-even analysis should serve as a *rough guide* to financial decision making.

Leverage Defined

B. The concept of **leverage** is also used to analyze the costs of operating and financing a business. Leverage is the existence of fixed costs as part of a firm's total costs.

Operating Leverage

1. **Operating leverage** results when a company has fixed operating costs.

a. The **degree of operating leverage** (DOL) is the percentage change in earnings before interest and taxes (EBIT) divided by the percentage change in units sold. In terms of sales price and volume and costs,

Measurement

$$DOL = \frac{x(p - v)}{x(p - v) - F_o} \qquad (15\text{-}2)$$

where x is output, p is sales price, v is variable costs per unit, and F_o is total operating fixed costs (be sure to exclude financing costs of interest and lease payments).

b. See problem 3 for an example using the above equation.

c. Operating leverage can also be expressed in terms of EBIT and F. Equation 15-2 then is written as:

Measurement

$$DOL = \frac{EBIT}{EBIT - F_f} \qquad (15\text{-}3)$$

d. Firms with a high F_o will have a high DOL. For these companies a change in sales will result in a greater response in EBIT than will occur in companies having a low F_o.

i. The airlines have high DOLs; the difference in profits between a half-full plane and a full plane is very large.

ii. Installing laborsaving machines increases fixed costs, reduces variable costs, and results in a higher DOL.

iii. A high DOL is good *if* sales rise, but it's bad if sales fall. This is because leverage magnifies, amplifies, and just plain makes the end results (income) bigger or smaller.

e. **Business risk** is influenced by the DOL, since a higher DOL will cause a greater variation in EBIT. Remember, however, that other influences on business risk include variability of sales and costs, so business risk and operating leverage are separate and distinct.

Financial Leverage

2. **Financial leverage** is the use of debt to help finance the business.

a. The **degree of financial leverage** (DFL) is the percentage change in earnings per share (EPS) divided by the percentage change in EBIT. It can be computed in terms of sales price and volume and costs. In the most simple form it is:

Measurement

$$DFL = \frac{EBIT}{EBIT - F_f} \qquad (15\text{-}4)$$

where F_f is total financial fixed costs (interest on debt and lease payments).

b. See problem 4 for an example using the above equation.

c. Firms with a high F_f (lots of borrowing) will have a high DFL. These companies will have higher fluctuations in EPS compared with similar firms that don't make extensive use of debt. A high DFL is good if EBIT is increasing, but—well, you know the story if things don't go as planned.

Overall Leverage

3. **Combined leverage** is the total leverage due to both operating and financing fixed costs.

a. The **degree of combined leverage** (DCL) is the percentage change in EPS divided by the percentage change in sales. In terms of sales price, volume, and costs,

Measurement

$$DCL = \frac{x(p - v)}{x(p - v) - F} \qquad (15\text{-}5)$$

where F is total operating and financial fixed cost.

b. See problem 5 for an example using the above equation.

c. The DCL can be increased by adding fixed costs in either the operating or the financing area.

d. In a format similar to Eqs. (15-2) and (15-4), DCL is calculated as:

Measurement

$$\boxed{DCL = \frac{EBIT + F_o}{EBIT - F_s}}$$

(15-6)

e. Note that EBIT is found in all forms of the equation that measures each of the three types of leverage. Recall that EBIT itself is computed from costs and the selling price and volume sold. So the six equations presented in this chapter are three basic expressions. The choice of which one to use depends on what form of leverage is being computed and what data are available.

COMPLETION QUESTIONS

Break-even   1. _____-_____ analysis is the study of the relationship be-
income   tween the selling price, the volume of production, the costs, and (*sales/income*).

income   2. Value of the firm is determined by the amount and variability of (*sales/income*).

leverage   3. A major influence on the amount and variability of earnings is (*EBIT/leverage*).

Fixed   4. (*Fixed/Variable*) costs do not vary as output changes.

fixed   5. Depreciation expense and rent on a building are examples of (*fixed/variable*) costs.

fixed, variable   6. Property taxes are (*fixed/variable*) costs, and income taxes are (*fixed/variable*) costs.

fixed   7. Costs may be (*fixed/variable*) between certain points of output, but outside that range they may change.

long, variable   8. In the (*short/long*) run all costs are (*fixed/variable*).

   9. Hesitancy about laying off people when production is first cut back tends
fixed, short   to make some labor costs (*fixed/variable*) in the (*short/long*) run.

output   10. The break-even chart shows costs and sales at different levels of (*output/financing*).

Decreasing   11. (*Increasing/Decreasing*) fixed costs will lower the break-even point.

Decreasing   12. (*Increasing/Decreasing*) variable costs will lower the break-even point.

higher   13. The (*higher/lower*) the contribution margin, the lower the break-even point.

   14. Nonlinear break-even analysis is used when variable costs per unit are
variable, incomes   (*constant/variable*). In these cases, (*incomes/sales*) are maximized at a specific output; increasing or decreasing production beyond this point will cause
fall   profits to (*fall/rise*).

zero	15. A business having no fixed production costs would have (*zero*/*infinite*) (*op-
operating	erating*/*financial*) leverage.
	16. If all other conditions are the same, the firm having the higher degree of
more	operating leverage (DOL) will be the (*less*/*more*) risky.
Capital	17. (*Capital*/*Labor*)-intensive firms would be expected to have higher DOLs
labor	compared with _____-intensive firms.
is not	18. Business risk (*is*/*is not*) synonymous with DOL. However, both concepts
EBIT	are concerned with variations in (*EBIT*/*sales*).
zero	19. A firm that uses equity only, to acquire its assets, will have (*zero*/*infinite*)
financial	(*operating*/*financial*) leverage.
debt, EPS	20. The use of (*equity*/*debt*) financing will increase fluctuations in (*EBIT*/*EPS*).
	21. The degree of combined leverage (DCL) is the percentage change in _____
EPS, sales	divided by the percentage change in _____.
increased, operating	22. DCL can be (*increased*/*decreased*) by adding _____or _____
financial	fixed costs.

PROBLEMS

1. A local 500-seat theater has annual fixed costs of $152,000. Many discount tickets are sold. The average price of admission is $4, and variable costs are $0.20 per customer.
   a. What is the contribution margin?

Solution

Step one

$$\text{Contribution margin} = p - v$$

$$= \$4 - \$0.20 = \$3.80$$

(This high margin is typical and is what makes theater owners so happy with packed houses.) *End of solution.*

b. Compute the break-even point.

Solution   **Step one**

$$x_b = \frac{F}{p - v}$$

$$= \frac{\$152,000}{\$4 - \$0.20} = 40,000 \text{ admissions}$$

c. What must be the average attendance to break even, based on 360 days of operation a year?

Solution   **Step one**

$$\frac{40,000}{360} = 111 \text{ admissions per day}$$

Step two   This would be 22 percent ($111 \div 500$) of capacity based on one showing per day.

d. What would be the income, before taxes, if the average daily attendance were twice the break-even point?

Solution   **Step one**   This would be 2 times 111 (or 222) customers per day, or 80,000 customers per year.

Step two

$$\text{Pretax income} = \text{sales} - \text{total costs}$$
$$= 80{,}000(\$4) - [\$152{,}000 + 80{,}000(\$0.20)]$$
$$= \$320{,}000 - \$168{,}000$$
$$= \$152{,}000$$

Step three Using the symbols in the outline, the answer can be found as follows:

$$\text{Pretax income} = x(p - v) - F_o$$
$$= 80{,}000(\$4 - \$0.20) - \$152{,}000$$
$$= \$152{,}000$$

Step four Note that the income is before taxes. To compute aftertax profits, multiply $152,000 by $(1 - \text{tax rate})$.

2. Auto Painters, Inc. (API), paints any car for $100. In the year just ended, the firm made $25,000 profit before taxes. The company had fixed costs of $75,000 and variable costs of $30 per paint job.
   a. How many cars did API paint last year?

Solution   **Step one**

$$\text{Pretax income} = \text{sales} - \text{total cost}$$
$$\$25{,}000 = \$100x - (\$75{,}000 + \$30x)$$
$$\$70x = \$100{,}000$$
$$x = 1429 \text{ cars}$$

   b. What was the break-even point for API?

Solution

$$x_b = \frac{F}{p - v}$$

$$= \frac{\$75,000}{\$100 - \$30} = 1072 \text{ cars}$$

Step two   If you forget the formula for the break-even point, try the following logic:
(a) At the break-even point income is zero.
(b) This means that sales equal costs.
(c) In symbols,

$$px_b = F + vx_b$$

$$x_b = \frac{F}{p - v}$$

which is the formula used in step one.

c. In the year just begun, API expects its variable costs to rise by one-third as a result of increases in labor and materials. What will be the break-even point this year?

Solution

Step one   The variable costs will rise by $10 (one-third of $30) to a rate of $40 per unit.

Step two

$$x_b = \frac{F}{p - v}$$

$$= \frac{\$75,000}{\$100 - \$40} = 1250 \text{ cars}$$

Step three   This is not too serious, because output last year was already 1429 paint jobs.

d. Suppose API decides to pass along the cost increase by raising its price. What would be the new rate if the firm wanted to maintain its income before taxes at $25,000 per year *and* if the total demand remained at last year's level?

Solution

Step one

$$\text{Pretax income} = \text{sales} - \text{total costs}$$

$$\$25,000 = 1429p - [\$75,000 + (1429 \times \$40)]$$

$$p = \frac{\$157,160}{1429} = \$110 \text{ per car}$$

Step two   The price increase would be 10 percent:

$$\frac{(\$110 - \$100)}{\$100} \times 100$$

e. Suppose the firm wanted to hold the line on price and push for more volume by staying open longer hours. How many paint jobs would be necessary to maintain profitability?

Solution

Step one

$$\text{Pretax income} = \text{sales} - \text{total costs}$$

$$\$25,000 = \$100x - (\$75,000 + \$40x)$$

$$x = \frac{\$100,000}{\$60} = 1667 \text{ cars}$$

Step two   This would be a 16.7 percent increase:

$$\frac{(1667 - 1429)}{1429} \times 100$$

3. The degree of operating leverage (DOL) is another way of analyzing sales and cost relationships.
   a. Calculate the DOL for the theater business described in problem 1 when the firm is operating at its break-even point.

Solution

Step one

$$\text{DOL} = \frac{x(p - v)}{x(p - v) - F}$$

$$= \frac{40,000(\$4 - \$0.20)}{40,000(\$4 - \$0.20) - \$152,000}$$

$$= \frac{152,000}{0} = \text{infinity}$$

Wow!

Step two   That is a pretty high DOL, but it could be expected from the definition of DOL in terms of operating earnings and output:

$$\text{DOL} = \frac{\% \text{ change in EBIT}}{\% \text{ change in units sold}}$$

At the break-even point, EBIT is zero, and so the percentage change from a zero base will always be infinite, resulting in an infinite DOL. The DOL is finite at all outputs other than the break-even point.

   b. What is the DOL for the theater operation when it has 80,000 admissions in a year?

Solution

Step one

$$DOL = \frac{80,000(\$4 - \$0.20)}{80,000(\$4 - \$0.20) - \$152,000}$$

$$= 2.0$$

c. Compute the DOL for the auto-painting concern described in problem 2e.

Solution

Step one API's variable costs were \$40 per car for the 1667 cars it hopes to paint.

Step two

$$DOL = \frac{1667(\$100 - \$40)}{1667(\$100 - \$40) - \$75,000}$$

$$= 4.0$$

d. Referring to the DOLs computed in problem 3b and 3c, which business would benefit more if actual sales were 10 percent above the expected levels?

Solution

Step one API has the higher operating leverage (4 versus 2 for the theater), and so its before-tax earnings would rise more.

Step two The increases in EBIT would be as follows: for the theater—2 times 10 percent, or 20 percent; for API—4 times 10 percent, or 40 percent.

Step three Remember that the DOL may be different at every level of output; thus it must be computed each time production changes.

4. In problems 1, 2, and 3 the analysis focused on the fixed costs related to operations. In this problem, attention is drawn to how the business is financed and to the fixed costs related to financing.

   a. Suppose the theater had no debt. What would be its degree of financial leverage (DFL)?

Solution

Step one With no debt, there is *no* financial leverage, which means that the DFL is 1.

Step two Using the formula DFL $= $ EBIT/(EBIT $-$ F_f)

$$F_f = 0$$

since there is no interest with no debt.

$$DFL = \frac{EBIT}{EBIT} = 1$$

(Note that DFL will never be below 1. Verify that this is also true for DOL.)

   b. Now suppose the owners wish to spend $600,000 remodeling the building using a bank loan at 12 percent interest. The estimated attendance for next year is 80,000 persons, and other data are as outlined in problem 1a. What is the DFL?

Solution

Step one

$$EBIT = sales - total \ costs$$
$$= 80,000(\$4) - [\$152,000 + 80,000(\$0.20)]$$
$$= \$152,000$$

Step two

$$\text{Fixed financing costs } F_f = 0.12(\$600,000)$$

$$= \$72,000$$

Step three

$$\text{DFL} = \frac{\text{EBIT}}{\text{EBIT} - F_f}$$

$$= \frac{\$152,000}{\$152,000 - \$72,000} = 1.9$$

c. What would happen to net income if the remodeling resulted in increasing attendance so as to increase EBIT by 20 percent?

Solution

Step one The percentage change in income is equal to the product of DFL and the percentage change in EBIT, and so income would increase by 1.9 times 20 percent, or 38 percent.

Step two In this case financial leverage is favorable, as it is whenever operating earnings are rising. If EBIT instead fell by 20 percent, then the financial leverage would magnify the decline, causing a drop in income of 38 percent.

5. Operating and financial leverage have been illustrated separately in problems 3 and 4. The overall effect can be examined by the degree of combined leverage (DCL).
   a. Compute DCL for the theater operation when 80,000 admissions x at $4 apiece p are expected with fixed operating costs F_o of $152,000, financing costs F_f of $72,000, and variable costs v of $0.20 a person. (These are the conditions outlined in problems 3b and 4b).

Solution

$$\text{DCL} = \frac{x(p - v)}{x(p - v) - (F_o + F_f)}$$

$$= \frac{80{,}000(\$4 - \$0.20)}{80{,}000(\$4 - \$0.20) - (\$152{,}000 + \$72{,}000)}$$

$$= 3.8$$

Step two   DCL also equals the product of DOL and DFL. From problems 2b and 3b, DOL = 2.0 and DFL = 1.9. Thus

$$\text{DCL} = (2.0)(1.9)$$

$$= 3.8$$

which verifies the result obtained in step one.

b. Suppose the admissions were 20 percent above the expected level of 80,000. What would happen to income?

Solution

Step one   The percentage change in income due to the combined effects of operating and financial leverage is the product of DCL and the percentage change in sales.

Step two   The income increase is 3.8 times 20 percent, or 76 percent.

Step three   This is a highly leveraged situation. If theater attendance rises, the owners will be in "fat city." If it falls, they'll be somewhere else.

Step four   We would need to know the company's income tax rate and the number of shares outstanding in order to compute earnings per share.

CHAPTER SIXTEEN

FINANCIAL FORECASTING AND PLANNING

QUINTESSENCE Financial forecasting leads to planning through budgets that provide the basis for controls on operations. This process helps establish and then accomplish the firm's goals. Trends, ratios, or statistical methods may be used in combination with judgment to develop forecasts of financial variables. These are combined and, along with other information such as expected changes in certain international conditions, are used to prepare pro forma balance sheets and statements of cash flows, and income. Careful forecasting and analysis allow the financial manager time to develop alternative solutions to problems that are anticipated and to steer the company on the course that has been set to maximize the value of the firm.

OUTLINE

I. What
   A. Techniques are available to help the financial manager make educated guesses about the firm's future financial condition. To do this requires forecasts of future performance and cash position at different points in time.
   B. Plans, budgets, and controls can then be developed so as to better meet objectives and cash needs.

II. Why
   A. Forecasting, planning, budgeting, and controlling help recover, sustain, and/or increase the profitability of the firm and reduce risk.
   B. These activities provide the basis for:
      1. Helping to set goals and implement them.
      2. Anticipating cash needs.
      3. Managing cash and investing temporary excesses in marketable securities to earn returns.
      4. Maintaining control over the firm's financial affairs and signaling changes in conditions.
      5. Making a favorable impression on lenders (who are good people to impress).

III. How

A. The first step is to *forecast individual balance sheet accounts*.

Trend Forecasts

1. **Trend forecasts** use historical data to predict the future.
   a. **No-change forecasts** use latest available figures as predictions.
   b. The more typical method is to project past *trends* and *seasonal patterns* into the future.

Forecast Sales First

2. Forecasts can also be made from the relationship of variables. In this method ratios are computed for each balance sheet account in relationship to a **base variable** (usually sales) using historical data.
   a. Future values of the base variable are forecast.
   b. Individual balance sheet categories are then forecast by multiplying the appropriate ratio by the base variable.
   c. As an example, suppose inventory averaged 6 percent of sales over the past five years. Sales are predicted to be $200 next year. The forecast for inventory would be 6 percent of $200, or $12.
   d. For forecasts over several years, the ratios are often more satisfactory than they are for the short run. Near-term predictions especially, as well as longer-range forecasts, require using considerable judgment to temper the projections.

Graphical and Statistical Aids

3. **Graphical** and **statistical methods** are more precise alternatives than **trend** and **ratio** projections.
   a. The simplest technique is to plot historical values of any two related variables. One is often the base variable, but other relationships can be used.
   b. A line of best fit is drawn, either by eye or by statistical method, to determine the relationship between the variables.
   c. The previously forecast value of one of these variables is used to predict the value of the other.
   d. This process is repeated until each account has been forecast. Sometimes two or more variables are used to predict one account.

4. Remember that no amount of complexity can assure absolutely accurate predictions. All methods of forecasting, no matter how sophisticated, should incorporate *judgment* into the final estimates.

International Conditions

B. Forecasting domestic and international environmental variables:

1. Incorporate the expected rates (in all countries where the firm has operations) of:

Inflation

   a. **Inflation**.

Interest

   b. **Interest**.

2. Estimates of the environmental variables can be obtained by examining prices of financial assets which reflect the aggregate of all forecasts.
   a. Current interest rates contain the estimate of future inflation.
   b. Commercial services offer specific forecasts.

Financial Forecasting

C. The next stage is to prepare a **comprehensive financial forecast** to tie together the predictions of the individual accounts.

Cash Flow

Balance Sheet

1. Procedures for developing the total picture are:
   a. The **cash flow method**, which forecasts future payments and disbursements of cash.
   b. The **balance sheet method**, which estimates the balance sheet accounts and the cash position. It is used for long-range planning.
2. First the sales forecast is made. (This may have already been done during the preparation of the forecasts of individual balance sheet accounts.)
3. A forecast of the income statement (**pro forma income statement**) is prepared by adding projections of other revenues to sales and then subtracting anticipated expenses to get taxable income, income taxes, and finally net profit.
   a. Preliminary projections of some accounts—such as interest on new debt, income from future security investments, and any dividend payments—will be made and later modified to fit the final version of the financial plans.
   b. Depreciation, which is not a cash flow, must be included in the expenses so that income taxes can be computed.

Cash Flow Forecasts

Identify Cash Flow Timing

4. In the next step, projections made earlier are used to estimate cash flows. Other expected cash receipts and payments such as sales of fixed assets, capital expenditures, loan payments, and dividends are included.
   a. Care must be exercised to identify the timing of each cash flow. For example, most sales are for credit, with the money being collected later. The cash flow is recorded at the time when the actual receipt is anticipated.
   b. Cash flow forecasts are most often done on a monthly basis, and other frequencies are used for additional planning purposes. Short-run needs are determined from weekly or even daily projections; long-range planning is prepared from annual forecasts.
   c. The forecast shows cumulative funds required at the end of each period. This indicates the amount of financing needed or the amount of extra funds available. With this information the financial manager can better plan for fund-raising and investment.

Balance Sheet Forecasts

5. The final step is to prepare a **supplemental balance sheet forecast** by adding changes in the accounts (as determined in the income statement and cash flow forecast) to beginning balances to develop ending balances. This is repeated each period by carrying forward the ending figures to serve as the base for the next period.
6. If only long-term forecasts are needed, the cash flow projection can be omitted and a **primary balance sheet forecast** prepared.
   a. First the pro forma income statements are developed to provide estimates of profits, dividends, and retained earnings.
   b. Individual balance sheet accounts are forecast using one of the single-variable methods.

c. The balance sheet is completed by entering the forecasted change in retained earnings and then balancing the statement, either by adding to cash, the amount by which liabilities and equity exceed assets, or by adding to funds required, the amount by which assets exceed the sum of liabilities and equity. These steps tell how much excess cash will be available for investing or how much additional cash will be required to meet anticipated needs.

Financing Plans and Budgets

D. The goals of the firm are made operational by **financial planning,** which uses the forecasts to prepare budgets, which in turn are used to control performance so as to achieve the goals.

1. There are two methods for helping to assure consistency between financial plans and company objectives:

Top-Down

  a. The **top-down approach** translates goals into activities that must take place in order for the objectives to be achieved. This method is especially useful for long-range planning.

Bottom-Up

  b. The **bottom-up approach** starts by having each separate area of the firm prepare forecasts and budgets. These are then combined to complete the total financial plan.

  c. Each method may require several revisions before the plans and budgets become finalized. Large firms often use both approaches to tell whether the original goals are realistic and to highlight parts of the company needing more attention.

Types of Budgets

2. Financial plans are implemented by preparing budgets that are formal statements of expected values of the firm's financial variables over a future period.

Capital

  a. **Capital budgets** tell when and how much will be spent on capital projects.

Operating Expense

  b. **Operating expense budgets** show breakdowns for various expense categories.

Cash

  c. The **cash budget** outlines when, where, and how much money will be used and the sources and timing of financing.

Financial Control

3. The other part of the financial planning and budgeting process is controlling the company's activities so that actual performance will approximate the overall plans.

  a. Each area is expected to operate within the confines of its budget.

  b. If actual results deviate from budget values, either action will be taken to bring operations back into line, or the budget will be revised to reflect changes, if this is the more logical alternative.

Planning Benefits

4. The forecasting, planning, budgeting, and controlling process helps a company accomplish what it wants to do. The process minimizes surprises by providing management with:

  a. A way of anticipating problems.

  b. The lead time to take actions aimed at alleviating troubles.

c. Feedback to determine how things are going in comparison with plans.

COMPLETION QUESTIONS

plans, budgets   1. Forecasts help establish (*plans/goals*) that are used to set (*ratios/budgets*)
controlling   that then serve as standards for (*maintaining/controlling*) operations.

planning   2. Careful financial _____ may help assure the availability of financing because of the favorable impression it makes on lenders.

3. When recognizing the fact that high and low points in many firms' sales
seasonal   historically occur at predictable times of the year, _____ patterns may be used in the forecast.

Trend   4. (*Trend/Ratio*) forecasts rely solely on historical data on the variable being forecast.

No-change   5. (*No-change/Ratio*) forecasts are used when the current value of a variable is the only information available.

Ratios   6. (*Historical levels/Ratios*) are most commonly used to forecast balance sheet accounts.

7. The variable that is used to predict values of other variables is called the
base   (*base/dependent*) variable.

sales   8. The most crucial variable to forecast is (*sales/assets*).

longer   9. Ratios for forecasting tend to be more satisfactory for (*shorter/longer*) time periods.

best fit   10. A line of (*best fit/seasonal patterns*) is used to establish the relationship of one variable to another.

11. The forecasted balance sheets and income statements are called the (*ex
pro forma   post/pro forma*) statements.

individually   12. Balance sheet accounts are usually projected (*individually/as a group*).

does not   13. Using complex statistical projection techniques (*does/does not*) assure accuracy in the forecasts.

14. The forecast of retained earnings comes from the (*balance sheet/income
income statement   statement*).

income statement   15. Depreciation is included in the (*trend/income statement*) forecast.

Accounts receivable	16.	(*Sales/Accounts receivable*) are usually the main source of cash receipts for a firm.
	17.	The major reason for making a forecast of depreciation is to figure (*income*
income taxes		*taxes/current assets*).
are not	18.	Capital expenditures (*are/are not*) forecast on the income statement.
cash flow	19.	Scheduled loan payments show up in the (*income statement/cash flow*) forecast.
longer	20.	Long-range planning calls for (*shorter/longer*) time periods between forecasts.
a need for	21.	If forecast figures for assets exceed those for liabilities plus equity, (*a need for/an excess of*) funds is predicted.
less	22.	Excess cash will be available if the forecast total for assets is (*greater/less*) than the total of liabilities plus equity.
	23.	The top-down and bottom-up approaches are used to ensure consistency
goals, plans		between the firm's _____ and _____.
long	24.	The top-down method is especially useful for (*short/long*)-range planning.
	25.	In the bottom-up approach, forecasts and budgets are first developed for the
individual areas		(*whole company/individual areas*).
capital	26.	The purchase of a new building would show up on the (*capital/expense*) budget.
expense	27.	The purchase of supplies shows up on the _____ budget.
cash	28.	The _____ budget shows all receipts and outlays.
actual	29.	Controlling operations relies on comparing (*projected/actual*) with budget figures.
	30.	Using financial forecasting, planning, budgeting, and controlling processes
anticipates		helps ensure management (*anticipates/is surprised by*) the future. Other
longer		advantages of the exercises include (*shorter/longer*) lead times for taking
plans		action and feedback for checking (*plans/goals*) against performance.

PROBLEMS

1. G Company's sales, in millions of dollars, over the 1986–1991 period were as follows:

	1986	1987	1988	1989	1990	1991
Sales	4.0	5.2	3.6	4.6	5.7	6.16

a. Determine the average annual compound rate of sales growth using 1986 and 1991 data.

Solution

Step one   The compound growth rate problem was discussed in Chapter 4. (Give yourself 20 points if you can remember "way back then.")

Step two

$$1991 \text{ sales} = 1986 \text{ sales} \times (F/P, \ i, \ 5)$$

$$(F/P, \ i, \ 5) = \frac{1991 \text{ sales}}{1986 \text{ sales}} = \frac{6.16}{4}$$

$$= 1.54$$

Step three   Looking in the five-year rows and the columns headed "F/P" in the tables in Appendix B of the text, we find the closest value to 1.54 in the 9 percent interest rate table.

b. Project 1992 and 1996 sales using the growth rate computed in problem 1a above.

Solution

Step one

$$1992 \text{ sales} = 1991 \text{ sales} \times 1.09$$

$$= \$6.16 \times 1.09$$

$$= \$6.71 \text{ million}$$

Step two

$$1996 \text{ sales} = 1991 \text{ sales} \times (1.09)^5$$

or

$$1996 \text{ sales} = 1991 \text{ sales} \times (F/P, \ 9\%, \ 5)$$

$$= \$6.16 \times 1.5386$$

$$= \$9.48 \text{ million}$$

c. Use the graphical approach to forecasting 1992 sales by drawing the line of best visual fit through the sales data over time.

Solution

Step one   Plot sales over time and extend the line of best fit for one year. See Fig. 16-1.

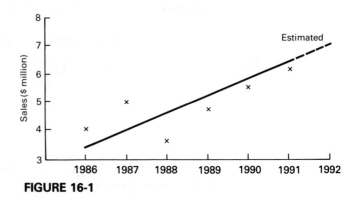

FIGURE 16-1

Step two   This indicates that sales will be approximately $7 million in 1992.

Step three   There are two major problems in this approach. First of all, each person will draw a different line of best visual fit. Who has the best eyesight? Use of statistical techniques (regression analysis) can avoid this problem. Second, there is nothing to say why 1986–1991 is the best period to base the forecast on—perhaps 1988–1991 would be better since it appears to show a more regular trend. Note the weakness in assuming that 1986 and 1991 are typical years to compute the compound growth rate—a different forecast would result if 1988 and 1991 were chosen. The projection differences grow considerably if a distant point (five years or more) is being forecast.

Step four   At this stage you may be seriously concerned about whether forecasting can be done with accuracy. It is very difficult, especially where growth is irregular. Remember the point in the earlier discussion about how important judgment is in forecasting? Perhaps the company underwent a major change in management or introduced a new product line in 1988. Then 1986 and 1987 would not be too relevant. The key is to be sure that the judgment factor is a part in any forecast.

2. Data for G Company's fixed assets for 1986 through 1991 (in millions of dollars) are 2.0, 2.5, 2.6, 2.7, 2.9, and 3.2. Using the sales given in problem 1, forecast fixed assets for the company in 1996 on the basis of the fixed-assets-sales ratio and estimated 1996 sales of $9.48 million.

Solution

Step one Compute the average fixed-assets ÷ sales ratio.

Year	Fixed assets	Sales	Fixed assets ÷ sales
1986	2.0	4.0	0.50
1987	2.5	5.2	0.48
1988	2.6	3.6	0.72
1989	2.7	4.6	0.59
1990	2.9	5.7	0.51
1991	3.2	6.16	0.52
1986–1991 average			0.55

Step two Check the average fixed-assets ÷ sales ratios:

$$\text{Fixed assets in 1996} = \frac{\text{fixed assets}}{\text{sales}} \times \text{sales in 1996}$$

$$= 0.55 \times \$9.48$$

$$= \$5.21 \text{ million}$$

Step three Looking at the fixed-assets ÷ sales ratios from 1986 to 1991, we find no apparent trend. Variation is normal, but trends are important to watch for since the projection should make use of the most likely ratio for the future. Again judgment plays a key role in the forecast—the process should not be automatic; it should not rely on some canned technique.

3. G Company's accounts receivable at the beginning of March were $150,000. Credit sales during the month amounted to $400,000. Collections for the same period totaled $200,000. What is the accounts receivable balance as of the end of March?

Solution

Step one The bathtub analogy is helpful here—the level of accounts receivable is increased by water flowing in (credit sales) and decreased by water flowing out (collections).

Step two

$$\text{Ending balance} = \text{beginning balance} + \text{credit sales} - \text{collections}$$

$$= \$150,000 + \$400,000 - \$200,000$$

$$= \$350,000$$

4. The experience of G Company has been to collect 5 percent of each month's sales during that month, 80 percent in the following month, and the last 15 percent in the month after that. Compute the accounts receivable balance for November and December if the beginning balance in November was $260,000 and sales data were as follows:

	Sales (Thousands of dollars)
September	200
October	450
November	400
December	600

Solution

Step one Compute collections for November and December. (We can't determine September or October figures because collections in those months will come, in part, from July and August sales.)

Step two

$$\text{November collections} = 15\% \text{ of September sales} + 80\% \text{ of October sales}$$

$$+ 5\% \text{ of November sales}$$

$$= 0.15(\$200,000) + 0.80(\$450,000)$$

$$+ 0.05(\$400,000)$$

$$= \$410,000$$

Step three

$$\text{December collections} = 0.15(\$450,000) + 0.80(\$400,000)$$
$$+ \ 0.05(\$600,000)$$
$$= \$417,500$$

Step four

$$\text{Accounts receivable ending balance} = \text{beginning balance} + \text{sales}$$
$$- \text{collections}$$
$$\text{November ending balance} = \$260,000 + \$400,000$$
$$- \$410,000$$
$$= \$250,000$$

Step five

$$\text{December ending balance} = \$250,000 + \$600,000 - \$417,500$$
$$= \$432,500$$

5. G Company's sales next year are estimated to be $10 million. Past experience indicates that the cost of goods sold will be 70 percent of sales, that operating expenses will be 10 percent of sales, that interest expense will be $0.4 million, and that the income tax rate will be 40 percent. Develop the pro forma income statement for next year.

Solution   **Step one**

G Company pro forma income statement
(Millions of dollars)

Sales	$10
Cost of goods (70% of sales)	7
Gross income	$ 3
Operating expenses (10% of sales)	1
Interest expense ($0.4 million)	0.4
Earnings before taxes	$ 1.6
Income taxes (40%)	0.64
Earnings after taxes	$ 0.96

6. When the pro forma balance sheet is developed, individual accounts are first forecast and then an account for cash or financing required is used to "balance" the statement. If the total of all assets for G Company, excluding cash, was predicted to be $25 million and the total of the liabilities and equity side was $20 million:
   a. What would be the entry for cash or funds required?

Solution

Step one   The "plug" or balancing account is determined by subtracting the liabilities and equity from assets:

$$\$25 \text{ million} - \$20 \text{ million} = \$5 \text{ million}$$

Step two   The difference is positive, which means that additional financing of $5 million is required. Stated more logically, projected asset needs exceed the projected financing sources, and so the firm must raise the difference, i.e., $5 million.

   b. How would the answer be affected if a minimum cash balance of $1 million were considered necessary?

Solution

Step one   This makes the problem more realistic, because if only $5 million were raised, as determined in problem 6a, the firm would expect to have a zero cash balance. This just wouldn't be practical.

Step two   The minimum cash needs are figured to be $1 million, and so this additional amount would have to be raised, making the total funds required $6 million.

   c. Suppose assets, excluding cash, had been $3 million less than the total computed from the predicted financing sources. How would this situation be interpreted?

Solution

Step one The difference between financial uses and sources is negative, and so the cash account would be the "plug."

Step two In this case the predicted cash balance would be $3 million. Too high, you say? OK, then, apply some of the $3 million to pay off some of the liabilities, pay more dividends, buy more plant, invest in marketable securities, etc. The point is that $3 million in cash is expected by the end of next year. Knowing this, the financial manager can help make plans to put part of it considered to be excess to some good use.

7. The retained earnings at the end of G Company's latest year of operation were $2.5 million. Sales for the next three years are forecast to be $10 million, $14 million, and $16 million, respectively. The firm expects to have a profit margin on sales of 10 percent and to have a dividend-payout ratio of 40 percent. What will be the balance in the retained earnings account three years hence?

Solution

Step one

$$\text{Sales} \times \text{profit margin} = \text{net income}$$

Step two

$$\text{Net income} \times \text{payout ratio} = \text{dividends}$$

Step three

$$\text{Net income} - \text{dividends} = \text{additions to retained earnings}$$

Step four

$$\text{Beginning retained earnings} + \text{additions to retained earnings}$$
$$= \text{retained earnings at end of period}$$

Step five Using beginning retained earnings of $2.5 million and following steps one to four, the following table can be developed (all figures are in millions of dollars):

Year	Sales × 0.10 = net income	× 0.40 = dividends	Additions to retained earnings	Retained earnings at end of period
1	10	1.0	0.4	0.6	3.1
2	14	1.4	0.56	0.84	3.94
3	16	1.6	0.64	0.96	4.90

Thus the retained earnings account is expected to be $4.9 million.

8. Ten percent of ISG Corporation's sales are for cash, and the remaining 90 percent are collected in the next month. Its material purchases follow the same pattern: 10 percent cash and 90 percent paid next month. What will be the balance in the cash account three months from now if today's balance is $40,000, collections and payments from the prior month are $110,000 and $22,000, respectively, and other events are as forecast below? (All figures are in thousands of dollars.)

Transaction	Month 1	Month 2	Month 3
Sales	100	150	120
Material purchases	30	20	40
Wage and salary payments	60	72	70
Rent payments	3	3	3
Tax payment		35	
Loan repayment	5		
Dividend payment			10

Solution

Step one The key to this problem is to convert sales and purchases to monthly cash receipts and expenditures and then simply add to, or subtract from, the beginning cash balance, just as you do with your checking account. Collections in each month are 10 percent of the month's sales plus 90 percent of the prior month's sales. Payments are figured in a similar manner.

Step two

	Month		
Transaction	1	2	3
Sales	100	150	120
Collections	10 + 110	15 + 90	12 + 135
Purchases	30	20	40
Payments	3 + 22	2 + 27	4 + 18

Step three The last step is to develop a table showing beginning cash, inflows, outflows, and ending cash.

	Month		
Item	1	2	3
Beginning cash balance	40	67	33
+ Collections	120	105	147
= Cash available	160	172	180
− Payments:			
Purchases	25	29	22
Wages and salaries	60	72	70
Rent	3	3	3
Taxes		35	
Loan	5		
Dividends	—	—	10
Total payments	93	139	105
= Ending cash balance	67	33	75

Step four The ending cash balance is $75,000. Note that at the end of the second month it dips to $33,000. If this were below the minimum desired level, some adjustments and/or borrowing would be necessary to bring the cash balance up to the proper level.

CHAPTER SEVENTEEN

INVENTORY AND ACCOUNTS RECEIVABLE MANAGEMENT

QUINTESSENCE   The decision process regarding current assets is basically similar to that for other investments; i.e., benefits and costs are determined and compared for alternatives. However, current assets are a special case because there are so many levels of investment and because they are reversible investments. For these reasons a net profit criterion is used in the benefit-cost analysis. The advantages of a high level of inventory include increased sales and lower costs of acquiring and ordering. These are offset by higher holding costs, higher costs of funds invested, and the risk that the market value of the inventory might decline below cost. Granting credit leads to more sales and accounts receivable. Countering this are higher costs of bad debts and the cost of funds tied up in accounts receivable.

OUTLINE   I. What
   A. This chapter describes risks, benefits, costs, and other characteristics of two of the major types of current assets: accounts receivable and inventories. Special problems are described when doing business abroad.
   B. The benefit-cost analysis is outlined for determining the optimum level of investment in each type of these assets. We want to know how much is enough, but we don't want too much.

II. Why
   A. Current asset management is time-consuming.
      1. The investment levels can change rapidly; most vary from day to day.
      2. There is a continuing need to monitor and compare actual balances against desired levels. The optimum levels also vary.
   B. Too much or too little of a current asset is costly.
      1. Excess amounts tie up funds. This costs money and exposes the firm to risks such as not being able to sell the inventory or collect the accounts receivable.

2. Insufficient amounts are too costly; too little inventory and/or accounts receivable may result in missed sales.

III. How

Basic Principles

A. The principles of current asset management are somewhat similar to the present value approach used for fixed assets (plant and equipment) as described in Chapters 8, 9, and 10.

1. However, the same procedure is impractical to use because there are too many alternatives to evaluate.

a. The frequent variations in the levels of inventories and accounts receivable result in an average amount being used for the investment figure.

b. Oftentimes the level in one current asset affects the amount of investment in another. In other words, the alternatives may be interdependent.

Include Cost of Capital

Reversible Investments

2. An equivalent alternative approach is to maximize average net profits with the cost of capital k treated as an annual dollar cost.

a. The net profit criterion is equivalent to the net present value method, because financing costs are included and because current assets are **reversible investments.** These are investments that, after being made, can be reversed; i.e., you can get your money back if you want to.

Maximize Profit

b. The general principle is to maximize net profit per period.

$$
\text{Net profit} = (1 - \text{tax rate}) \times (\text{annual cash revenues} - \text{annual cash costs}) - k \times \text{investment} \qquad (17\text{-}1)
$$

c. Another way to view the decision is to compute the cash flow needed to provide an NPV of zero. This then is the maximum amount required to justify the proposed investment.

Minimize Costs

d. For some problems it is easier to minimize costs.

$$
\text{Total cost} = (1 - \text{tax rate}) \times \text{annual cash costs} + k \times \text{investment} \qquad (17\text{-}2)
$$

Types of Inventory

B. Managing the level of **inventories** involves deciding what level to maintain and how much to acquire each period in order to maintain the desired level.

1. Three major types of inventory are:

a. **Raw materials,** which are goods purchased to make a product.

b. **Work-in-process,** which consists of partially finished goods in the production process.

c. **Finished goods,** which are products ready for sale.

2. The level of inventories in different industries varies greatly. Manufacturing firms have significant amounts of all three types; wholesalers and retailers have finished goods only.

Average Inventory Investment

3. The average inventory investment is equal to the cash outlay C needed to acquire each unit times the order size Q divided by 2. (This is simply the cost per unit times the average number of units on hand.)

   a. There are four types of costs associated with inventories:

Acquisition Costs

   i. **Acquisition costs** are the cash costs per period of acquiring inventory. They are equal to the cost per unit C times the rate at which inventory is being used up. (This is the usage rate S.) The acquisition cost varies as a result of **quantity discounts.** Quantity discounts are given to pass on the supplier's cost savings from filling large orders. This means that cost per unit C declines as the order size Q increases. If the usage rate S is constant, the acquisition cost will be less for larger orders.

Order Costs

   ii. **Order costs** include payments for transportation, moving into storage, any equipment setups, and clerical functions. These payments are approximately the same for each order, and so order costs equal the usage rate S times the cost per order f divided by the order size Q.

Holding Costs

   iii. **Holding costs** are expressed as a percentage h of the average dollar investment in inventory. These costs include storage costs, property taxes in the inventory, and other miscellaneous charges.

Cost of Funds

   iv. The **cost of funds** is the cost of capital rate k times the average level of inventory investment. The value for k is an aftertax rate, but all other costs are before-tax figures.

   v. The different types of inventory costs are summarized in the table below.

Cost	Formula	Effect on cost if order size is increased
Acquisition	CS	Decreases
Order	$\dfrac{fS}{Q}$	Decreases
Holding	$\dfrac{hCQ}{2}$	Increases
Funds	$\dfrac{kCQ}{2}$	Increases

Order-Size Effects

   b. Total aftertax inventory cost with a tax rate (τ) is

$$\text{Inventory cost} = (1 - \tau)\left(CS + \frac{fS}{Q} + \frac{hCQ}{2}\right) \\ + \frac{kCQ}{2}$$ (17-3)

i. The problem is to find the order size Q that minimizes total costs.

ii. Since the average inventory investment I equals $CQ/2$, Eq. (17-3) can be rewritten as

$$\text{Total cost} = (1 - \tau)\left(CS + \frac{fCS}{2I} + hI\right) + kI$$ (17-4)

If this equation is used, the objective is to find the level of inventory investment I that minimizes total costs. Once this level has been found, the order size Q can easily be calculated.

Cost Trade-Offs

iii. Note the trade-offs indicated in the right-hand column of the preceding table; two types of costs are reduced with larger orders, while the other two are increased. Smaller, more frequent orders mean lower levels of investment, which result in lower holding costs and costs of funds. However, quantity discounts will be missed, and order costs will be up. The opposing cost forces are balanced by computing each cost at different order sizes (or inventory levels), adding up the costs, and then choosing the order size (or inventory level) that gives the minimum total cost.

iv. In the special case when no quantity discounts are available, the **economic order quantity**, EOQ, is calculated as

EOQ

$$\text{EOQ} = \sqrt{\frac{2(1 - \tau)fs}{(1 - \tau)hC + kC}}$$ (17-5)

(See Appendix 17A of the text for the derivation and problem 7 in the *Study Guide* for an example of the use of this equation.)

Inventory Benefits

4. In practice, inventories are often kept at a level *above* the minimum cost point because of other benefits associated with having larger inventories. These are the result of variations in the usage rate and in the time it takes for an order to arrive.

Avoid Stockouts

a. Higher inventories mean that **stockouts** will be minimized. This is good, because they may result in missed sales, loss of good-

Safety Stocks

will, or even shutting down of the production process. **Safety stocks** are the amount of increase in the inventory needed to protect the firm in the event of unanticipated demand or slow-downs of deliveries.

   i. The greater the uncertainty concerning usage and/or delivery times, the higher the safety stock.

   ii. The stockout cost is estimated at different levels of safety stocks.

   iii. The chances that a stockout may occur diminish as the safety stock increases, but this is offset by higher holding costs and costs of funds.

Optimum Stock

   iv. The *optimum* safety stock is the amount at which safety stock costs are minimized, as shown in the following equation:

$$\text{Safety stock costs} = (1 - \text{tax rate}) \times (\text{expected stockout costs} + \text{holding costs}) + \text{costs of funds} \qquad (17\text{-}6)$$

   v. Stockout costs, especially loss of goodwill, are difficult to estimate, and so safety stocks are often set by rules of thumb and managerial judgment.

Customer Service

  b. *Marketing policies* influence the level of inventories, especially of finished goods. Customers often prefer doing business where a complete line of goods is available, as opposed to places where the selection is limited. The wider variety helps sales, but it runs inventory costs up.

Speculation

  c. In periods where costs of items purchased for inventory are rising rapidly, firms have an incentive to increase their inventories. This extra investment is called **inventory speculation.** Its potential benefits are offset by higher holding costs and the risk of being caught with large stocks of slow-moving items.

Risks

5. The **risk factor** must be included in the inventory decision.

  a. The major risk is the chance that the market value of the inventory will fall below cost as a result of:

Technology

   i. **Technological improvements,** which often result in cost and price reductions. Most of us have bought some item that we could have purchased later for much less, e.g., personal computers and digital watches. We feel bad—and so do businesses that experience the same situation.

Styles

   ii. **Style changes,** which can also cause drops in market values. Many people have realized a good buy on miniskirts and wide ties. They are happy, but the sellers that were caught in a bind by these developments don't feel too great.

   iii. A rapid rise or fall in the prices of goods such as agricultural commodities.

iv. Other losses, such as those caused by spoilage, shrinkage, and theft.

Measuring Risks

b. Risks can be incorporated into the inventory analysis by adding an allowance for them into the holding costs and/or by increasing the cost of capital rate, as suggested for the treatment of risk in capital budgeting.

International Considerations

6. For multinational corporations (MNCs) a complicating factor is the location of the inventory.
   a. The inventory should be stored close to:
      i. Production facilities in the case of raw materials.
      ii. Sales, when finished goods are involved.
   b. Political and regulatory considerations may cause exceptions:
      i. To minimize expropriation risk the MNC should keep inventories in the more stable countries.
      ii. Tariffs, taxes, etc., also create incentives to shift inventories to countries different from those that make sense in strict financial terms.

Accounts Receivable

C. **Accounts receivable** is the total of all credit extended by the firm to its customers.
   1. The dollar amount has two components:
      a. The cash outlays the company has made to provide the goods for sale. This is the actual investment that the firm has in its accounts receivable.
      b. The difference between the selling price and the cash outlay. This is the markup, or gross margin.

Credit Decisions

2. Credit is granted to individuals and firms (also governmental bodies) on the basis of the seller's assessment of the customer's likelihood of payment—you can charge your purchase from me *if* I think you'll pay for it later.

Retailers

3. Consumer credit
   a. Smaller merchants rely on credit cards issued by banks and others. Larger operations have their own credit.
   b. The firm's exposure to loss is limited to the amount of credit offered to a customer.

Risk Assessment

   c. In **risk assessment,** the chance of nonpayment is evaluated against the benefit gained by extending credit, i.e., more sales.
      i. Interest charges normally apply to balances extending beyond 30 days.
      ii. The firm gathers information from the customer and from credit bureaus or credit agencies.
      iii. On the basis of these data and the firm's experience and judgment, customers are assigned to one of a set of **risk groups.** The higher-risk classes have the higher expected percentage losses and therefore are granted relatively less credit.

Credit for Business Terms

4. **Business credit** is sales by one firm to another according to specific **credit terms,** which include:
   a. The **type of account,** which is usually an **open account.** Here the buyer pays later for the goods.
   b. The **credit period,** which specifies when payment is due.
   c. The size of the **discount** offered from the invoice price for prompt payment.
   d. The **period** during which the buyer can pay and still get the discount.
   e. The **credit limit** in terms of dollars.

"The Five C's"

5. Credit evaluations, which are aided by information available from credit agencies such as Dun and Bradstreet, are based on customer attributes—"the five C's of credit."
   a. **Character**—desire to repay.
   b. **Capacity**—ability to repay.
   c. **Conditions**—the economic situation surrounding the customer.
   d. **Capital**—net worth.
   e. **Collateral**—assets pledged.

Net Profit Is Used to Set Policy

6. Alternative credit policies are evaluated by the incremental effects on net profit. Too tight policies mean missed sales; too loose policies mean more bad debts, so a rationale for optimal restriction is needed.
   a. Additional accounts receivable and cash revenues are estimated for the proposed change in credit policy.
   b. Increases in cash expenses, including acquisition costs, bad-debt losses, collection expenses, and holding and order costs are subtracted from the cash revenues expected to be generated by the policy change.
   c. The difference is multiplied by 1 minus the tax rate to get aftertax net revenues.
   d. The total of the incremental cash investment in accounts receivable plus additional inventory required at the estimated sales gain is multiplied by the cost of capital to get the cost of added funds.
   e. The cost of more funds is subtracted from net new revenues after tax to give net profits.
   f. The above steps are summarized in the following equation:

Calculation

$$\text{Net profit} = (1 - \text{tax rate}) \times (\text{added cash revenues} - \text{added cash expenses}) - \text{cost of capital} \times \text{added investment}$$

(17-7)

   g. The process is repeated for other credit policies, and the one that yields the maximum net profit is recommended.

Risk Factors

7. Accounts receivable are relatively low-risk assets.
   a. Bad-debt losses are reasonably predictable and are subtracted from expected revenues.
   b. The major risk lies in the possibility that a significant number of customers may suddenly get into financial difficulties.
   c. Credit insurance is available for protection against unusual losses.

Foreign Receivables

   d. **Foreign accounts receivable** have additional risks.
      i. It is more difficult to determine creditworthiness of firms abroad due to differences in business practices, etc.
      ii. It is more difficult and expensive to collect from nonpaying customers because of differences in foreign legal systems. Note that foreign credit risks can be eliminated by using letters of credit as part of the transactions (see Chapter 19).
      iii. Accounts receivable denominated in a foreign currency carry a foreign exchange risk. This can be avoided by demanding payments in the home country currency.
   e. Accounts receivable need to be *monitored* by checking on:
      i. The average collection period and comparing it with stated credit policy.
      ii. An aging schedule to identify how many of and how long the accounts are past due.
      iii. The *levels* and *trends* in the above measurements as well as what is happening to the ratio of bad-debt losses to credit sales.

COMPLETION QUESTIONS

decreases 1. Too much or too little investment in current assets (*increases/decreases*) profits.

net present value 2. The (*net present value/payback*) approach to investing in current assets is
variable impractical to use because the investment levels are too (*constant/variable*)
many and because there are too (*many/few*) alternatives to evaluate.

net profit 3. The _____ _____ criterion used to evaluate current
net present value assets is equivalent to the _____ _____ _____ method used to evaluate fixed assets.

reversible 4. Current assets are (*reversible/risky*) investments, which means they can be converted into cash relatively easily.

net 5. Current asset decisions are based on maximizing _____
profits, total costs _____ or minimizing _____ _____.

raw materials	6. The types of inventory are _____ _____ ,
work-in-process	_____-_____-_____ , and
finished goods	_____ _____ .
cost	7. The average inventory investment is equal to the (*selling price/cost*) per unit times the average number of units on hand.
order size	8. The average quantity of inventory is equal to the (*daily production/order size*) divided by 2.
acquisition	9. The product of the cost per unit and the usage rate is the (*acquisition/order*) cost.
holding, funds	10. If the order size is increased, the two types of costs that will also increase are (*acquisition/holding*) and (*funds/order*).
acquisition	11. Quantity discounts affect _____ costs.
acquisition ordering	12. The higher the level of inventory, the lower the costs of (*funds/acquisition*) and (*holding/ordering*).
above, minimum	13. Variations in the demand for inventory and in delivery times cause firms to maintain actual inventory levels at (*above/below*) the (*minimum/maximum*) cost point.
safety stocks	14. In order to protect against stockouts, _____ _____ are often held.
lower	15. The more predictable the usage and the delivery times are, the (*lower/higher*) will be the safety stock.
stockouts	16. Loss of goodwill and interruptions in the production process may be caused by _____ .
increase	17. A policy of offering a wide variety of products for sale will (*increase/decrease*) the investment in inventory.
more	18. In periods of rapid inflation there is a tendency toward (*more/less*) inventory speculation.
fall below	19. The major risk consideration in inventory decisions is the chance that the market value of the inventory might (*rise above/fall below*) cost.
holding, funds cost of capital	20. An allowance for inventory risk can be made by adding to (*acquisition/holding*) costs or to (*order/funds*) costs. The latter cost adjustment is made by increasing the (*net present value/cost of capital*).
production	21. MNCs try to keep raw material inventories close to the point of (*production/sales*).

small   22. An MNC that has a plant in an unstable foreign country will tend to have (*large/small*) inventories in that country.

higher   23. The (*lower/higher*) a firm's markup, the lower will be the cash investment that it has in accounts receivable in comparison with the amount actually recorded as accounts receivable.

24. A firm that experiences no bad-debt losses from its credit sales probably
stringent   has too (*lax/stringent*) credit standards.

increased   25. The benefit of liberal credit terms is _____ sales.

26. The accounts receivable for a firm that supplies only one industry would be
more   considered (*less/more*) risky than those of a company whose customers are in many different fields.

Smaller   27. (*Larger/Smaller*) merchants typically do not have their own credit cards.

Capacity   28. (*Capacity/Character*) is the ability of a customer to pay debts.

capital   29. A measure of financial strength of a customer is (*collateral/capital*).

eliminated   30. Foreign credit risk can be (*maximized/eliminated*) using letters of credit to finance transactions.

PROBLEMS

1. A $1000 investment will result in three years of annual cash inflows of $800 and annual cash expenses (excluding taxes) of $200. Assume that the tax rate is 40 percent, the cost of capital k is 12 percent, and the salvage value is $1000.
   a. Calculate the net present value (NPV) of this investment.

Solution

Step one This looks like a standard capital budgeting problem—and it is. The reason it is included in this chapter is to show that using the net profit criterion employed to evaluate costs and benefits in current investment decisions is equivalent to using NPV in fixed-assets investment decisions.

Step two

$$\text{Net cash inflows before taxes} = \$800 - \$200$$

$$= \$600 \text{ per year}$$

Step three

$$\text{Taxes} = 0.40 \times \$600 = \$240$$

Step four

$$\text{Cash flow after taxes} = \$360$$

Step five What about depreciation? It is initial investment minus salvage value spread over the project life, or

$$\frac{\$1000 - \$1000}{3} = 0$$

In current assets no depreciation occurs because the investments are reversible. You can usually get your money back any time.

Step six

$$\begin{aligned}
\text{NPV} &= \text{present value of all cash inflows} - \text{present value} \\
&\quad \text{of cash outflows} \\
&= \$360 \ (P/A, \ 12\%, \ 3) + \$1000 \ (P/F, \ 12\%, \ 3) - \$1000 \\
&= \$360 \ (2.4018) + \$1000 \ (0.7118) - \$1000 \\
&= \$576
\end{aligned}$$

b. Compute the net profit per year.

Solution

Step one

$$\begin{aligned}
\text{Net profits} &= (1 - \text{tax rate}) \times (\text{cash revenues} - \text{cash costs}) \\
&\quad - k \times \text{investment} \\
&= (1 - 0.4) \times (\$800 - \$200) - 0.12 \times \$1000 \\
&= \$240 \text{ per year}
\end{aligned}$$

Step two   Note that the adjustment for taxes was applied only to the cash flows. The cost of capital is an aftertax figure, and so no tax adjustment is necessary for figuring the cost of funds.

c. Calculate the NPV of the profits and compare it with the NPV of the investment figures in problem 1a.

Solution

Step one

$$\text{NPV of profits} = \$240 \ (P/A, \ 12\%, \ 3)$$
$$= \$240 \ (2.4018)$$
$$= \$576$$

Step two   This is the same as the NPV of the cash flows calculated in problem 1a. This exercise confirms the proposition that NPV and net profit are equivalent measures of costs and benefits when reversible investments are being analyzed.

Step three   Remember that we can work just as well with costs only. We select either the alternative that provides the maximum level of profits *or* the alternative that provides the minimum level of costs.

2. Suppose the investment outlined in problem 1 was actually a situation for Terry-the-Tireman's tire business. He plans to keep an average inventory of $1000 on hand, which will generate a before-tax net cash flow of $600 per year. He is considering increasing his average inventory to $2000, and he estimates that the net cash flow would be $750 per year. Which plan would provide the greater profits, assuming a 40 percent tax rate and a cost of capital of 12 percent?

Solution

Step one   In problem 1 we found the net profit with the $1000 investment to be $240 per year.

Step two   With the $2000 inventory investment,

$$\text{Net profits} = (1 - 0.4) \times \$750$$
$$- 0.12 \times \$2000$$
$$= \$210 \text{ per year}$$

Step three   This means that the additional inventory does not help; in fact, profits decline. The best choice, given the above data, is to maintain an average inventory of $1000.

3. Sarah's Hat Shop sells an average of 100 hats per month. Her current inventory policy is to maintain an average investment of $500 in the hats, which cost $10 apiece.
   a. What is the number of hats in each order, and how frequently should the orders be placed?

Solution

Step one   The average investment I is half the price per unit C times the order size Q.

$$I = \frac{CQ}{2}$$

$$\$500 = \frac{\$10Q}{2}$$

$$Q = 100 \text{ hats}$$

Step two   Since the usage rate S is 100 hats per month, a new order must be placed every month.

   b. What is the annual acquisition cost?

Solution

$$\text{Acquisition cost} = CS$$
$$= \$10 \times 100$$
$$= \$1000 \text{ per order}$$
$$\text{Annual cost} = 12 \times \$1000$$
$$= \$12,000$$

c. If it costs $10 to write up each order, what are the annual order costs?

Solution

Step one   The amount of each order cost f is $10; thus with monthly orders, the annual order cost would be $120 (12 × $10).

Step two   Using the following formula:

$$\text{Order costs} = \frac{fS}{Q}$$
$$= \frac{\$10 \times 12 \times 100}{100}$$
$$= \$120$$

Step three   Note that the usage rate S must correspond to the time period being analyzed. A 100-hat-per-month rate is equivalent to 1200 hats per year.

d. What would be the annual holding costs if they are 3 percent of the average investment?

Solution   **Step one**

$$\text{Holding costs} = hI$$
$$= 0.03 \times \$500$$
$$= \$15 \text{ per year}$$

e. If the cost of capital k is 10 percent per year, what is the cost of funds?

Solution   **Step one**

$$\text{Cost of funds} = kI$$
$$= 0.10 \times \$500$$
$$= \$50$$

f. If the tax rate is 50 percent, what is the total aftertax cost of this inventory policy?

Solution   **Step one**

$$\text{Total cost} = (1 - \text{tax rate}) \times (\text{acquisition} + \text{order} + \text{holding})$$
$$+ \text{cost of funds}$$
$$= (1 - 0.5) \times (\$12{,}000 + \$120 + \$15) + \$50$$
$$= \$6117.50$$

4. Determine whether Sarah's Hat Shop has the optimal inventory level by using data given in problem 3 to compute total costs at order sizes of 50, 150, 200, and 250 hats.

Solution

Step one The following table can be prepared using the procedure outlined in the solution to problem 3.

			Annual dollar costs of			
Order size	Acquisition = CS	Order = fS/Q	Holding = hl	Subtotal after tax	Funds = kl	Total
50	12,000	240	7.50	6,123.75	25	6,148.75
100	12,000	120	15.00	6,067.50	50	6,117.50
150	12,000	80	22.50	6,051.25	75	6,126.25
200	12,000	60	30.00	6,045.00	100	6,145.00
250	12,000	48	37.50	6,042.75	125	6,167.75

Step two The minimum cost is with an order size of 100 hats, which represents an average inventory of $500.

Step three Note the constant $12,000 of acquisition costs. This is so because a constant cost per unit was assumed, no matter what the order size. See the next problem for the effect of quantity discounts.

5. Suppose the hat supplier offers a quantity discount to Sarah's Hat Shop according to the following schedule:

Purchase quantity	Price per unit
50	$10.00
100	9.80
150	9.65
200 and above	9.55

What order size will minimize *total* costs as outlined in problem 3?

Solution

Step one Acquisition costs vary as a result of the quantity discounts. This also affects the holding cost and the cost of funds since the inventory investment is the product of the order quantity and the price per unit.

Step two The table below is developed as the table in problem 4 was.

Order size	Annual dollar costs of					
	Acquisition $= CS$	Order $= fS/Q$	Holding $= hI$	Subtotal after tax	Funds $= kI$	Total
50	12,000	240	7.50	6,123.75	25.00	6,148.75
100	11,760	120	14.70	5,947.35	49.00	5,996.35
150	11,580	80	21.71	5,840.85	72.37	5,913.22
200	11,460	60	28.65	5,774.32	95.50	5,869.82
250	11,460	48	35.81	5,771.90	119.37	5,891.27

Step three The minimum cost is achieved at an order size of 200 units, which means that the average investment will be $\dfrac{(9.55 \times 200)}{2}$, or $955.

6. Stewart Nail Distributor, Inc., prides itself on quick service, which it achieves by maintaining a large inventory so as to fill its orders promptly. The firm is concerned that it has too high an investment in inventory, and so a special study has been conducted to determine the costs and benefits of different safety-stock levels. Assuming a tax rate of 40 percent, a holding cost of 3 percent per year, a 10 percent cost of capital, and annual stockout costs as shown below, what should the safety stock be?

Average safety-stock investment	$600,000	$500,000	$400,000	$300,000
Annual stockout costs	0	$ 10,000	$ 25,000	$ 50,000

Solution

Step one The trade-off for reducing inventory is lower holding costs and lower costs of funds but more missed sales.

Step two

$$\text{Total costs} = (1 - \text{tax rate}) \times (\text{holding costs}$$
$$+ \text{stockout costs}) + \text{cost of funds}$$

The costs of a $500,000 safety stock are

$$\text{Total costs} = (1 - 0.4) \times (0.03 \times \$500,000 + \$10,000)$$
$$+ 0.10 \times \$500,000$$
$$= \$65,000$$

Step three Applying the same equation to other safety-stock levels yields the following results:

Safety stock	Total costs
$600,000	$70,800
500,000	65,000
400,000	62,200
300,000	65,400

Step four Total costs are minimized by having a safety stock of $400,000.

7. Bonnie's Fabric Store deals with a supplier who does not give quantity discounts. What would Bonnie's optimal order size be if she receives her major cloth item in 50-yard bolts at $100 per bolt, sells 60,000 yards per year, estimates each order costs $20 to prepare, has holding and capital costs of 5 and 12 percent per year, respectively, and has a 30 percent income tax rate?

Solution

Step one Since acquisition costs are constant, this problem can be solved using the economic order quantity model.

$$\text{EOQ} = \sqrt{\frac{2(1 - \tau)fS}{(1 - \tau)hC + kC}}$$

where

Usage rate $S = 1200$ bolts per year
Cost per order $f = \$20$
Holding cost $h = 5\%$
Capital cost $k = 12\%$
Price per bolt $C = \$100$
Tax rate $\tau = 30\%$

Step two Plug the values into the formula and solve:

$$EOQ = \sqrt{\frac{2(1 - .3)(20)(1200)}{(1 - .3)(.05)(100) + .12(100)}}$$

$$= 46.6, \text{ or } 47 \text{ bolts per order}$$

8. Mary L Corporation is considering changing its practice of sending out bills to its credit accounts at the end of each month to a procedure of billing customers on a rotating basis, with different groups of people being billed every day on a monthly cycle. It is estimated that, as a result, the average collection period will be cut from forty-five to thirty days.
   a. What will be the new level of accounts receivable if the firm's annual sales are $24 million?

Solution

Step one Accounts receivable are thirty days' or one month's, sales of $2 million (1/12 × $24). *End of solution.*

   b. What is the cash investment in accounts receivable if the total of the acquisition costs, plus stocking and selling costs, averages 60 percent of the sales price?

Solution

Step one The cash outlay by the firm in its accounts receivable is $1.2 million (0.60 × $2).

Step two The other 40 percent of the accounts receivable represents accounting profit.

9. Lisa and Jennifer have recently purchased a store specializing in women's and children's apparel. The previous owner had, over twenty-five years, built the business from a small boutique into one of the larger and better stores in the area. During the past ten years the credit policy had been changed twice—from no credit to limited credit and from limited credit to

open credit. Lisa and Jennifer are trying to determine whether to maintain the open credit policy or return to one of the previous policies. Suppose you are a financial consultant and they have asked for your recommendation based on a cost-benefit analysis of the data listed below:

Credit policy	Sales	Inventory	Accounts receivable	Bad-debt and collection costs
No credit	100	10	0	0
Limited credit	150	15	20	5
Open credit	250	25	100	25

The cost of goods sold is 70 percent of sales, the cost of capital is 10 percent, the income tax is 40 percent, and no interest is charged on past-due accounts.

Solution

Step one The advantages of granting credit are higher sales, which are offset by higher costs due to bad-debt and collection expenses, larger investment in inventory, and larger accounts receivable.

Step two The cost of goods sold is 70 percent of sales, and so the net revenues at different credit policies are as shown below:

Credit policy	Sales	Cost of goods sold	Bad-debt and collection costs	Net revenues	
				Before tax	After tax
None	100	70	0	30	18
Limited	150	105	5	40	24
Open	250	175	25	50	30

Step three The cash investment in accounts receivable is 70 percent of sales, and so the cost of funds is as shown below:

Credit policy	Accounts receivable	Inventory	Cash investment	Cost of funds
None	70	10	80	8
Limited	105	15	120	12
Open	175	25	200	20

Step four

$$\text{Profits} = \text{net revenues after tax} - \text{cost of funds}$$

Credit policy	Net revenues	Cost of funds	Profit
None	18	8	10
Limited	24	12	12
Open	30	20	10

Step five This indicates that the most profitable policy would be to grant limited credit.

CHAPTER EIGHTEEN

CASH MANAGEMENT

QUINTESSENCE

Managing is a process of speeding up collections and slowing down disbursements. Cash balances are maintained at necessary levels to cover transactions and to compensate banks for services. Excess cash above needs is invested in marketable (money market) securities to earn a return and to provide a safe and ready reserve of liquid assets. Cost-benefit analysis compares the expenses incurred to add efficiency with the interest earnings from investing the idle funds. Efficient management of cash flow includes use of such techniques as lock boxes, preauthorized and depository transfer checks, electronic payments, concentration banks, payments netting, and cash pooling.

OUTLINE

I. What
   A. Cash balances should be minimized to provide amounts needed for doing business, for having a margin of safety, and for compensating banks for services they render.
   B. Many techniques and systems are available to efficiently manage cash flows.
   C. Excess funds are invested to earn the highest return that goes with safety and liquidity needs.
   D. Multinational corporations (MNCs) use sophisticated information management systems to pool and invest funds in countries offering good short-term investment opportunities.

II. Why
   A. Cash facilitates trade but offers no returns itself. Too much or too little is costly.
   B. Effort spent on cash management provides relatively high returns—a few people can make efficient arrangements yielding significant benefits.
   C. The complexities of international trade create challenges for cash managers.

III. How

Cash Management

   A. **Cash management** involves managing cash balances (some currency, but mainly demand deposits), cash flows (receipts and collections), and short-term investments (securities) and short-term borrowing.

275

Cash Cycle	1. The firm's **cash cycle** traces operations that result in cash flows from beginning to the end of the normal and repetitive process of buying and selling the company's products.
	a. Purchases are recorded as inventory and as accounts payable when goods are received.
Payment Period	b. The **average payment period** (accounts payable balance divided by purchases per day) measures the length of time the firm waits before paying its suppliers.
Disbursement Period	c. The **disbursement time** indicates how many days it takes from the point when a check is mailed until it clears the bank.
Inventory Period	d. The **average inventory period** is equal to the inventory divided by the cost of goods sold per day. It is the average number of days inventory is on the shelf before being sold.
Collection Period	e. The **average collection period** is equal to the time from when the goods are sent until the check is written (**customer payment period**) and received through the mail (**mail time**). Added to this is the time it takes the firm to record the check and deliver it to its bank (**processing time**) and have it available for use (**availability time**).
Cash Cycle Period	f. The **cash cycle** is the overall period from the point when the firm pays its suppliers for inventory to the point after the goods are sold, the cash is collected, received, and is actually available for use by the firm.
Managing Cash Flows	2. The objectives of **cash flow management** are to:
	a. *Accelerate collections* (including the internal processing and bank availability times).
	b. *Slow down payments.*
Float	3. **Float** is money in the process of being collected. It is *free credit*.
Collection Float	a. Businesses try to minimize **collection float** (the amount of free credit they provide to other firms) by:
Lock Box	i. Establishing a **lock box** system. This is a special post office box in a city where the company has many customers. The local bank picks up the checks and has them cleared so mail, processing, and availability times are reduced.
Preauthorized Checks	ii. Having customers use **preauthorized checks,** which dramatically cut the delays because the checks are issued by the firm and are payable to itself.
	iii. Making major efforts to record and deposit payments as quickly as possible.
	iv. Negotiating with their bank to provide as close to instant availability of the funds as possible.
	b. It is important to note that the amount of cash shown on the balance sheet is equal to the available cash balance plus currency, plus checks deposited but not yet available, plus checks in hand but not yet deposited, minus checks written but not yet cleared.
Disbursement Float	c. **Disbursement float** is money in the process of being paid out.

Controlled Disbursement Zero Balance Accounts

Automated Clearinghouses

Managing Cash Balances Compensating Balances

Transaction Balances

Concentration Bank Depository Transfer Checks Cost-Benefit Analysis

It is analogous to collection float and is measured by the time from mailing the check to the point when the cash actually leaves the firm's account. The strategy for maximizing this time is called **controlled disbursement,** which involves:

  i. Maintaining **zero balance accounts.** The firms still write checks on these accounts. The banks have funds wired to them at the end of each day in amounts that exactly cover what has been presented for payment during the day.

  ii. Checks are often written and mailed from locations that are distant from the supplier or other party being paid.

  iii. On the other hand, many firms make some payments electronically through **automated clearinghouses.** While this reduces disbursement float it does save paperwork and creates better relations with suppliers.

  d. Efficient cash flow management calls for appropriate efforts to speed up and slow down the income and outgo, particularly for larger firms where the dollar amounts are substantial.

4. Firms maintain cash balances (checking accounts) to handle transactions and to pay for the bank services.

  a. **Compensating balances** are amounts kept on deposit in the bank to pay it for the loan and other services rendered.

    i. Most bank loan agreements require a certain minimum deposit to be maintained.

    ii. The amount is computed by dividing the annualized bank service charge by the bank's earnings credit rate. The latter figure is typically tied to a money market rate (e.g., the 90-day Treasury bill rate).

  b. **Transaction balances** are held to facilitate payments.

    i. The amount is influenced by the uncertainty of the daily cash receipts and disbursements. The more unpredictable these are, the greater the balance needed.

    ii. If the balance is kept too low, the shortage will cause costs to be incurred, necessitating borrowing or the sale of securities.

    iii. If the cash balance is too high, the firm will miss the opportunity to invest the excess funds and earn interest.

  c. Large firms try to keep their cash balance at no more than that required by the compensating balance. Excess cash is automatically "swept" into an overnight repurchase agreement that earns interest. Companies with deposits at a number of banks will have excess cash wired daily to a **concentration bank.** Sometimes **depository transfer checks,** which cost only a few cents, are used to move funds between banks.

5. The basic approach to analyzing cash management alternatives is to compare the cost (fees, salaries, and equipment) of gaining more efficiency with the benefits (interest) derived from the cash released.

Investing Excess Cash

6. **Excess funds** are invested temporarily or longer.
   a. Cash availability varies because of seasonal patterns and because of the business cycle.

Precautionary Motive

   b. Some firms like to have a ready reserve to meet unexpected cash needs. This **precautionary motive** can be mitigated by arranging for bank credit.
   c. Excess funds are also needed to make large planned payments such as taxes or dividends.

Money Market Securities

7. Most investments are made in **money market securities** with maturities coinciding with cash needs.
   a. The key characteristic of these investments is that they can be sold quickly with little chance of loss.
   b. Typical investments include Treasury bills, commercial paper, banker's acceptances, and certificates of deposit. (Review the descriptions of these in Table 18-5 of the text.)
8. Sometimes firms accumulate and invest cash for longer periods, as in the case of financing future acquisitions. Security purchases may be long-term bonds or common stock.

International Cash Management

B. **International cash management**
1. The MNC has the same objectives as the domestic firm:
   a. Minimize collection float.
   b. Avoid excessive cash balances.
   c. Maximize earnings on short-term investments commensurate with safety of principal.

Complications

2. Complicating factors in various nations include:
   a. Differences in banking practices.
   b. Tax regulations.
   c. Changing government restrictions.
   d. Exchange rate fluctuations.
   e. Collections from around the world.
   f. Underdeveloped electronic funds transfer systems.
3. Because of longer float periods and greater access to money markets in different countries, MNCs have substantial incentives for making extra efforts to improve cash management.

Payments Netting

4. **Payments netting** involves the use of centralized payment information to cancel out cross-payments thereby avoiding transaction expenses.
   a. In other words, MNCs try to avoid having their affiliates send and receive payments around the world until each subsidiary nets the accounts payable and receivable from each of its trading partners.
   b. Some countries, such as Japan, have restrictions on payments netting.

Cash Pooling

5. MNCs use **cash pooling.**
   a. This centralizes the cash account in one place to meet the combined precautionary cash balance needs of several subsidiaries.

**Management
Information
Systems**

b. Less total cash is needed for the group compared to the sum total required for each operation.
c. The central location chosen is based on the nation offering the best combination of safety, liquidity, and yield. This includes such characteristics as a good money market, a stable currency, and low tax rates.
6. Sophisticated management information systems are vital to the success of international cash management.

COMPLETION QUESTIONS

higher
1. A company that experiences wide variations in the amount of sales and collections will tend to have (*lower/higher*) demand deposit balances.

checking
2. Firms often maintain minimum _____ account balances to compensate banks for some of their services.

speed up
slow down
3. The principle of cash management is to (*speed up/slow down*) collections and to (*speed up/slow down*) payments.

decrease
4. Shifting from month-end billing to the billing of customers throughout the month will (*increase/decrease*) the average accounts receivable balance.

nationwide
5. A lock box system may help a firm with (*nationwide/local*) customers.

concentration
6. A cash management practice involves transferring a firm's funds from accounts in many banks to a single (*correspondent/concentration*) bank.

float
7. Money in the process of being collected is called _____.

Collection
8. (*Collection/Disbursement*) float time can be reduced using preauthorized checks.

increase
9. Zero balance accounts are used to (*increase/decrease*) disbursement float.

precautionary
checking
10. The (*transactions/precautionary*) motive for holding cash has to do with the firm's (*checking/savings*) accounts.

marketable securities
11. Available cash that is in excess of minimum requirements is invested in _____ _____ .

transactions
12. The desire to maintain a ready reserve of liquid assets to meet unexpected needs is called the _____ motive.

quickly
loss
13. Liquid assets are those that can be sold _____ with little chance of _____ .

less
14. Common stocks are (*less/more*) liquid than commercial paper.

invested
15. Cash management benefits are measured by earnings on cash (*invested/borrowed*).

minimize

balances
16. MNCs try to (*maximize/minimize*) collection float and avoid excess cash (*balances/earnings*).

differences
17. Complications for international trade include (*differences/similarities*) in banking practices and governmental laws and regulations.

18. The practice of offsetting a subsidiary's bills due to and due from the parent firm is called _____ _____.

payments netting

pooling
19. The idea similar to using concentration banks is called cash _____.

more
20. Sophisticated management information systems are (*less/more*) important for MNCs compared to domestic firms.

PROBLEMS

1. Jodidaniel, a travel and tour agency, maintains an average cash balance of $10,000 on its books. Its annual sales are $1,460,000. Its disbursements, which average $1900 daily, have a float of five days. What is the average cash balance according to the bank records if the bank requires one day after checks are deposited to make the funds available?

Solution

Step one The average daily sales are:

$$\frac{\$1,460,000}{365} = \$4000 \text{ per day}$$

Step two Added to the book balance is the disbursement float which is

$$4 \text{ days} \times \$1900 \text{ per day} = \$7600$$

Step three Subtracted from the book balance is the availability float which is

$$1 \text{ day} \times \$4000 \text{ per day} = \$4000$$

Step four The bank's records would show an average daily balance of

$$\$10,000 + \$7600 - \$4000 = \$13,600$$

2. How would the bank balance be affected if Jodidaniel didn't deposit checks until the day after they were received?

Solution

Step one By delaying making its deposits by one day the average balance would decrease by $4000 to a figure of $9600. *End of solution.*

3. How much in additional expenses could Jodidaniel pay to have its checks deposited the same day they arrive if the company could earn 10 percent on temporary investments?

Solution

Step one If a person were hired to deposit the checks the day of arrival, the firm would have an average of $400 available for investment.

Step two This would earn 10 percent of $4000, or $400 per year.

4. Langroise Corp. estimates that its next year's sales will be $73 million. It sells to customers around the country and has an average accounts receivable balance equal to thirty days' sales. The financial manager estimates that instituting a lock box system will cause the accounts receivable balance to decline to twenty-five days' sales.
   a. What will be the reduction in accounts receivable?

Solution

Step one

$$\text{Sales per day} = \frac{\$73 \text{ million}}{365} = \$200,000$$

Step two   Accounts receivable:

$$30 \text{ days} \times \$200,000 = \$6,000,000$$

$$25 \text{ days} \times \$200,000 = \$5,000,000$$

$$\text{Reduction} = \$1,000,000$$

b. Assuming that funds can be reinvested at 5 percent, how much could the firm pay to the banks to operate its lock box system?

Solution

Step one   The faster check clearing frees up $1 million, which the company could invest at 5 percent to earn

$$0.05 \times \$1 \text{ million} = \$50,000$$

Step two $50,000 is the maximum amount that could be paid to the banks. If the banks perform the service for less, it would be profitable; if they charge more, it would not.

CHAPTER NINETEEN

SHORT-TERM FINANCING

QUINTESSENCE In analyzing costs of each type of short-term financing, the effective interest costs should be computed. In addition, an appraisal should be made of the potential impact on the firm's credit rating and of the reliability, restriction, and flexibility characteristics of each source. The cost of trade credit, which is the most widely used type of short-term financing, is the cost of forgoing cash discounts. The cost of bank loans is increased by compensating-balance requirements. Commercial paper is one of the lowest-cost sources, but it is unreliable if a firm encounters difficulties. Weaker firms may have to pledge accounts receivable or inventory as collateral in order to secure credit. These arrangements increase financing costs. In international trade, credit risks are large but can be minimized with letters of credit and banker's acceptances. Foreign exchange risks can be eliminated using the forward market or money market instruments.

OUTLINE

I. What
   A. Analyzing short-term financing possibilities involves an evaluation of costs and benefits with reference to total dollar costs, impacts on credit rating, reliability, restrictions, and flexibility.
   B. Short-term financing sources include trade credit, bank loans, and secured borrowing.
   C. Multinational corporations often use banker's acceptances and foreign exchange.

II. Why
   A. Virtually all firms rely on short-term financing.
   B. The financial manager must decide which particular types of short-term sources can best meet forecasted requirements for funds.
   C. International trade creates special financing problems.

III. How

Aspects to Consider
   A. There are five aspects to consider for each source of short-term financing. These are costs, in terms of either dollars or restrictions, and impacts related to the future reliability and availability of funds.

283

Costs	1. The dollar **cost** of financing is minimized by choosing the source with the lowest annual interest rate.
Credit Impact	2. The effect on the firm's **credit rating** may be more for some sources than for others.
Reliability	3. The **reliability** of continued borrowing is greater for those types of financing that are more likely to be available whenever needed.
Restrictions	4. Some sources will have more **restrictions** than others.
Flexibility	5. The **flexibility** is the ease of increasing or decreasing the amounts used.

B. The three major sources of short-term financing, in declining order of importance, are **trade credit, bank loans,** and **commercial paper.** The first and third types are unsecured; bank loans can be either secured or unsecured.

Trade Credit

1. **Trade credit** arises when one firm buys from another and does not pay immediately. This interfirm debt is recorded as accounts receivable for the supplier and accounts payable for the buyer.

   a. Trade credit is an almost automatic financing source, expanding and contracting as purchases rise and fall.

   b. Terms tend to be similar within each industry, but it is still important to evaluate each supplier's credit conditions.

   i. A "picture" of some of the credit terms is shown below:

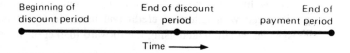

FIGURE 19-1

   ii. Of major concern is the cost of forgoing the cash discount as measured by

Cost of Forgoing Cash Discounts

$$\text{Annual interest rate} = \frac{\text{percent discount}}{100 - \text{percent discount}} \times \frac{365}{\text{payment period} - \text{discount period}} \qquad (19\text{-}1)$$

   iii. The supplier offering terms with the lowest annual interest rate is preferred if payment is delayed until the end of the payment period and if other things such as product quality and service are the same.

iv. If payments are made within the discount period, trade credit has provided free financing from the time when the goods are received to the point when payment is made.

v. The rate computed in Eq. (19-1) is the cost of using trade credit financing *when the discount is missed*. It can be compared with the costs of other types of short-term credit to determine the cheapest source. For example, taking out a bank loan at 10 percent would be preferred over using trade credit if the latter cost 15 percent.

vi. While trade credit is flexible and convenient, it is limited to the volume of purchases, and it does not provide cash for other needs.

vii. Firms that are late in paying their bills may develop a poor credit rating. This can be very costly, because alternative sources of financing may become unavailable and suppliers may stop granting credit and start demanding cash, either COD or even CBD (Cash Before Delivery).

Bank Loans

2. **Bank loans** are the second major source of short-term financing for business and are typically established with a note (IOU) that may be payable on demand or at the end of a certain time period.

Seasonal

a. **Seasonal loans** are **self-liquidating** because they are used to finance items, like inventory and accounts receivable, that are soon converted into cash to repay the loan.

Credit Line

i. **A line of credit** is an informal agreement by a bank to lend a business up to a certain maximum amount anytime during a period of typically one year or less. In most of these arrangements, the loan must be repaid entirely at some point during the year.

Revolving Credit

ii. In a **revolving credit** agreement a bank, for an extra fee, makes a legal commitment to extend credit up to a specified amount anytime during a period of usually several years.

Compensating Balance

iii. **Compensating balances** are typically a part of bank lending. They are a requirement for a company to maintain a minimum average demand deposit balance. They increase the cost of the loan *if* the balance required is above the amount normally kept on deposit. Sometimes the borrower must pay a lower rate on the unused part of the loan. The effective interest rate can be computed by dividing the annual costs (interest plus fees) by the amount that is actually available for discretionary use. Further complications of the bank arrangements can be incorporated into this general equation.

Interim Financing

b. **Interim,** or **bridge, financing** loans are made to cover the need for long-term financing before it is available. Examples are short-term loans for construction. These loans are repaid when the project is completed and permanent financing is obtained.

Prime Rate

      c. Interest rates on bank loans are negotiated, with the **prime rate** going to businesses having the highest credit rating. (Major firms can sometimes borrow at less than prime.) Riskier borrowers pay higher rates, but banks refuse even to lend to the most risky customers. There are three different ways to pay interest:

Ordinary Interest

        i. Interest charges paid *at the loan maturity* are called **ordinary interest,** and the rate quoted is the true interest rate.

Discount Loans

        ii. In **discount loans,** the interest charges are deducted from the amount borrowed *at the beginning* of the loan. The true interest rate is higher than the rate quoted because the firm does not have use of the full amount borrowed.

Floating Rates

        iii. In **floating rate loans,** the interest rate varies as often as daily. It is fixed in some preset relationship such as prime plus 2 percent and the rate floats up and down whenever the prime rate changes.

Commercial Paper

  3. **Commercial paper** is a short-term (270 days or less) marketable security issued by large businesses having excellent credit ratings.

    a. These IOUs are lower-cost sources than bank loans, but not everyone can raise funds this way—only the biggest and best can do so.

    b. Most issuers of commercial paper have to arrange lines of credit with banks to help assure repayment of the commercial paper when it matures.

    c. Investors in commercial paper include other firms, small banks, and financial institutions.

    d. About half of the paper is sold directly to investors by a few finance companies such as GMAC and GE Credit.

    e. The impersonal nature of the commercial paper market means that a company can find this source of credit unavailable if financial difficulties arise. Banks tend to be more loyal to their customers and more willing to stand behind them in time of trouble.

Secured Borrowing

C. **Secured borrowing** is used by firms whose credit rating is not high enough to qualify them for unsecured loans.

  1. Assets, called **collateral,** are pledged as security for the loan. If troubles occur, the lender has first claim on the collateral.

Accounts Receivable

  2. **Accounts receivable** serve as excellent collateral.

    a. Under a **general lien** the firm pledges all its accounts receivable for a loan of up to approximately 75 percent of the receivables outstanding.

    b. An alternative approach is for the lender to first review the receivables, rejecting those judged to be too risky. Since this procedure leads to higher-quality collateral, the lender will lend a higher percentage of face value—perhaps 90 percent or more, compared with a lesser amount under the general lien approach.

Factoring	c. The cost of accounts receivable lending is high because both borrower and lender must keep close track of the receivables.
	d. **Factoring** is the *sale* of accounts receivable.
	i. The factor, who is the buyer, usually performs credit and collection services, thereby relieving the firm of the need to maintain a credit department.
	ii. However, factors are not in business for their health only, and so they pass their costs on to the firm, making this source of financing fairly expensive.
Credit Cards	e. **Bank credit cards** provide retailers with a source of financing using accounts receivable. This is similar to factoring, *except:*
	i. The accounts receivable come from consumers instead of businesses.
	ii. The credit card customer doesn't identify with the store as strongly as one business does with another that has factored its accounts receivable. For this reason many large retailers have kept their own charge account systems rather than replace them with bank credit cards.
Inventory Loans	3. Inventory items that have a ready market are often used as loan collateral. Raw materials and finished goods such as grains, chemicals, new cars, and lumber are acceptable security, whereas perishable goods, work-in-process, and items of widely fluctuating values are not suitable.
	a. Under a **general lien,** the firm pledges all its inventory as collateral.
Floor Planning	b. In a **floor planning** arrangement, specific goods are identified and pledged as security. Cars, farm equipment, and other durable goods are the most common examples. The lender, which can be a bank, finance company, or the manufacturer, is repaid when an item is sold.
Warehousing	c. Because the lender must periodically verify the existence and condition of the pledged inventory, a third-party specialist, called a **warehousing company,** is sometimes hired to provide control via a warehousing arrangement.
	i. In a **field warehouse** this third party controls the pledged inventory at the borrower's premises.
	ii. Tighter control results when the pledged goods are stored in a **public warehouse.** This adds costs for moving goods in and out of storage and makes them less accessible to the borrower. This type of secured arrangement is the most expensive of all—there just are no free lunches.
Financing Complexities	D. **Financing international trade** is more complex than financing domestic business because of risks of foreign exchange fluctuations, the increased difficulty of credit evaluation and bill collection, and the longer shipping times.

Foreign Exchange Risk

1. The **foreign exchange risk** is due to the potential movements of exchange rates between order and payment dates.
   a. There is no foreign exchange risk (or credit risk) if payment occurs when the order is placed.
   b. When payment is delayed, the exporter is exposed to foreign exchange risk if the goods are invoiced in the importer's currency and vice versa.

Forward Contract

   c. Foreign exchange risk can be eliminated by having whoever is exposed to the risk sell a **forward contract** to deliver the currency of the trading partner when payment is made.
   d. Another method of avoiding foreign exchange risk is to use the **money market.**
      i. The party exposed to the risk creates an offsetting liability or asset in the foreign currency.
      ii. The idea is to either borrow or invest now and then make or receive payments at the settlement date so as to offset the loan or the investment.
   e. The key to understanding these transactions is to remember that goods flow from exporter to importer and that payments flow in the opposite direction and involve an exchange of currencies either *now* or *later*. This process costs money, especially if risks are to be avoided.

Letters of Credit

2. **Letters of credit** are used to facilitate international trade.
   a. They specify that a bank will pay for the goods if certain conditions are met.

Irrevocable Import Letter of Credit

   b. In an **irrevocable import letter of credit,** the importer arranges for its bank to authorize another bank (often one near the exporter) to pay the exporter for the goods if the exporter presents sales, shipping, etc., documents.
      i. The bank's credit has been substituted for the importer's credit so far as both the exporter and its bank are concerned.
      ii. Banks trust banks because they usually keep their promises and therefore have excellent credit reputations.
   c. A letter of credit can be used to obtain financing.

Time Draft

      i. A **time draft** (a check) is made payable by the exporter at the future date specified in the letter of credit.

Banker's Acceptance

      ii. If the exporter's bank stamps "accepted" on the draft, it becomes a **banker's acceptance,** which is a legal obligation of the bank and is negotiable in money markets.
      iii. The exporter can sell the acceptance or use it as collateral for a low-cost loan.

COMPLETION QUESTIONS

costs

1. The critical factors to analyze for short-term financing sources are _____,

availability

either in terms of dollars or in terms of restrictions, and benefits that are related to the _____ of funds.

trade

2. The most important source of short-term financing is _____

credit, unsecured

_____. It is (*secured/unsecured*) interfirm debt.

payable

3. Accounts (*receivable/payable*) show the amount of trade credit used by a firm.

discount

4. Trade credit is free when payments are made within the (*discount/payment*) period.

cash

5. The cost of trade credit is the cost of forgoing the _____ discount.

higher

6. The (*lower/higher*) the cash discount, the higher the cost of trade credit.

shorter

7. The (*shorter/longer*) the payment period, the higher the cost of trade credit.

purchases, does not

8. Trade credit is related to (*sales/purchases*). It (*does/does not*) provide cash to pay other bills.

9. Firms incurring a bad credit reputation will experience their accounts (*re-*

payable, less

ceivable/payable) becoming (*less/more*) of a source of financing.

Bank loans

10. (*Bank loans/Commercial paper*) may be secured or unsecured.

self-liquidating

11. Seasonal loans are _____-_____ because they are

cash

used to finance items that are soon converted into _____ to repay the loan.

line of credit

12. In order to keep a(n) _____ _____ _____ from becoming long-term financing, banks require firms using this source to be out of debt at least one time during the year.

13. An extra fee is charged for a legal commitment by a bank to lend under a

revolving credit

_____ _____ agreement.

14. The requirement in a bank loan to maintain some minimum level in the

compensating balance

checking account is called a _____ _____. This may

higher

result in a (*lower/higher*) cost for the loan.

Interim

15. _____ financing is used to bridge the gap between the need for,

long

and availability of, (*short/long*)-term financing.

16. The interest rate charged by banks to their most creditworthy customers is

prime rate

called the _____ _____.

Ordinary	17. (*Ordinary/True*) interest is paid along with principal when the loan (*originates/matures*).
matures	
discount	18. In _____ loans, interest is deducted at the outset of the loan. This (*raises/lowers*) the true interest rate.
raises	
Floating, prime	19. _____ rate loans have interest rates that vary as the (*prime/discount*) rate changes.
nine	20. Commercial paper has a maturity of _____ months or less.
less	21. Commercial paper usually costs (*more/less*) than a bank loan.
commercial paper	22. In time of trouble (*bank credit/commercial paper*) is the first source of financing to dry up.
do not	23. Small firms (*do/do not*) issue commercial paper.
more	24. Secured borrowing is (*more/less*) expensive than unsecured financing.
receivable	25. As a rule, accounts (*receivable/payable*) are a better source of collateral than inventory.
general lien	26. Under a (*bond indenture/general lien*), all accounts receivable are pledged.
higher	27. If the lender can select from the receivables, a (*lower/higher*) percentage of the amount pledged will be lent.
sold, factoring	28. Accounts receivable are (*sold/bought*) instead of pledged in a _____ arrangement. This is typically a (*low/high*) cost of financing, because the _____ often performs credit and collection services.
high	
factor	
retailers	29. Bank credit cards are used by (*retailers/wholesalers*) for financing that is somewhat similar to _____.
factoring	
their own	30. Some large firms that sell to the public use (*bank credit card/their own*) charge account systems so as to maintain a stronger customer identification with the firm.
canned	31. An example of inventory suitable as loan collateral is (*fresh/canned*) peaches.
is not	32. High-fashion clothing inventory usually (*is/is not*) acceptable loan security.
	33. The dealer's stock of cars or farm equipment might be financed by a (*public warehouse/floor planning*) arrangement. The lender could be a bank, a finance company, or the (*customer/manufacturer*).
floor planning	
manufacturer	
inventory	34. Control of pledged (*accounts receivable/inventory*) by a warehousing company on the borrower's premises is done through a (*public/field*) warehousing arrangement.
field	
monetary	35. Exchange rate (*monetary/conversion*) risk is the result of alterations in balance sheet accounts caused by movements in exchange rates.

36. If foreign exchange rates shift, the competitive position of a firm is affected. This is known as the exchange rate (*business/government*) risk. — *business*

37. By paying when ordering, the importer (*avoids/adds to*) foreign exchange risk. In this case the burden of financing is placed on the (*buyer/seller*). — *avoids*, *buyer*

38. Goods flow from _____ to _____, and payments flow from _____ to _____. — *exporter, importer*, *importer, exporter*

39. In a(n) _____ _____ _____ the credit of a (*bank/government*) is used in place of the credit of a firm. — *letter of credit*, *bank*

40. A letter of credit may be used in financing international trade by creating a(n) _____. — *draft*

41. (*Time/Sight*) drafts are used for payments to be made after the order date. — *Time*

PROBLEMS

1. Musselman Variety has an average accounts payable balance of $10,000.
   a. If it is purchasing an average of $200 per day from its supplier, how long is this firm waiting to pay its bills on the average?

Solution

Step one Accounts payable equal purchases per day times the number of days bills are outstanding, or

$$\text{Days outstanding} = \frac{\$10,000}{\$200}$$

$$= 50$$

   b. Suppose the supplier in problem 1a has net 50 terms. If another supplier offers credit terms of net 60, what would be the advantage of buying from the other source?

Solution

Step one The new accounts payable balance would increase to $12,000 (60 × $200).

Step two This represents an additional $2000 of free financing, assuming that the prices, quality, and other features of the goods are the same. This source of financing is limited to the purchase of goods, but it does permit the firm to use cash for other purposes.

    c. Suppose a third vendor offers the same goods, services, etc., and offers credit terms of 3/15, net 60. Which supplier should be chosen?

Solution

Step one The cost of credit from the first supplier is zero for fifty days. It is zero for sixty days from the second supplier, and for the third vendor it is

$$\text{Annual interest rate} = \frac{3}{100 - 3} \times \frac{365}{60 - 15} = .251, \text{ or } 25.1\%$$

Step two Vendor 3 is used only if the firm's borrowing cost is higher than 25.1 percent. Musselman Variety should borrow funds if it can raise them for less than 25.1 percent and pay this supplier cash on the fifteenth day after purchase.

2. ABC Construction Corporation has been granted a $500,000 line of credit from its bank. The interest rate on funds borrowed is 1 percent above the prime rate (currently at 7 percent), and the bank requires a compensating balance of 15 percent of the amount actually borrowed plus 10 percent of the unborrowed portion.
    a. What are the compensating balances when ABC has borrowed $300,000 and secondly, when the full credit line is used?

Solution

Step one When $300,000 is borrowed, $200,000 of credit is unused; thus the compensating balance would be 0.15 × $300,000 + 0.10 × $200,000 = $65,000.

Step two When the full line of credit is borrowed, the compensating balance would be 0.15 × $500,000 = $75,000.

b. Suppose the firm borrows $300,000 on its line. What is the effective interest rate paid if it keeps an average working balance of $25,000, irrespective of any compensating-balance requirements?

Solution

Step one When ABC borrows $300,000, its compensating balance, as figured in problem 2a, is $65,000.

Step two The firm normally keeps $25,000 in its bank account, and so it must have an additional $40,000 ($65,000 − $25,000) on deposit, which reduces the funds available from the loan to $260,000 ($300,000 − $40,000).

Step three The interest rate is prime plus 1 percent, or 8 percent. The interest paid, on an annual basis, is $24,000 (0.08 × $300,000).

Step four The effective rate per year is $24,000/$260,000 × 100 = 9.23 percent.

c. Assume that ABC wants to formalize its bank borrowing by establishing a revolving credit arrangement. If all other terms remain the same except that the bank charges an additional fee of 1 percent on the unused credit, what is the cost of borrowing $300,000 for one year?

Solution

Step one The only change from problem 2b is the additional fee of $2000 (0.01 × $200,000).

Step two The effective annual rate is:

$$($24,000 + $2000)/$260,000 \times 100 = 10 \text{ percent}$$

3. Compare the financing costs of First National Bank, which charges 10 percent ordinary interest, with those of First State Bank, which quotes a 9 percent rate on a discount basis.

Solution

Step one For comparison purposes, interest rates are usually converted to the same basis as the ordinary rate.

Step two The discount loan rate of First State Bank is the amount of interest charged divided by the actual funds available. For a $1000 loan this would be $90/($1000 − $90) × 100 = 9.89 percent.

Step three This is lower-cost financing, compared with the 10 percent ordinary interest at First National Bank.

Step four Step two could be worked for any loan amount or solved using percentages; the answer would always be 9.89 percent.

4. What is the effective annual rate for $20 million of commercial paper that can be sold for 7 percent if it must be accompanied by a backup line of credit that costs 1 percent of the credit line and requires a deposit balance of $1 million over normal balances?

Solution

Step one The cost per year is (0.08 × $20 million) or $1,600,000.

Step two The funds available, in millions of dollars, are $20 (amount borrowed) − $1.6 (interest—commercial paper interest is discounted) − $1 (additional compensating balance) = $17.40.

Step three The effective interest rate is $1.6/$17.40 × 100 = 9.2 percent.

CHAPTER TWENTY

WORKING CAPITAL MANAGEMENT

QUINTESSENCE   Current assets minus current liabilities equals net working capital. The short-term accounts are managed for the purposes of meeting production and sales requirements, minimizing financing costs, and producing liquidity. The interests of the business are best accomplished by matching the maturity of the financing source with the length of the financing need. The yield curve shows the costs of short- and long-term borrowing. It is used to aid in making financing decisions involving trade-offs between risks and costs. The interrelationships of sales, working capital, and expansion projects need to be evaluated for capital budgeting as well as for the specific decisions of amount and type of current assets and current liabilities.

OUTLINE
  I. What
    A. The management of working capital decisions relating to:
      1. Current assets and current liabilities.
      2. The amount of long-term financing used to pay for current assets.
    B. The **matching principle** specifies that short-term needs be financed with short-term sources and that long-term needs be paid with long-term sources.
    C. Yield curves aid in short- versus long-term financing decisions.
  II. Why
    A. Current assets and current liabilities must be analyzed as interrelated decisions.
    B. Matching the length of sources and uses exposes the firm to less risk and results in lower financing costs.
    C. Growth in sales normally requires additional financing.
  III. How

Working Capital
    A. **Working capital** is current assets minus current liabilities, which is also called net working capital. It is the long-term financing portion of short-term needs. (Think about this statement—remember that the *balance* sheet means the net working capital will be "balanced" with an equal amount in the long-term liabilities or equity accounts.)

1. Long-term debt agreements may specify the maintenance of a minimum amount of net working capital.
2. The level and management difficulty of working capital is determined by:
   a. Basic characteristics of the business—lots of inventory for a retailer, not much for an electric utility (you can't store juice).
   b. The complexities involved in controlling each of the current accounts in a company—a bowling alley is simple compared with a department store.

Relationships with Sales

3. Current assets are interrelated among themselves as well as with current liabilities.
   a. Increased sales lead to more accounts receivable, inventory, cash, purchases to build the inventory, and resulting additions to accounts payable.
   b. To analyze the impacts of a change in the level of a particular account the expected cash flows resulting from the shift are compared with the change in the investment. Present value calculations are used, and if more accuracy is desired, the precise timing of each cash flow is taken into account.
   c. **Pro forma** financial statements are also used to help make decisions.

Matching Principle

B. The principle of matching the maturity of the source of funds with the time period of use is based on minimizing risk and cost.
   1. If long-term needs are financed with short-term loans, the firm will have to refinance many times. This adds a risk that new borrowing will be unavailable or available only at higher costs. Transaction costs from repeated borrowings will also be higher.
   2. If short-term needs are financed with long-term sources, there will be times when a company will have excess funds that may have to be invested in low-yielding securities.

Permanent Working Capital

   3. Financing fixed assets and **permanent working capital** with long-term sources *is desirable*. This need is equal to the difference between the minimum investment in current assets needed to sustain current sales and the permanent current liabilities that are tied directly to sales.

Yield Curves

   4. The **yield curve** helps explain the trade-off between risk and financing cost.
      a. This graph is a plot of interest rates for different maturities of debt.

Influences

      b. The shape of the yield curve is determined by:
         i. The current level of short-term interest rates.
         ii. Investors' and borrowers' expectations of future rates.
         iii. Risk premiums for investors to own longer-term debt.

Risk Premium for Long-Term Debt

      c. The curve is typically upward-sloping, which means long-term rates are usually higher than short-term rates. This relationship is normal because:

i. An increase in interest rates causes long-term securities to decline in price more than the drop in short-term debt values. The longer maturities are more risky and should offer higher returns.

ii. Interest and principal payments are more uncertain the further in the future they are—again, more risk dictates higher returns (interest rates).

Risk and Return Trade-Off

d. An upward-sloping yield curve indicates investors believe interest rates are increasing. This results because people buy short-term securities, forcing prices up and yields down. They plan to reinvest in long-term bonds later when interest rates have risen.

e. The typical risk premium on long-term debt presents a *dilemma*.

i. Short-term debt is cheaper, but

ii. Short-term debt is riskier. Interest rates and the firm's ability to refinance are uncertain, and too much short-term debt would result in low or negative net working capital, which lenders don't like to see.

Liquidity

5. **Liquidity** is the ability to raise cash by converting assets or by taking advantage of unused but available credit.

a. **Planned liquidity** is based on forecasts of cash flows.

b. **Protective liquidity** is needed to meet unexpected cash demands. The nature of the industry and the particular firm will determine how conservative the liquidity level will be.

Risk and Return

6. There is a trade-off between the level of investment in current assets and the amount of short-term financing.

a. Aggressive policies call for lower amounts of working capital by keeping cash and equivalent (short-term investments) to a minimum and using lots of short-term financing.

b. Conservative policies opt for safety at a cost of forgone returns.

c. Recall the importance of the nature of the business in determining appropriate levels of working capital.

i. What is highly risky in one type of operation may be OK in another.

ii. Industry norms can serve as a rough guide to working capital policies.

Working Capital and Growth

7. Working capital needs must be included in the appraisal of proposed business expansion (capital budgeting).

a. Add the additional current assets required.

b. Subtract the current liabilities that are automatically generated.

c. Using the changes in working capital will be approximately correct. For better accuracy, the timing of the cash flows must be used.

COMPLETION QUESTIONS

matching 1. The _____ principle specifies that short-term needs be financed
short   with _____-term sources.

net working 2. Current assets minus current liabilities equals _____ _____
capital   _____.

increased 3. Increased sales are typically accompanied by (*increased/decreased*) bank
decreased   loans and (*increased/decreased*) cash balances.

4. If short-term financing were used for long-term needs, financing costs and
increase   risks would likely (*increase/decrease*).

is 5. It (*is/is not*) advisable to finance permanent working capital with long-term
   sources.

short 6. Temporary working capital should be financed with _____-term
   sources.

yield 7. The _____ curve is a plot of interest rates versus debt maturities.

higher 8. Long-term rates are typically (*lower/higher*) compared with short-term rates.

lower 9. An increase in interest rates will cause (*greater/lower*) price declines in
   short-term debt as opposed to long-term debt.

upward 10. Yield curves are usually (*upward/downward*)-sloping.

11. A downward-sloping yield curve indicates investors are expecting interest
decline   rates to (*rise/decline*).

Liquidity 12. _____ is the ability to raise cash.

Planned 13. (*Planned/Protective*) liquidity is based on forecasts of cash flow.

Protective 14. (*Planned/Protective*) liquidity is needed to meet unexpected cash demands.

increase 15. Normally, working capital needs for capital budgeting projects will (*increase/
   decrease*) the amount of the investment.

16. Examples of natural increases in current liabilities that accompany expanded
payable   sales are accounts and wages (*receivable/payable*).

1. Liquidity, Inc.'s balance sheet is as follows (in thousands of dollars):

Assets		Liabilities and net worth	
Cash and securities.......	$ 400	Bank loan................	$ 800
Accounts receivable	1,200	Accounts payable	1,100
Inventory	900	Long-term bonds.........	2,200
Net plant	4,500	Owners' equity...........	2,900
Total	$7,000	Total	$7,000

What is Liquidity, Inc.'s working capital (net working capital position)?

Solution

Step one The sum of current assets is

$$\$400 + \$1200 + \$900 = \$2500$$

Step two Net working capital equals current assets minus current liabilities (this is the same as working capital in common parlance).

$$(\$400 + \$1200 + \$900) - (\$800 + \$1100) = \$600$$

2. Sales for Liquidity, Inc., are forecast to be $6 million next year. Accounts receivable and inventory are typically 24 and 18 percent of sales, respectively. How much additional financing will be required?

Solution

Step one The accounts receivable next year will be 24 percent of $6 million, or $1,440,000.

Step two The year began with $1,200,000 in accounts receivable, so the increase is $1,440,000 − $1,200,000, or $240,000.

Step three   By similar logic, the increase in inventory is (.18 × $6,000,000) − $900,000, or $180,000.

Step four   Additional financing for these two terms is $240,000 + $180,000, or $420,000.

3. Given the information in problems 1 and 2, how much spontaneous trade credit will be generated if purchases average 22 percent of sales?

Solution

Step one   The accounts payable will be 22 percent of $6 million, or $1,320,000. This is an increase of $220,000 over last year's level of $1,100,000.

Step two   Needs of $420,000 exceed the spontaneous amount by $200,000, which is the additional financing that would be required.

4. What would be likely ways to finance Liquidity, Inc.'s needs?

Solution

Step one   The *matching* principle should be a major determining factor of the type of financing. If sales were expected to remain at $6 million or above, or if the firm felt liquidity should be increased, some permanent source such as long-term debt or equity could be chosen. If sales were expected to fluctuate or if the amount of liquidity could be reduced, then temporary financing could be employed. Bank loans would be one of the most likely sources of short-term financing. *End of solution.*

5. The Sporthaus sells boating and waterskiing equipment in the summer and snow-skiing equipment in the winter. Monthly cash flows, in thousands of dollars, for the coming year are forecast as follows:

	Jan.	Feb.	Mar.	Apr.	May	June	July	Aug.	Sept.	Oct.	Nov.	Dec.
Inflow	30	15	30	20	25	30	35	30	60	40	45	65
Outflow	50	40	50	45	15	15	30	65	35	40	40	15

Assuming next year to be typical, how much "permanent" and how much temporary financing is needed by this firm?

Solution

Step one The permanent financing is the minimum cash requirement during the forecast period—needs above this amount are temporary.

Step two The cumulative cash position reveals the financing needs:

Outflow	Jan.	Feb.	Mar.	Apr.	May	June	July	Aug.	Sept.	Oct.	Nov.	Dec.
Net cash flow	(20)	(25)	(20)	(25)	10	15	5	(35)	25	0	5	50
Cumulative cash flow	(20)	(45)	(65)	(90)	(80)	(65)	(60)	(95)	(70)	(70)	(65)	(15)

Step three The minimum needed, which is the permanent financing, is $15,000 (in December). All other months require more financing.

Step four The maximum amount of temporary financing occurs in August. Assuming that $15,000 of permanent financing would be acquired, the firm will need to borrow a short-term amount of ($95 − $15), or $80,000.

Step five The permanent type of financing should be secured from some long-term loan or the sale of common stock. The temporary financing would probably come from a line of credit. The short-term loan would be repaid in December, at the point of minimum need.

CHAPTER TWENTY-ONE

LEASING

QUINTESSENCE　Companies want assets because they can use them to produce the goods and services that they sell. Assets can be purchased or rented by a lease agreement. A variety of leases are available: operating leases are short-term and not entered on the balance sheet; financial leases are longer-term, capitalized on the balance sheet and noncancelable; the lessor (owner) provides maintenance in a maintenance lease; an asset is sold by the user and leased back from the buyer in a sale and leaseback; and a third party finances the asset in a leveraged lease. Multinational corporations use leases to take advantage of different tax rates and currency controls in different countries. The analysis of lease or buy decisions begins by computing net present values of each alternative. Other factors to evaluate for each situation are the cash drain, the effect on borrowing capacity, restrictions that accompany the asset acquisition, who bears the risk of obsolescence, and how the tax benefits of owning are reflected in the lease payments. Competition for leasing customers and the many different parties involved means that each factor must be considered for every particular deal—generalizations are not appropriate.

OUTLINE
I. What
　A. A lease is a contract that specifies that the user of an asset (the lessee) will pay the owner (the lessor) a rental for the right to use the asset.
　B. Major types of leases include operating, financial, sale and leaseback, full-service, and leveraged leases.
　C. The net present value method is used for analyzing the costs and benefits of lease versus buy decisions.
　D. Alleged advantages and disadvantages of other considerations must be examined on a case by case basis.

II. Why
　A. "Just because you like beer, why buy a brewery?" This was the theme of a leasing company's ad that pointed out the idea that it's what the assets produce that is wanted, not the title to the assets themselves. Leasing is a way of acquiring the *use* of assets without having to own them.

303

B. The popularity of leasing has increased greatly throughout the world.
   1. One-fifth of all new equipment in the United States is leased.
   2. Entire plants may be leased.
C. An evaluation of leases requires careful analysis of the numbers via present value calculations *and* an appraisal of the qualitative impacts of leasing versus buying alternatives.

III. How

Leasing Participants

A. In addition to the lessee and lessor, a lender may supply the money in a **leveraged lease** arrangement, or a **lease packager** may be involved in an arranging role.
   1. Manufacturers set up approximately 50 percent of all equipment leases.
   2. Banks act as lenders for 33 percent. The remainder of equipment leasing is done by independent leasing companies.
B. There are five major types of leases offered by various leasing organizations, lease packagers, and manufacturers.

Operating Lease

   1. An **operating lease** for such items as computers and vehicles is for an indefinite, although usually short, period. Maintenance and other services may be provided by the lessor. Operating leases are not capitalized (entered on the balance sheet).

Financial Lease

   2. A **financial lease** involves an intermediate- or long-term commitment by the lessor and lessee. These leases can cover real estate, airplanes, and office and construction equipment.
      a. Maintenance is usually not provided by the lessor.
      b. Equipment leases are arranged by banks, finance companies, and leasing companies who buy assets wanted by businesses and then lease those assets to them.
      c. Options to renew or purchase allow the lessee to continue use of the asset after the initial lease expires.
      d. Financial leases are like debt: missing the payments results in serious trouble.

Sale and Leaseback

   3. A **sale and leaseback** enables a firm to convert an asset into cash. Under such an arrangement the company sells one of its assets to another party and then leases it back from that buyer. Sale and leaseback arrangements are financial leases and are most often used with real estate.

Full-Service

Net Lease

   4. In **full-service leases (maintenance leases)** the lessor provides the maintenance. They are short-term, like operating leases, but are the opposite of **net leases,** which have the lessee pay for maintenance, insurance, and property taxes.

Leveraged Lease

   5. A **leveraged lease** is a **third-party lease** in which the lessor borrows from a lender (the third party) to acquire the asset and then applies the lease rentals to repay the loan.
      a. Depreciation benefits are allocated to the lessor.
      b. With costly items, a **trust** is often created to buy the asset with equity funds from the lessor and debt monies obtained by selling

mortgage bonds. This helps to further limit the lessor's liability, because the lessee guarantees the bonds.

Tax Factors
1975 Act

C. Taxation issues are key factors in leasing.

1. Compliance with 1975 tax law provisions is required to enable the lessee to deduct lease payments and to permit the lessor to claim normal benefits of ownership through depreciation. To qualify:

   a. The lessor must always have a 20 percent investment in the asset value during the life of the lease.

   b. The asset's residual value must be at least 20 percent of its original cost and the lease period must be at least one year or 20 percent of the estimated life, whichever is longer.

   c. If the lessee is given an option to buy the asset when the lease expires, the purchase must be *voluntary* and based on fair market value.

   d. The lessee may not participate in financing the acquisition of the asset.

   e. The lessor must anticipate a profit, beyond the tax benefits, from the lease.

1981 Act

2. The Economic Recovery Tax Act of 1981 redefined the qualifications for tax treatment of leases for *corporate borrowers:*

   a. At least a 10 percent investment.

   b. A minimum term of at least the asset's class life under the Accelerated Cost Recovery System.

   c. A maximum term of no more than the greater of:

      i. 90 percent of the asset's expected useful life or

      ii. 150 percent of the Asset Depreciation Range class life for the asset.

True Lease

3. The changes of qualifications for a **true lease** in 1981 resulted in many sale and leaseback arrangements. Assets were sold by companies with low or nonexistent profits to firms having considerable amounts of taxable income.

1986 Act

4. The corporate alternative minimum tax (AMT), created by the **1986 Tax Reform Act,** established a new incentive for leasing and offset the elimination of the investment tax credit.

   a. A firm that is subject to the AMT can lease from a company that is not.

   b. The depreciation benefits gained by the lessor can be passed on in the form of lower lease rentals.

Accounting Aspects
Capital Lease

D. There are two alternatives of **accounting for leases:**

1. A **capital lease** treats the lessee as the owner.

   a. This means the lessee's balance sheet will show the present value of all future lease payments as an asset and as a liability.

   b. To qualify for this accounting treatment:

      i. Ownership must transfer to the lessee at the end of the lease.

      ii. The cost at time of transfer must be nominal.

iii. The lease term must be at least 75 percent of the asset's useful life.

iv. The present value of all lease payments must be at least 90 percent of the fair market value of the asset.

Operating Lease

2. Leases that are not capital are considered as **operating leases** and are not "capitalized" on the balance sheet.

International Leasing

E. **International leasing** involves a lessor in one country and a lessee in another.

1. Both parties are often subsidiaries of an MNC.

2. Typically, a business in a low tax rate country will lease from a firm in a high tax rate nation with each company being able to realize the depreciation benefits of ownership.

3. Expropriation risk may be reduced by operating leased assets that are owned outside the politically unstable country.

4. Sometimes exchange controls can be circumvented because lease payments will still be allowed.

Lease or Buy Analysis

Purchase Expenses

F. **Lease** or **buy analysis** is based on the *net present value of the cash flows* associated with each alternative.

1. Compute the NPV of purchasing the asset. Expenses include:
   a. Costs of maintenance.
   b. Any interest charges incurred.
   c. Income taxes after allowing for depreciation.
   d. Estimated salvage value. (This is actually a recovery of part of the initial investment.)

Lease Expenses

2. Compute the NPV of leasing the asset. The cash flows are determined by subtracting cash expenses, lease payments, and income taxes from the revenues generated by the asset.

3. Choose the option with the highest NPV if it is zero or above. (Otherwise the NPV would be negative, meaning the asset should not be acquired by any means since it does not earn the minimum required rate of return.)

Selecting Discount Rates

4. The discount rates used in the NPV calculations should reflect the risks involved that are *greater* for the leasing situation.
   a. The *net* cash flows generated each year in the purchase option are amounts that must be considered as available for equity *and* any debt used to buy the asset.
   b. The net cash flows generated in the case of leasing are available to equity *only*, because the lease payments have already been deducted when the net cash flows were computed.
   c. Remember, it is the *net* cash flows that are being used to estimate the benefits from leasing or from buying the assets.
   d. Since the cash flows generated in the purchase option are available to cover *both* equity and debt, they represent a less risky situation.

Use Higher Rate for Leasing

   e. This means that a higher discount rate should be applied in evaluating a lease compared with the appropriate rate to be used for a purchase. (This is further explained in footnote 13 in the textbook.)

5. See problem 1 at the end of this chapter for an illustration of the calculations described above.

G. Other things to consider in lease or buy decisions are:

Other Factors
Cash

1. **Cash availability,** which is not affected differently by either choice *unless* the company can lease the asset but cannot borrow the necessary funds to buy it.

Debt Capacity

2. Because leasing and borrowing are considered to be similar by lenders, there is no significant reason why leasing might increase the **borrowing capacity** of a firm.

Convenience

3. Leasing does have the advantage of **convenience,** because assets can be leased for a short time at a known cost with relatively few legal efforts required and no sales taxes are involved.

Restrictions

4. **Restrictions** may be imposed by lenders to help improve the firm's capacity to repay the debt. Lessors also establish controls to protect their own interests, namely, the leased assets. The marketplace normally reflects these constraints. Any benefits from having no restrictions will result in higher costs.

Obsolescence

5. The **risk of obsolescence** is passed on to the lessee through higher lease payments *unless* the lessor is better able to find economic uses for outmoded assets and unless competition causes lessors to reflect their efficiency in a lowering of their charges.

Salvage

6. The anticipated **salvage value** is reflected in lease payments; the higher the salvage value, the lower the lease payments. The advantage of either buying or leasing depends on whose guess concerning the salvage value turns out best, *but* no one can accurately predict the future, and so this consideration is usually not treated as a benefit to either party at the time of the decision.

Taxes

7. **Tax benefits** of depreciation belong to the owner, which favors buying over leasing *unless* competition forces lessors, who are also owners, to pass on these benefits. It is possible to have your cake and eat it too. Tax benefits can work to the advantage of both lessor and lessee when the owner is in a higher tax bracket than the renter and they share in these reduced taxes. It works this way because the deductions help the owner more than the renter. Competition for customers causes the owner to pass on part of this benefit.

8. None of the above considerations can be categorically said to favor either buying or leasing. Each decision must be individually analyzed; there may be some definite advantages to one form or the other, but it all depends on the parties involved and the particular deal.

COMPLETION QUESTIONS

lessor
lessee

1. The owner of the asset is the _____, and the user is the _____.

use of
title to

2. Most firms are interested primarily in the (*use of/title to*) an asset, as opposed to the (*use of/title to*) it.

Operating

3. (*Operating/Financial*) leases are relatively short-lived.

Financial

4. (*Operating/Financial*) leases are similar to debt.

asset
cash

5. A sale and leaseback enables a firm to convert a(n) (*asset/liability*) into (*cash/profit*).

short, operating
lessor

6. A full-service maintenance lease is (*short/long*)-term, like a(n) _____ lease; the (*lessor/lessee*) provides the maintenance.

leveraged, lessor

7. A(n) _____ lease is a third-party lease in which the (*lessor/lessee*) acquires the asset by borrowing from a lender.

encouraged

8. The Economic Recovery Tax Act of 1981 contained provisions that (*encouraged/discouraged*) companies to make sale and leaseback arrangements.

expropriation

9. Leasing of assets by a foreign subsidiary of an MNC is a way of avoiding (*expropriation/financial*) risk.

present values, buy

10. Net (*profits/present values*) are used in analyzing lease or _____ decisions, because the choice should be based on the contribution of net

cash flows

(*profits/cash flows*) to the welfare of the firm.

purchased

11. When the asset is (*purchased/leased*), costs of operation, including depreciation and interest associated with any debt financing used, are deductible expenses.

lessor

12. Depreciation is deductible from taxes due from the (*lessor/lessee*).

lessor

13. Salvage value is a cash inflow to the (*lessor/lessee*).

discount

14. The (*yield/discount*) rate used to evaluate a lease is the required rate of return on assets of comparable risk.

more

15. Cash flows associated with a lease are typically (*more/less*) risky than those in a purchase.

positive

16. The preferred choice between leasing and buying is the alternative that results in the highest (*positive/negative*) net present value.

less

17. Leasing results in (*more/less*) of a cash drain only if the company can lease the asset but cannot borrow funds to buy it.

better, may not	18. On the surface, leasing looks (*better/worse*) because it (*does/may not*) add debt to the capital structure.
is not	19. In most cases, borrowing capacity (*is/is not*) greater if a firm leases instead of buys its assets.
present value	20. For leased assets that are included on the balance sheet, the liability would be the _____ _____ of the lease payments.
higher	21. If restrictions are not imposed on the firm by lenders or lessors, (*higher/lower*) costs to the firm will normally result.
higher	22. A high risk of obsolescence will normally be reflected in (*higher/lower*) lease payments.
does not	23. The fact that the lessor gets the tax advantages of taking depreciation (*does/does not*) favor buying over leasing.
buyer, seller	24. If the (*buyer/seller*) is in a higher tax bracket than the (*buyer/seller*), it may be desirable to arrange a lease.
smaller	25. The greater the salvage value, the (*smaller/larger*) the lease payments will be.
is not	26. It (*is/is not*) possible to generalize about whether each consideration in lease or buy decisions favors one route or the other.

PROBLEMS

1. Walter's Grocery is going to install a sign in front of the store. The installed price is $10,000, or the sign can be leased for $4500 per year, including maintenance. If the sign were purchased, maintenance expenses would be $2666 per year. The lease runs for the estimated life of the sign, which is ten years. Assuming no salvage value, straight-line depreciation, discount rates of 10 percent for leasing and 8 percent for buying, and an income tax rate of 40 percent, should Walter lease or buy the sign?

Solution

Step one In this problem, the decision to acquire the sign has already been made. Theoretically, the justification should be based on a positive net present value of the costs and benefits of estimated additional sales that will result from the new sign, but Walter is convinced that the new sign will be worth it. This means that the decision concerning how to acquire it will be based on which alternative costs the least.

Step two The costs of purchasing are as follows:

Years	Maintenance	Depreciation	Total expense before tax	Tax savings = tax rate × expenses	Cash expenses = tax + maintenance
1–10	$2,666	$1,000	$3,666	−$1,466	$1,200

$$\text{Present value} = \text{cost of sign} + \text{present value of expenses}$$
$$= \$10,000 + \$1200 \times (P/A, 8\%, 10)$$
$$= \$10,000 + \$1200 \times 6.7101$$
$$= \$18,052$$

Step three The costs of leasing are as follows:

Years	Lease expense	Aftertax expense
1-10	$4,500	$2,700

$$\text{Present value} = \$2700 \times (P/A, 10\%, 10)$$
$$= \$2700 \times 6.1446$$
$$= \$16,590$$

Step four The present value of the leasing costs is lower, and so it should be favored.

Step five If the net benefit from increased business could be estimated, this information would be used. The net present value of each option could then be computed, and the choice would be whichever alternative provided the highest positive net present value. The difficulty with the sign decision as analyzed here is that we have assumed that a new sign will result in a positive net present value.

2. Now suppose that Walter has second thoughts about even acquiring the sign at all. He wonders what is the minimum amount of new business the sign must attract in order to be economically justified. He figures that his variable costs amount to 90 percent of sales. Give yourself a triple star if you can answer Walter's question.

Solution

Step one The principle involved here is that the additional net cash inflow must be at least equal to the cash outflow.

Step two Since leasing was determined in problem 1 to be the lower-cost alternative, the cash outflows are $2700 per year.

Step three Variable costs are 90 percent of sales S, and so the additional cash inflows before taxes will be $0.1S$ each year. (Remember that fixed costs don't change.) The aftertax cash inflows will be $0.1S \times .6$, or $0.06S$.

Step four The minimum annual sales needed are figured from the equation showing cash inflows equal to cash outflows, or

$$0.06S = \$2700$$
$$S = \$45,000$$

Step five Now Walter can sleep better if he thinks the sign will bring in more than this amount of new business each year.

3. Kathleen's Kamper Kits, Inc., is considering the purchase of land and a building for $1 million. The property can be leased for 18 years for an annual rental of $100,000 for the first 5 years and $150,000 for years 6 through 18. The estimated aftertax sales price of the property is $750,000 at the end of the lease. The building is depreciable at an annual rate of $50,000. Assuming that lessee pays maintenance and that KKK pays property taxes of $15,000 per year and has an income tax rate of 40 percent, should the investment be made if a minimum aftertax return of 15 percent is required?

Solution

Step one Determine cash flows as follows:

Item	Years 1–5	Years 6–18	Year 18
Lease income	$100,000	$150,000	
Less property tax	(15,000)	(15,000)	
Less depreciation	(50,000)	(50,000)	
Equals taxable income	$ 35,000	$ 85,000	
Income tax (40%)	14,000	34,000	
Net cash flow	71,000	101,000	$750,000

Step two

$$\text{The net present value} = -\$1,000,000 + \$71,000 \times (P/A, 15\%, 5)$$
$$+ \$101,000 \times (P/A, 15\%, 13) \times (P/F, 15\%, 5)$$
$$+ \$750,000 \times (P/F, 15\%, 18)$$
$$= -\$1,000,000 + \$71,000 \times 3.3522$$
$$+ \$101,000 \times 5.5831 \times 0.4972$$
$$+ \$750,000 \times 0.0808$$
$$= -\$421,000$$

Step three Because the NPV is negative, the return is less than the minimum of 15 percent, and so the purchase should be rejected.

4. A nonprofit hospital is considering acquiring $225,000 in x-ray equipment that leases for $40,000 per year on a ten-year lease. What is the implied rate of return used by the lessor if any salvage value is ignored?

Solution

Step one The lessor sets the lease payments as the amount needed to provide a present value equal to the cost of the machine when the cash flows are discounted at the required rate of return.

Step two

$$\$225,000 = \$40,000 \times (P/A, i, 10)$$
$$(P/A, i, 10) = 5.625$$

This factor indicates an interest rate of approximately 12 percent.

Step three If the hospital can borrow at less than 12 percent, it should buy the x-ray machine. Taxes don't affect its decision, because it is nonprofit and doesn't pay any taxes.

5. Art's Boating Company has a chance to pay $5000 per year for a thirty-year lease to a lakefront site for a marina. What would be the asset and liability on ABC's balance sheet if the lease were to be capitalized at 10 percent?

Solution

Step one The present value of the lease payments would be

$$\text{Present value} = \$5000 \times (P/A,\ 10\%,\ 30)$$
$$= \$5000 \times 9.4269$$
$$= \$47,135$$

Step two This amount would be entered as an asset, "leased property under capital lease," and also as "capital lease obligations" on the liabilities side of the balance sheet.

CHAPTER TWENTY-TWO

CONVERTIBLES AND WARRANTS

QUINTESSENCE

Companies need to offer a variety of securities to be able to attract funds at minimal cost. Convertibles and warrants have a special appeal to investors because they offer them an option to acquire common stock. Convertible bonds and convertible preferred stock have an investment value based on the future interest and principal or dividend payments. They also have a conversion value related to the market price of the stock into which they can be converted. The actual market price of the convertibles will always be at or above one of these support values, and so these securities offer a relatively safe return and a potential opportunity for gain. From the firm's standpoint, the conversion privilege, which is a "sweetener" for investors, will result in savings in interest and dividend payments. Warrants offer a similar attraction except that they do not entitle the holders to interest, dividend, or voting privileges and they are exercised by paying additional cash to the firm for the shares.

OUTLINE

I. What
  A. This chapter describes characteristics of convertibles and warrants, which are security alternatives to bonds, preferred stock, and common stock.
  B. Methods are outlined for valuing these securities that can be converted into common stock of the issuing firm.

II. Why
  A. Convertibles and warrants can be used by a company to raise funds.
  B. The financial manager must know what makes these securities appeal to investors.

III. How

Exchange for Common
Conversion Price

  A. Convertible bonds and convertible preferred stock can be exchanged at the owner's option for shares of common stock.
    1. The rate of this exchange can be expressed in terms of the **conversion price,** which is the price or rate at which the convertible security can be traded for common stock. Another way of stating this is to

Conversion Ratio

      specify the **conversion ratio,** which is the number of common shares received in exchange for the convertible security.

315

a. The linkage between the conversion price and the conversion ratio is through the **par value** of the convertible security.
  i. The par value is the amount of purchasing power in the conversion process. It is a constant amount (usually $1000 for bonds) that may be used to "buy" common stock.
  ii. Either the conversion price *or* the conversion ratio is specified, and the other term is computed from the following equation:

Calculation

$$\text{Conversion price} = \frac{\text{par value}}{\text{conversion ratio}} \qquad (22\text{-}1)$$

b. The terms of the conversion are often adjusted over time either by raising the conversion price or by reducing the conversion ratio. Also, appropriate adjustments are made whenever a stock splits or a stock dividend occurs.

Valuation

2. The **value** of a convertible security is influenced by its worth as an issue having no conversion feature and by the worth of the convertible privilege.

Investment Value

a. The **investment value** is the worth of the security excluding any contribution from the conversion option.
  i. For a convertible bond, this is the sum of present values of the interest and principal. (See problem 3.)
  ii. For a convertible preferred stock, this is the present value of the future dividend payments.

Conversion Value

b. The **conversion value,** which is separate from the income features of the investment value, is the market value of the stock that would be received if the securities were converted.
  i. It is equal to the conversion ratio times the market price of the stock.
  ii. The higher the stock price, the higher the conversion value.
  iii. Conversion value can be above or below the investment value, depending on whether the stock price is high or low.

Market Value

c. The **market value** or actual price of the convertible security will not fall below certain points.
  i. It will always be at or above the investment value because of the conversion privilege. The conversion privilege has a value that may be almost nil if the stock is likely to be depressed for a long period, or the conversion right may have considerable value if the stock is high or is considered very likely to go up. In other words, the additional advantage of the conversion feature can be substantial, and it can never be negative.
  ii. The market value of the convertible security will always be at or above the conversion value because the security can be traded for stock that can actually be sold for this amount.

<table>
<tr><td>

Floor Price

</td><td>

iii. Points *i* and *ii* mean that the market value will never fall below a **floor price** as set by either the investment value or the conversion value. If the stock price is high, the effective floor is the conversion value. If the stock price is low, the floor is set by the investment value.

</td></tr>
<tr><td>

Conversion Premium

</td><td>

iv. The amount by which the market value exceeds the floor price is the **conversion premium.**

v. Study Figure 22-2 in the text for a helpful review of this section.

</td></tr>
<tr><td>

Dilution

</td><td>

3. The **dilution effect** of conversion refers to the drop in earnings per share (EPS).

  a. This results in having more shares outstanding after the conversion takes place.

  b. In a few cases, the EPS actually rises because the bond interest or preferred dividend payments on the convertible securities are eliminated upon conversion and this more than compensates for the increase in the number of shares.

</td></tr>
<tr><td>

Appraising Convertibles

Upside Potential Price Floor

</td><td>

4. Convertibles can be appraised from both the buyer's and the seller's viewpoints.

  a. These issues are attractive to investors because they provide a relatively safe investment—a fixed-income security with a price floor and a potential for a large gain if the stock price rises.

</td></tr>
<tr><td>

Lower Income Yield

</td><td>

  b. However, the investor sacrifices to gain this opportunity because the income yield on a convertible security is usually less than what would be paid on a nonconvertible issue. Also, convertible bonds are often subordinated to other debt of the company.

</td></tr>
<tr><td>

Potential for Bargain-Priced Common

</td><td>

  c. From the firm's viewpoint, convertibles appear to be attractive because of the lower yield.

    i. However, if the stock price rises, the effect will be to have sold common stock at a bargain price since the convertibles will be exchanged at a rate that is below the increased stock price. This is not good.

    ii. If the firm's stock doesn't appreciate in value, conversion will not take place, and the firm will have sold its fixed-income securities for relatively low yields. This may be good.

</td></tr>
<tr><td>

Flotation Cost Savings

</td><td>

  d. A real benefit does accrue to the firm in the sense of reduced flotation costs when convertibles are sold and later converted if the alternative was to sell convertibles and refund them with the proceeds from the sale of new common stock. This would involve extra fees to refund the convertible securities and additional flotation costs connected with the common stock offering.

</td></tr>
<tr><td>

Forcing Conversion

</td><td>

5. Companies include a **call provision** with convertible issues so that these security holders can be "forced" to convert into common stock.

  a. Firms force conversion by offering investors a choice of receiving a conversion value that is greater than the call price.

</td></tr>
</table>

b. This is done by waiting until the conversion value is above the call price and then calling the issue for redemption.

c. Investors thus convert into common stock to avoid receiving less than they would if they allowed their securities to be redeemed for the call price. (See problem 6.)

Warrants
Option Price

B. **Warrants** are options to buy a specified number of shares of a firm's common stock at a specified price, called the **option** or **exercise price.**

1. They are similar to convertible securities except that when a warrant is turned in, the option price must be paid in *cash* to acquire the common stock.

2. Warrants are like stock rights except that they are sold to any investor or issued in a package with bonds or preferred stock. Rights, on the other hand, are issued without charge to all existing common stockholders.

3. Warrants expire at a given date, except for a few that are perpetual.

Theoretical Value

4. The **theoretical value** of a warrant equals the difference between the market price of the common stock and the option price times the number of shares that can be purchased with each warrant.

a. This is the discount on the common stock allowed to the warrantholder, if the warrantholder exercises the warrants.

b. The theoretical value is zero if the market value of the common stock that the warrant allows the warrantholder to purchase is at or below the option price. A warrant can never have a negative value.

Market Value

c. The market price of the warrant will always be at or above its theoretical value because the option to buy common stock is worth at least zero and often more.

Premium

i. The difference between the market price and the theoretical value is called the **premium** on the warrant.

ii. The premium declines as the stock price increases beyond the option (exercise) price.

No Dividends

d. Holding a warrant is somewhat equivalent to holding the common stock except that warrantholders never receive dividends, cannot vote, etc.

High Risk/Return
Potential

e. An advantage of owning warrants is that they usually trade at a lower price level than the common stock.

i. This means that they have a relative degree of protection against a downside loss—they have less far to fall compared with the common stock.

ii. This also means that they can realize a proportionately greater gain for a given increase in the stock price. (See problem 7 for an illustration of this point.)

Usage

5. Warrants have been frequently used by small, dynamic firms and more recently by larger corporations.

a. Warrants are issued with bonds, with preferred stock, or even with common stock.

b. Investors find warrants attractive because, compared with common stock, their potential percentage gain is greater. This usually offsets the sacrifice of giving up dividends and voting rights.

c. An advantage for the firm is the realization of cash for the warrants even if the stock price falls later on. A disadvantage is (as in the case of convertibles) having, in effect, to sell equity at a discount if the market price for the stock rises substantially by the time the new equity money is received by the company.

COMPLETION QUESTIONS

Convertible   1. _____ securities have the added feature of being able to be

common   traded in for (*preferred/common*) stock.

common   2. The conversion into (*preferred/common*) stock occurs at the option of the

investor   (*issuer/investor*).

price   3. Investors prefer a low conversion (*price/ratio*) or a high conversion

ratio   _____.

price, ratio   4. The product of the conversion (*call/price*) and the conversion _____

par   equals the (*market/par*) value of the security.

upward   5. It is common for the conversion price to be adjusted (*upward/downward*) over time.

investment   6. The (*conversion/investment*) value of a convertible bond is the present value

interest, principal   of the _____ and _____ payments from that bond.

conversion   7. The _____ value of a convertible security is its worth based on

common stock   the market price of the firm's _____ _____.

high, conversion   8. If the stock price is (*low/high*), the _____ value will be above the investment value.

market, below   9. The (*market/par*) value of a convertible security will never be (*below/above*) either the investment or the conversion value.

premium, market   10. The conversion (*value/premium*) is the amount by which the bond (*market/par*) value exceeds the floor price.

dilution   11. The _____ effect of conversion occurs when earnings per share

more   change as a result of (*more/fewer*) shares being outstanding.

loss, gain	12. Convertible securities are attractive to investors because they offer a limited potential for _____ and a large potential for _____ .
lower	13. Convertible securities usually offer (*lower/higher*) yields from interest compared with the yields offered by nonconvertible securities.
rising	14. A (*rising/falling*) stock price increases the likelihood of investors' exercising the conversion option.
debt	15. After a convertible bond is converted, (*debt/equity*) will be reduced and
equity	(*debt/equity*) will increase.
call	16. To force conversion, the convertible security must have a (*call/sinking fund*)
above, call	provision, and the conversion value must be (*below/above*) the _____ price.
warrant	17. The difference between exercising a (*warrant/call*) and exercising a convertible security is that cash must be paid to the company for the new shares.
Warrants	18. _____ differ from stock rights in that the former are sold to
given to all	anyone, whereas rights are (*given to all/sold to some*) existing stockholders.
A few	19. (*Most/A few*) warrants are perpetual.
theoretical	20. The _____ value of a warrant is equal to the difference between
stock, option	the _____ price and the _____ price of the com-
shares	mon stock times the number of _____ that can be purchased with each warrant.
zero	21. The theoretical value of a warrant is _____ when the stock price
below	is equal to or (*below/above*) the option price.
do not	22. Warrantholders (*do/do not*) receive dividends or have the right to
vote	_____ .
below	23. Warrants sell in a price range that is (*above/below*) the level of the common stock.
more	24. Warrants become (*less/more*) valuable as the stock price rises.
option	25. If the stock price falls below the _____ price, warrants will not be exercised.

PROBLEMS

1. What is the conversion price for a $1000 par convertible bond if the conversion ratio is twenty shares per bond?

Solution

$$\text{Conversion price} = \frac{\text{par value}}{\text{conversion ratio}}$$

$$= \frac{\$1000}{20}$$

$$= \$50$$

Step two This means that the bond can be converted into twenty shares at the rate of $50 per share.

2. What is the conversion ratio for a $25 par convertible preferred stock that can be exchanged for common stock at the rate of $10 per share?

Solution

Step one

$$\text{Conversion ratio} = \frac{\text{par value}}{\text{conversion price}} \qquad \text{that}$$

$$= \frac{\$25}{\$10}$$

$$= 2.5 \text{ shares}$$

Step two This means that a share of this convertible preferred stock can be exchanged for 2.5 shares of common stock.

3. PH Co. has a $1000 par, $6\frac{1}{2}$ percent convertible bond outstanding that matures twenty years from today and offers investors the right to convert the bond into twenty-five shares of common stock.
   a. What is the investment value of this bond if other bonds that are not convertible but that are similar to this issue in every other respect are selling to yield 8 percent?

Solution

Step one   The investment value or theoretical value is the present value of the interest and principal payments, discounted at the yield to maturity appropriate for the same-risk straight bonds, ignoring the conversion feature.

Step two   This discount rate is 8 percent. The coupon or interest rate is $6^1/_2$ percent, which provides $65 per year for a $1000 par bond.

Step three   The investment value of this bond is

Investment value = $65 × (P/A, 8%, 20) + $1000 × (P/F, 8%, 20)

= $65 × 9.8181 + $1000 × 0.2145

= $852.68

b. What is the conversion value when the PH common stock is trading at $30 per share?

Solution

Step one   The conversion value is the conversion ratio times the market price per share of the common stock.

Conversion value = 25 × $30

= $750

End of solution.

4. Using the same terms described in the preceding problem:
   a. Determine the floor on the market price of PH Co.'s convertible bond.

Solution

Step one   The floor price is the greater of either the investment value *or* the conversion value.

Step two   Since the investment value is higher, the floor or minimum bond price is $852.68

b. What is the conversion premium on this bond if it is actually selling at $905?

Solution

Step one   The conversion premium is the excess of the market value over the floor provided by either the investment or the conversion value.

$$\text{Conversion premium} = \$905 - \$852.68$$

$$= \$52.32$$

Step two   In this situation the investment value is higher than the conversion value, but the bond still sells for a premium because the conversion privilege is deemed worth something extra. The premium is $52.32.

c. What would be the likely market value of the convertible bond if the PH common stock was selling for $70 per share instead of $30 per share?

Solution

Step one   The only change is the stock price, and so the investment value remains the same—it varies only when market rates of interest move.

Step two   The change in the stock price will be reflected in the conversion value and the bond price.

$$\text{New conversion value} = 25 \times \$70$$

$$= \$1750$$

Step three   The main contributor to the bond value is now its conversion feature. The bond market price would be at least $1750. The conversion premium, however, would likely be very small since owning the convertible bond is more like owning common stock when the actual stock price is well above the conversion price.

    d. What is the floor on the convertible bond price when the stock is $70 per share?

Solution

Step one   The effective floor price, whenever the stock price exceeds the conversion price, is the investment value.

Step two   The investment value, as previously determined, is $852.68.

Step three   This means that a purchaser of the convertible bond has some protection against loss because if the stock were to fall drastically, the bond would not decline so far. For example, if the stock fell from $70 to $5 per share, which is a drop of 93 percent, the bond would fall only to its investment value, which is a 51 percent drop [($1750 − $852.68)/$1750].

5. YZ Corporation has a $20 million 7 percent convertible bond issue outstanding that is convertible into ten shares for each $1000 par value bond. If earnings before interest and taxes are estimated to be $15.4 million this year, what would be the dilution effect on the earnings per share if the entire bond issue were converted into common stock? The company currently has 1 million shares outstanding, and its income tax rate is 40 percent.

Solution

Step one   The dilution effect of conversion is shown by comparing the earnings per share (EPS) before and after conversion.

Step two   The amount of change in EPS will depend on the amount of interest paid on the bonds (which will be eliminated upon conversion) and on the number of new shares issued for the old bonds.

Step three Converting the bonds will result in 200,000 more shares since there are twenty thousand $1000 par bonds in the $20 million issue and each bond can be traded in for ten shares.

Step four

	Before conversion	After conversion
Earnings before interest and taxes	$15,400,000	$15,400,000
Interest (0.07 × $20,000,000)	1,400,000	—
Earnings before taxes	$14,000,000	$15,400,000
Taxes (40%)	5,600,000	6,160,000
Earnings after taxes	$ 8,400,000	$ 9,240,000
Number of shares outstanding	1,000,000	1,200,000
EPS	$8.40	$7.70

Step five The dilution calculations in the above table show that EPS will decline from $8.40 to $7.70.

6. Filbert Co. has a convertible bond outstanding with a conversion price of $25. The $1000 par bond is callable at $1100 now, and the common stock is currently quoted at $35 per share. Would the firm be able to "force" conversion of this issue?

Solution

Step one Forcing conversion is accomplished not by twisting the arm of investors but by offering them two choices—one for more money than the other.

Step two We need to determine the value of each choice.

Step three If investors send in their bonds asking for cash, they will receive $1100 for each $1000 par bond.

Step four The conversion value equals the conversion ratio times the stock price, as follows:

$$\text{Conversion value} = \frac{\$1000}{\$25} \times \$35$$

$$= \$1400$$

Step five The 40 shares of stock could be sold for this amount less charges for commissions totaling a few dollars.

Step six The choice is then between $1100 and $1400. All investors will convert their bonds into stock without feeling any real pressure.

7. Each Nagel Company warrant entitles the holder to purchase three shares of Nagel common stock for $22 per share.
   a. What is the theoretical value of each warrant when the market price of the stock is $20 per share?

Solution

Step one The theoretical value equals the difference between the market price and the option price times the number of shares per warrant.

$$\text{Theoretical value} = (\$20 - \$22) \times 3$$

$$= -\$6$$

Step two This can't be negative, because it would mean you would be paying $6 to someone to take the warrant off your hands.

Step three Warrants can never have a negative value, but they can be worthless. In this case their theoretical value is zero.

   b. What is the theoretical value if the stock is $25 per share?

Solution

Step one

$$\text{Theoretical value} = (\$25 - \$22) \times 3$$

$$= \$9$$

End of solution.

c. What is the premium if the warrant sells for $10?

Solution

Step one The premium is $10 − $9, or $1 per warrant. *End of solution.*

d. Compare the exposure to loss by investing in the warrants as opposed to exercising the option and buying the stock.

Solution

Step one The maximum potential loss in purchasing a warrant is $10, whereas the exposure to loss by investing in three shares of stock is $66 ($22 × 3).

Step two In addition, the relative or percentage gain when the stock goes up will be greater in a warrant than the percentage return realized in stock.

Step three These two observations are major reasons why investors find warrants attractive in spite of the fact that investors receive no dividend or voting rights.

CHAPTER TWENTY-THREE

HOLDING COMPANIES, MERGERS, AND CONSOLIDATIONS

QUINTESSENCE   Businesses can be joined together in a holding company in which one firm controls others by ownership of their stock. They can also be combined in mergers or consolidations, where the result is a single surviving company. The potential advantages of business combinations are savings resulting from elimination of duplication and/or economies of scale in such areas as production, research, marketing, financing, management, and accounting. Benefits may also occur from tax savings. A company can purchase the physical assets of another firm or acquire the stock of that firm. Payments are made in the form of cash or securities. The transaction is nontaxable to the sellers only if they receive voting shares as compensation. The terms of an acquisition are influenced mainly by the estimates of cash flows or earnings per share on a with- and without-merger basis. The purchase method of accounting may result in lower taxes for the merged operation than when taxes are computed under pooling of interests accounting.

OUTLINE

   I. What
   A. Multicorporate organizations are those in which two or more firms are joined together under the control of a single management.
   B. Advantages of these arrangements, their formation, the potential problems faced, and accounting treatments are discussed in this chapter.

   II. Why
   A. A group of corporations provides economies of larger-scale operations.
   B. These combinations result in more investment opportunities.
   C. Businesses can grow externally as well as internally.

   III. How

**Holding Company
Subsidiaries**
   A. A **holding company** is a corporation having effective control over one or more other firms, called **subsidiaries.**
   1. Control is achieved by owning a substantial block (usually 20 percent or more) of the subsidiary's stock.

329

2. A disadvantage of the holding company arrangement is the possibility of added taxes on profits.
   a. This is minimized somewhat by a provision that excludes up to 80 percent of interfirm dividends from taxation.
   b. If the subsidiary is 80 percent or more owned by the holding company, there will be no taxes on the interfirm dividends.

Merger

B. In a **merger** or **consolidation,** previously separate companies are brought together in a single corporation.

1. In a merger, one of the combining firms survives ($A + B = A$); in a consolidation, a new company is formed ($A + B = C$). The financial issues for both types of combination are essentially the same, so only the term "merger" will be used in the following discussion.

Horizontal
Vertical

2. A **horizontal combination** is the merger of firms in similar lines of business, a **vertical combination** is the merger of companies engaged in different stages of production of the same type of product, and a **conglomerate** is a grouping of dissimilar firms.

Conglomerate
Divestiture

3. A **divestiture** (spin-off) is the sale or division of a subsidiary.

Leveraged Buyout

4. In a **leveraged buyout** (LBO), private investors acquire the stock of a publicly held firm, or a subsidiary, with the financing based on borrowing on the assets of the acquired business.
   a. In recent years, high debt to equity ratios have caused much controversy over LBOs.
   b. LBOs have given management extra incentives to run the firm more efficiently.

5. The procedure for a merger is as follows:

Negotiations

   a. The merger begins with negotiations between the different firms' managements.

Approvals

   b. The terms of their agreement must be approved first by the respective boards of directors and then by stockholders. (Usually a two-thirds favorable vote is required.)
      i. Note the difference between this and a holding company arrangement, where neither the directors nor the shareholders vote. The shares are simply sold, by individual investors, to the holding company.

Proxies
Tender Offer

      ii. When one company doesn't want to be acquired, the other firm may solicit **proxies** from the shareholders of the resisting company. Alternatively, a **tender offer** could be made—this is the more common case in unfriendly takeover attempts.

Antitrust

6. **Antitrust** laws require the Federal Trade Commission, the Justice Department, and often other agencies to block mergers if the result would be immediate, or even potential, reduction in competition.
   a. The courts are often involved in applying the laws.
   b. The Justice Department actions ordering the splitting up of AT&T and the decision to drop the IBM antitrust case have had

major impacts on competition in the communications and computer industries.

Exchange of Assets

7. If an acquisition does not occur by vote of the merging firm's shareholders or by the outright purchase of shares, assets of one company can be bought by another.

   a. The acquiring firm's stockholders do not vote in these cases, and the other company's shareholders vote only if a major portion of its assets are being sought.

   b. Securities and/or cash may be used for the purchase.

Tax-Free Exchange

   i. For an acquisition to be **tax-free,** a major part of the payment must be in the form of voting shares of common or preferred stock. (Actually, taxes are postponed until the stock that shareholders received is sold.)

Taxable Exchange

   ii. In a taxable exchange both the selling firm and its shareholders pay taxes on any gains they receive.

   iii. The **1986 Tax Reform Act:**

      (a) Repealed the General Utilities doctrine, which had placed limits on the amount of gain that a corporation would pay taxes on. This action makes tax-free exchanges relatively more attractive than before.

      (b) Limits the tax loss carryforwards that the acquiring company is eligible to receive.

      (c) Prevents a company from deducting, for tax purposes, any premiums and related expenses paid in the process of buying back shares from stockholders. (The premium is commonly referred to as greenmail in the context of takeover attempts.)

   iv. The postponing of taxes in the tax-free exchange usually more than offsets the benefits of higher depreciation that result in the taxable transactions.

Trends

8. Merger activity has been cyclical, with many cases occurring in the 1920s and late 1960s. Shifts are due to:

   a. Changes in governmental policy regarding:

      i. Antitrust action.

      ii. Tax treatment of business combinations.

   b. Exceptionally good or bad performance of conglomerates that had grown through mergers.

   c. Varying availability of desirable merger candidates.

Reasons for Mergers
Operating Economies

9. Reasons for a merger include:

   a. **Operating economies** that result from **synergies:**

      i. Elimination of duplication of production and management costs.

      ii. More effective research programs.

      iii. More efficient marketing efforts in terms of advertising and offering a complete product line.

iv. Savings as a result of consolidating financial activities such as accounting, credit and billing, and raising funds.

v. A more dominant market position, although this is typically temporary because of antitrust regulation.

vi. A gain due to cross-fertilization of ideas and managerial expertise (2 + 2 = 5).

vii. Experience has been mixed, resulting in some very successful companies; most eventually failed and realized they could not "do everything." Expansion into familiar fields is the current guideline.

Taxes

b. Two **tax considerations** that favor mergers between companies:

i. Inheritance taxes are minimized when shares in one company are sold by the heirs to another firm, as opposed to selling them in the marketplace.

ii. Losses in one company can be offset against gains and income in another company.

External Growth

c. Opportunities to **grow externally** by providing new areas for expansion:

i. External expansion is *more rapid* and usually *less risky* than internal growth.

ii. Sometimes it is impossible to expand internally. For example, patents may prohibit a firm from introducing a product made by another company. The answer may be to merge with this company.

iii. Remember, however, that the acquiring firm generally pays for what it gets, so external expansion is not necessarily cheaper.

Portfolio Diversification

d. *Reducing risk* or the fluctuation in earnings by **diversification:**

i. This reduction in earnings fluctuation is most likely to occur if the merging firms are in different lines of business (low correlation between each stream of earnings).

ii. However, *investors can diversify on their own* by buying shares in different companies. While this involves higher transaction costs, it does mean that *the main justification for a merger lies instead in operating economies and tax benefits*.

iii. The advantage of lower risk is a lower probability of bankruptcy, which will in turn increase the value of the firm's shares.

iv. In closely held family corporations, diversification is often easiest if done by the firm rather than the owners themselves.

Gains to Sellers

10. Sellers experience significant gains from mergers but buyers do not. Two qualifications to this general statement are:

a. Acquiring firms are typically larger than the acquired so the impact is minimal on the buyer.

b. Buyers' costs incurred in the acquisition process are ignored in the studies, but if they were included, the merger activities might actually create losses.

Cost-Benefit Analysis
Cash Purchase

11. In merger negotiations, both buyer and seller seek terms that will permit them to be better off.
   a. In a **cash purchase** the buyer finds the deal acceptable if the present value of the future aftertax cash flows from the acquired firm exceeds the price paid plus the present value of any of the seller's debts.
      i. The seller's stockholders must feel that the cash they are receiving is worth more than any benefits that would be theirs as a result of the future performance of their existing firm without the merger.
      ii. The acquisition price is usually above the selling firm's pre-merger stock price.

Stock Purchase

   b. If a **stock purchase** is involved, values on a pre- and postmerger basis are figured by estimating earnings per share and then by applying an appropriate price-earnings ratio.
   c. Which company gets the bigger share of the merger benefits depends on the following (book values do not have any impact):
      i. The number of other merger candidates available.
      ii. The number of merger-hungry firms—successful small companies are actively sought by larger firms.
      iii. The expected growth rates of earnings of the companies.
      iv. The amount of liquid assets in the firm being acquired.

Accounting Treatment
Purchase

12. The two methods of accounting for mergers differ mainly in the valuation of the assets of the acquired firm.
   a. In the **purchase** method, the assets are valued at the price paid for the acquisition (market value of the stock offered). The liabilities of the selling firm are combined with those of the buyer and the assets are depreciated according to their restated values. Incomes are combined from the merger date *forward*.

Pooling of Interests

   b. In the **pooling of interests** approach, both assets and liabilities of the acquired company are simply added to those of the buying firm. Incomes of the two companies are combined for *all time periods*.
   c. In most cases the purchase price is greater than the book value (assets minus liabilities).
      i. The depreciation base is higher under the purchase method. This results in greater depreciation charges for the merged companies, which means lower taxable income and lower taxes but higher cash flow, which is good. (See problem 4.)

Goodwill

      ii. When the acquiring firm pays more for another firm's assets than the amount those assets could be sold for individually, a premium called **goodwill** is created. It must be amortized over a period of years, which reduces income. These charges are not deductible for tax purposes (bad news).

    iii. The reduction of earnings from goodwill occurs in the purchase method of accounting but not under pooling of interests, because book values are used in the pooling of interests methodology.

Accounting Standards

  d. The accounting profession limits the use of the pooling of interests method to cases where:

    i. The acquired firm receives payment in a single transaction in the form of voting common stock.

    ii. The combined firm retains most of the acquired assets for at least two years after the merger.

COMPLETION QUESTIONS

holding
subsidiaries

1. A (*holding*/*conglomerate*) company has control over one or more other firms, called (*partners*/*subsidiaries*).

less

2. Effective control may be achieved with (*less*/*more*) than 50 percent of a company's shares.

tender offer
above

3. A(n) _____ _____ is an offer to purchase shares in another company. The price specified is usually (*above*/*below*) the prevailing market price for those shares.

30

4. If a holding company owns less than 80 percent of a subsidiary, it must pay taxes on up to _____ percent of the dividends it receives from that subsidiary. If 80 percent or more of the stock is owned, the tax on the dividends is _____ percent.

0

higher

5. Earnings of a holding company have a (*lower*/*higher*) degree of leverage than earnings in a situation where the firms are separately owned.

6. When firm *A* joins firm *B* to form firm *C,* the combination is a(n)

consolidation, merger

_____. *A* + *B* = *A* represents a _____ situation.

7. If Grandma's Pie Company and Grandpa's Cookie Corporation joined, it

horizontal

would be a (*horizontal*/*vertical*) combination.

8. The merger of U-Plant-Em Trees Corporation with We-Cut-Em Lumber

vertical

Company is a(n) _____ combination.

9. Travel Tours, Ltd., merging with A-Z Meatpackers is an example of a(n)

conglomerate

_____ combination.

10. When a few investors borrow funds to acquire a public firm, it is called

leveraged buyout   a(n) _____ _____.

11. An advantage of the holding company route to acquisition is that shareholders

do not   of the firm being acquired (*do/do not*) vote on the matter.

Decreases   12. (*Increases/Decreases*) in antitrust actions will promote mergers.

has not   13. Merger activity (*has/has not*) increased steadily over the past fifty years.

External   14. (*External/Internal*) growth can be faster and less risky than (*external/*

internal   *internal*) growth.

synergy   15. An expected benefit of _____ occurs when "2 + 2 = 5." This

says that the results of a merger may be beneficial as a result of the cross-

expertise   fertilization of ideas and management (*costs/expertise*).

diversification   16. The fluctuations in earnings of a firm can be reduced by (*diversification/*

decreases   *growth*) which (*increases/decreases*) the probability of bankruptcy.

17. Because investors can buy stocks of different companies, the main advan-

operating, tax   tages to mergers are _____ economies and _____

benefits.

Losses, gains   18. _____ in one operation can be used to offset _____ in

lower   another, which results in (*lower/higher*) total taxes for the two businesses.

19. Property owned by a firm can be purchased outright or acquired by buying

stock, are not   the (*debt/stock*) of that firm. The seller's stockholders (*are/are not*) required

to approve the purchase of their firm's assets.

shares   20. Control of the property can be gained for less money if (*shares/assets alone*)

are purchased.

cash   21. The selling stockholders are subject to taxes when they receive (*stock/cash*).

22. If the sellers believe the buyer's shares are overpriced, they may prefer a

taxable   (*taxable/nontaxable*) transaction.

voting   23. Taxes on the sellers can be postponed if they receive (*voting/nonvoting*)

securities as payment.

24. Payments to buy back shares from stockholders in a takeover attempt are

greenmail   referred to as _____.

25. When cash is offered as payment, the merger proposal is evaluated on a

net present value   (*net present value/earnings per share*) basis.

26. When stock is paid to the seller, the deal is analyzed by the effect on (*net*

earnings per share   *present value/earnings per share*) with and without the merger.

27. Shareholders of both firms can be benefited by a merger as a result of _____ of scale and _____ benefits.

28. If the number of merger-hungry firms is high, the terms of the merger will tend to favor the (*buyer/seller*).

29. Book values (*are/are not*) usually very important considerations in setting merger terms.

30. Assets of the acquired firm tend to be valued (*lower/higher*) on the acquiring firm's books in the purchase method of accounting.

31. Taxes paid by the merged entity will usually be (*lower/higher*) if pooling of interests accounting is used than if the purchase method is used.

32. The pooling of interests method (*can/cannot*) be used when the merger transaction is taxable to the seller.

PROBLEMS

1. AA Corporation owns 55 percent of the shares in BB Company and 81 percent of the shares in CC Company. Assuming that AA is in the 40 percent tax bracket, how much tax would be paid if AA received $1 million in dividends from each of its subsidiaries?

Solution

Step one   Interfirm dividends are up to 80 percent tax-free unless the parent company owns 80 percent or more of the subsidiary, in which case they are totally nontaxable.

Step two   In this case AA owns more than 20 percent but less than 80 percent of BB. The taxes paid on the BB dividend would be $0.40 \times 0.20 \times \$1,000,000 = \$80,000$.

Step three   The taxes paid on the CC dividend would be *zero* since it is 81 percent owned by AA.

2. Suppose that AA Corporation has no operations itself and that its only holding is in BB Company, which expects to earn and pay dividends of $5 million if next year is good or $2 million if it is bad. AA has $6 million of a 7 percent debt issue outstanding and $4 million in equity. What will be the return on equity under the good- and bad-year assumptions?

Solution

Step one   AA has no other income, which is typical for a holding company, and so its fortunes are entirely dependent on the results of its subsidiary. In this case, the dividends from BB must be treated as ordinary income, i.e., the dividend exclusion does not apply.

Step two   AA's income statement (ignoring all expenses except interest and taxes) is as follows (dollar amounts are in millions):

	Good year	Bad year
Dividend income (55% of BB dividends)	$2.750	$1.100
Interest (0.07 × $6)	.420	.420
Taxable income	$2.330	$ .680
Taxes (40%)	.932	.272
Net income	$1.398	$ .408
Return on equity (net income/$4)	35%	10%

Step three   Notice the effect of leverage. The subsidiary's profits jump 2.5 times (5/2) in a good year, and the holding company's profits increase 3.4 times (1.398/0.408).

3. J Company has broken even each year since its formation except this year, when it expects to lose $1 million. K Corporation has always been profitable, and this year it expects to earn $2 million before taxes. What would be the taxes paid by each firm without a merger and the taxes paid if they were merged, assuming a 40 percent tax rate?

Solution

Step one   J Company would pay no taxes and would have this $1 million loss to carry forward to offset income in the next fifteen years.

Step two   K Corporation would pay $800,000 (0.4 × $2,000,000).

Step three   The J-K Corporation would have taxable income of $1,000,000 and a tax of $400,000 (0.4 × $1,000,000).

Step four   The advantage of a merger is to make use of the tax loss immediately instead of having to wait until some later date when it could be offset against income. This assumes pooling of interests accounting is used. Under the purchase method, only future incomes (losses) can be combined.

4. What would be the difference between H Corporation's acquiring I Company for $10 million under the purchase method of accounting and its acquiring I Company using a pooling of interests procedure? Use straight-line depreciation, no salvage value, and an average life of twenty years for the assets, which are valued on I's books at $5 million. I Company has no liabilities, and its pretax cash flow is estimated to be $2.3 million each year for the next twenty years. The tax rate is 40 percent, and the appropriate discount rate is 14 percent.

Solution

Step one   A major difference between the two methods of accounting for business combinations is in the value at which the assets are placed on the books of the acquiring firm. This results in different amounts of depreciation, which affects taxes and, in turn, cash flows.

Step two   In the purchase method of accounting, the assets are valued at cost to the acquiring firm, which is $10 million. Depreciation then is $500,000 per year ($10,000,000/20).

Step three   Under a pooling of interests, the cost basis is $5 million, so the depreciation is $250,000 per year ($5,000,000/20).

Step four   The aftertax or net cash flows contributed by I Company under each accounting method are as follows (dollar amounts are in millions):

	Purchase	Pooling of interests
Pretax cash flow	$2.30	$2.30
Depreciation	.50	.25
Taxable income	$1.80	$2.05
Taxes (40%)	$ .72	$ .82
Net cash flow	$1.58	$1.48

Step five   The net present value under a purchase method is:

$$\text{Net present value} = \$1.58 \times (P/A,\ 14\%,\ 20) - \text{initial outlay}$$

$$= \$1.58 \times 6.6231 - \$10$$

$$= \$0.464 \text{ million}$$

Step six The pooling of interests NPV is:

$$\$1.48 \times 6.6231 - \$10 = -\$0.198 \text{ million}$$

Step seven This result indicates that the acquisition is advisable (positive NPV) if the purchase method of accounting is used, whereas the deal would not be advisable (negative NPV) under a pooling of interests procedure. In order to qualify for the purchase method of accounting, H Company would have to offer some combination of cash and bonds to I Company shareholders.

5. East, Inc., and West, Ltd., are negotiating the terms of a merger that is expected to result in cost savings so as to produce a combined profit of $5 million. Other data for these firms are shown below:

	East	West
Estimated earnings	$3 million	$1 million
Shares outstanding	1 million	0.5 million
Earnings per share	$3	$5
Price-earnings ratio	10	10
Market value of the firm	$30 million	$10 million

The discussions have narrowed the offers down to West stockholders' receiving 200,000 or 300,000 shares from East. If the merged company sells at 10 times earnings, giving it a market valuation of $50 million, what would be the probable final terms of the merger?

Solution

Step one Since the earnings of the combined East-West businesses are estimated to be greater than the total earnings of the individual firms, each party to the merger could be benefited. This is an example of synergy. An analysis of the impact on each set of shareholders, patterned after Exhibit 23-4 in the text, follows:

(a)	Number of East shares issued to West shareholders	200,000	300,000
(b)	Exchange ratio [(a) ÷ 500,000]	0.4	0.6
(c)	Number of East shares outstanding after the merger [1,000,000 + (a)]	1,200,000	1,300,000
(d)	Postmerger fraction of ownership by West [(a) ÷ (c)]	1/6	3/13
(e)	Value of West shareholdings [(d) × $50,000,000]	$8,333,333	$11,538,462
(f)	Postmerger fraction of ownership by East [1,000,000 ÷ (c)]	5/6	10/13
(g)	Value of East shareholdings [(f) × $50,000,000]	$41,666,666	$38,461,538

Step two If West shareholders accepted 200,000 East shares, the value of the West holdings would drop from $10 million to $8.3 million. East shareholders would experience a rise in their market value from $30 million to almost $42 million. This proposal would heavily favor East, and so the negotiation would probably have to result in about 300,000 East shares being given to West in order for everyone to be satisfied.

Chapter 2

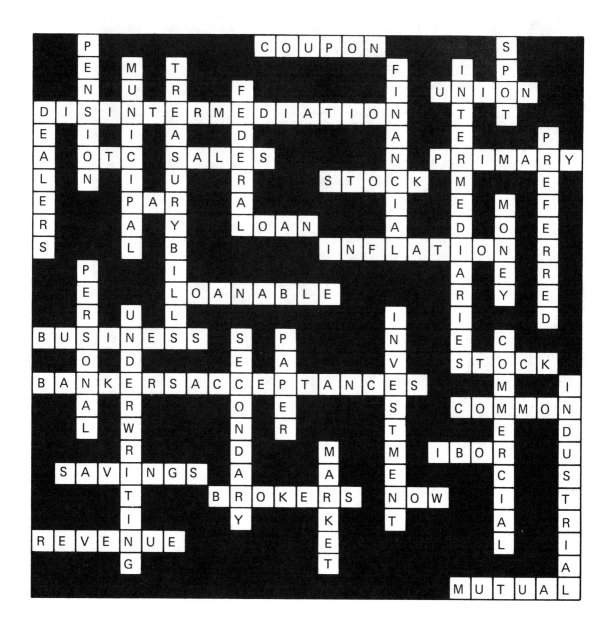

Chapter 6

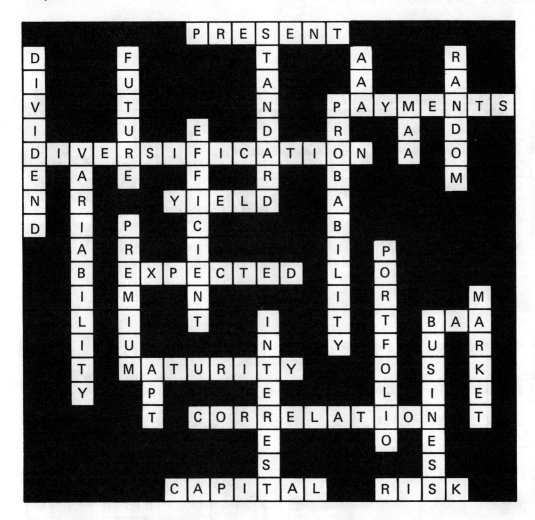

Chapter 11

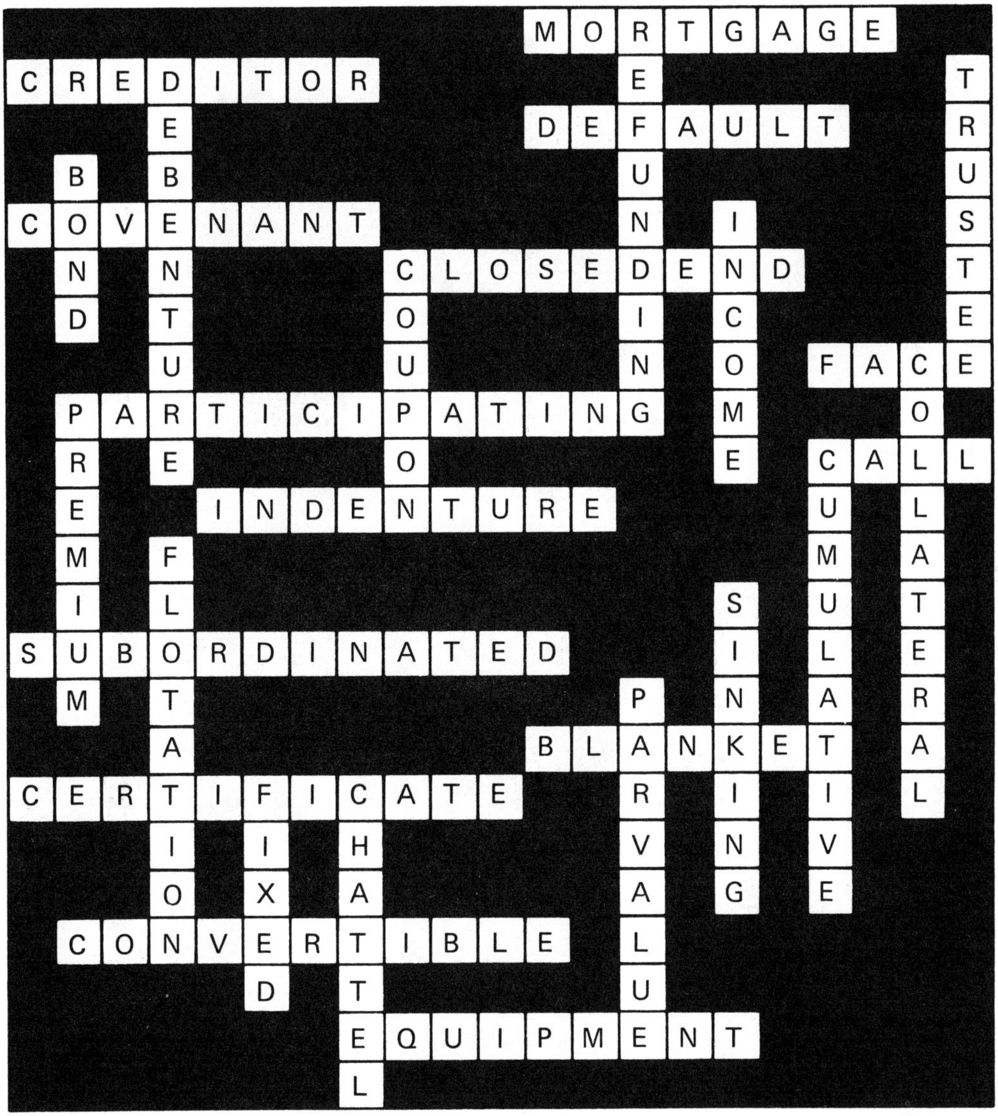
MORTGAGE
CREDITOR
DEFAULT
COVENANT
CLOSEDEND
FACE
PARTICIPATING
CALL
INDENTURE
SUBORDINATED
BLANKET
CERTIFICATE
CONVERTIBLE
EQUIPMENT
REFUNDING
TRUSTEE
DEBENTURE
BOND
INCOME
COUPON
COLLATERAL
PREMIUM
FLOTATION
SINKING
CUMULATIVE
PARVALU
FIXED
CHATTEL